FODOR'S
BRAZIL
1988

Editor: Audrey Liounis
Area Editor: Edwin Taylor
Contributor: Joanna Berkman
Drawings: Michael Conway, Lazlo Roth, Michael Kaplan
Maps and City Plans: C.W. Bacon, M.S.I.A., John Hutchinson, Dyno Lowenstein, Leslie S. Haywood, Jon Bauch Design

Edwin Taylor is an American journalist with ten years of experience writing on Brazil. A resident of Rio de Janeiro, Taylor was the founding editor of Brazil's English-language daily newspaper, the Latin American Daily Post, *and is today editor and publisher of Brasilinform, an English-language information service on Brazil which publishes newsletters.*

Joanna Berkman, a Boston-based freelance writer, has been a reporter for the Boston Herald, *a social science researcher for Abt Associates in Cambridge, and has taught in the Expository Writing Program at Harvard. She studied Portuguese language and culture at the University of Lisbon and has lived in and written about Brazil.*

FODOR'S TRAVEL PUBLICATIONS, INC.
New York & London

Copyright © 1987 by Fodor's Travel Publications, Inc.

All rights reserved under International and Pan-American Copyright Conventions. Published in the United States by Fodor's Travel Publications, Inc., a subsidiary of Random House, Inc., New York, and simultaneously in Canada by Random House of Canada Limited, Toronto. Distributed by Random House, Inc., New York.

No maps, illustrations, or other portions of this book may be reproduced in any form without written permission from the publisher.

ISBN 0-679-01474-8
ISBN 0-340-41788-9 (Hodder & Stoughton)

MANUFACTURED IN THE UNITED STATES OF AMERICA
10 9 8 7 6 5 4 3 2 1

CONTENTS

Foreword   v

Map of Brazil, vi–vii

Introduction to Brazil   1

Planning Your Trip   21

Before You Go: What it Will Cost, 23; Sources of Information, 23; Travel Documents and Customs, 23; When to Go, 25; Packing, 25; Special Events, 26; Tours, 26; Tips for British Visitors, 29

Getting to Brazil: By Air, 29; By Sea, 31; By Car, 32

Staying in Brazil: Money Matters, 33; Accommodations, 34; Dining Out, 34; Tipping, 35; The Language, 36; Business Hours and Holidays, 36; Telephones, 37; Mail, 37; Newspapers, 37; Conversion Table, 38; Electric Current, 39; Photography Tips, 39; Useful Addresses, 39; Health and Safety, 40; Sports, 41

Traveling in Brazil: By Air, 43; By Rail, 43; By Bus, 43; Car Rentals, 44

Leaving Brazil: Customs Returning Home, 44

EXPLORING BRAZIL

Rio de Janeiro   49
Map of Rio de Janeiro, 59
Map of Rio's Beach Neighborhoods, 62
Excursions from Rio, 90

São Paulo   99
Map of São Paulo, 107
The State of São Paulo, 117

The South   123
Rio Grande do Sul, 124
Paraná and Santa Catarina, 129

Central-South Brazil   133
Brasilia, 134
Map of Brasilia, 138–139
Minas Gerais–Belo Horizonte and the Historical Cities, 143

Central-West Brazil   149
The Pantanal, 150
Goias, 153

Bahia   159
Salvador, 160
Map of Salvador, 164

iii

CONTENTS

Excursions from Salvador, 166
The State of Bahia, 174

The Northeast 179

The Amazon 191

Tourist Vocabulary 208

Index 210

FOREWORD

Brazil is a country so large and diverse that little can be called typically Brazilian. Traveling here can mean spanning centuries and cultures, from the antiquated Portuguese and African atmosphere of Bahia to the excitement of Rio de Janeiro or the bustle of modern São Paulo. In Brazil you will find everything you expected and more than you ever dreamed existed.

While every care has been taken to ensure the accuracy of the information contained in this guide, the publishers cannot accept responsibility for any errors which may appear.

All prices quoted in this guide are based on those available to us at the time of writing. In a world of rapid change, however, the possibility of inaccurate or out-of-date information can never be totally eliminated. We trust, therefore, that you will take prices quoted as indicators only, and will double-check to be sure of the latest figures.

Similarly, be sure to check all opening times of museums and galleries. We have found that such times are liable to change without notice, and you could easily make a trip only to find a locked door.

When a hotel closes or a restaurant produces a disappointing meal, let us know, and we will investigate the establishment and the complaint. We are always ready to revise our entries for the following year's edition should the facts warrant it.

Send your letters to the editors of Fodor's Travel Publications, 201 E 50th Street, New York, NY 10022. Continental or British Commonwealth readers may prefer to write to Fodor's Travel Guides, 9–10 Market Place, London W1N 7AG, England.

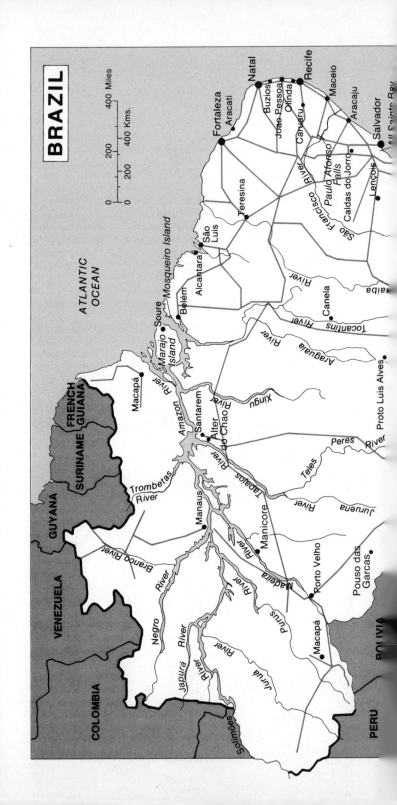

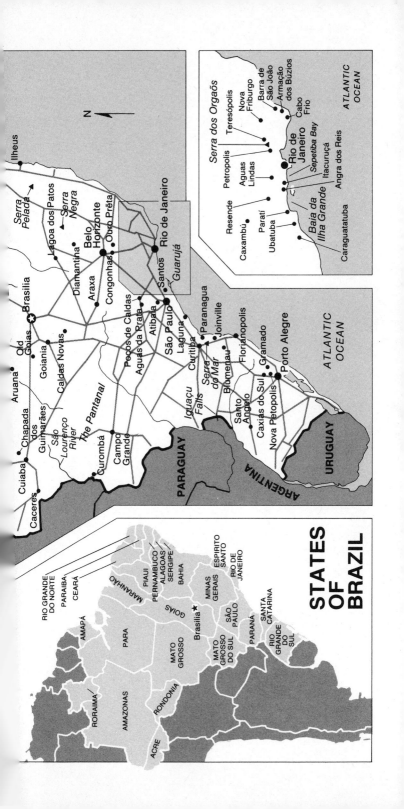

INTRODUCTION TO BRAZIL

Brazil is so big and covers so many square miles through all sorts of terrain that it is impossible to make generalizations about what is "typically" Brazilian. From the pine forests and frosts of the south to the steamy cities along the Equator, Brazil is a study in extremes and contrasts.

Because of its peculiar combination of wealth and industrial might in the south, Third World poverty and hunger in the northeast, urban wealth and sophistication in São Paulo and Rio de Janeiro, wildlife preserves in the Pantanal, and aboriginal tribes in the Amazon territories and interior, the Brazilian cultural continuum includes the polar opposites of the societal spectrum, as well as every variation in between.

The struggle between development and conservation, progress and preservation of the past, national pride and openness to the contributions of other countries, is played out here in plain view. The clash of opposites is manifested in almost every phase of life. The Pantanal and the Amazon, acknowledged universally as great natural storehouses of flora and fauna, must contend with the mining and agricultural interests that would deplete or destroy these very resources. Brazilians decry the cultural imperialism of the United States and the power of the International Monetary Fund, yet they listen to American music almost more avidly than to their own and English terms pepper their Portuguese as symbols of imported ideas. Women are beginning to

2   **BRAZIL**

move into the work force and find their own identity outside of traditional roles, yet men are still strongly macho.

Accompanying these modern dilemmas is the romance of the pioneer: Brazil still has a sense of its own frontier because the largely undeveloped interior still *is* a frontier, a kind of continental Alaska within everyone's reach. A new wave of Gold Rush fever has struck, sending thousands of prospectors into the jungle to gamble on striking it rich. Undiscovered Indian tribes and unexplored territory exist to a degree now unimaginable in the United States or Europe.

At the social level, destitute urban slums called "favelas" grow up right next to the most luxurious mansions. Wealthy socialites and movie stars rub elbows with their maids and workers during lavish Carnival parades where everyone participates equally in the magic. Yet, in practical terms, the great divide between rich and poor remains as unbridgeable as ever and Brazil continues to be a nation with very few "haves" and countless "have nots."

These extremes are perhaps the only constants in a nation of coexisting inconsistencies. Regional differences remain profound, providing a set of internal subcultures that with time will no doubt be lost to interstate highways, shopping malls, chain restaurants, and national media. The forces of modernization are hard at work in Brazil, but they must resist the powerful pull of the past and so haven't progressed as far as they have elsewhere. The distinctions and distinctiveness of Brazil still endure.

A Glance at Brazil's History

Brazil was discovered in 1500, just eight years after America. How Columbus missed this giant of the Western Hemisphere and touched down upon little San Salvador remains one of the mysteries of that era. Spain was badly in need of new territories and when they put all their money on Columbus they made a mistake, for Portugal was also in need and backed a sea captain named Pedro Alvares Cabral. The Portuguese king was in a landgrab race for the new colonies with the Spanish rulers, and both of them wanted as much as they could get in the shortest amount of time. There were great things coming out of India that could be sold to fill the royal coffers, later to be converted into ships and arms and manpower to dash across the seas again and grab more land.

When Cabral sighted Brazil he thought that he was seeing India, but upon landing and finding none of the expected Maharajas or a road clearly marked "Cathay," he reasoned that he had discovered some place new. He thought it was an island and sent out a search party to walk around once and come back again. What Cabral had stumbled upon was, of course, not an island, but the biggest hunk of land to be claimed in the entire New World.

The Tupi natives were friendly, much to everyone's surprise and pleasure; and after celebrating Mass, Cabral left a few men to watch his new country and then hurried back to Portugal.

The Portuguese referred to the new colony as "The Island of Santa Cruz" (Holy Cross); later when their error was discovered they called

INTRODUCTION 3

the new colony "Land of Santa Cruz." But with the coming of merchant ships from the mother country and the vast exporting of a hard wood called "brazil," the people of Portugal began to refer to the place as "The Land of Brazil." From there it was an easy step to calling it simply Brazil.

The Portuguese were interested in trade, and the long coastal lands of their new-found colony were richer agriculturally than anything the Spanish had been able to claim.

Farmers arrived from Portugal to set up huge sugar and spice farms. They plowed from the present-day city of Olinda down almost to Rio. The land was rich, the nights cool, and there was lots of elbow room. But workers were scarce, and imitating their Spanish enemies, they set out to enslave the local Indians.

The natives—there were many different tribes which were being lumped together under the heading "Indian"—were not accustomed to toiling long, hot afternoons in cane or cotton fields and died off rapidly. Some escaped enslavement by fleeing deeper into the jungle. Later, slaves from the bulge of west Africa were brought in. Swooping down along the Guinea coast and as far south as Angola, Portuguese slave traders attacked villages, killed off the weak, and shackled the strong. The trip to Brazil was long and rough and many died on the way, but those that managed to survive the voyage were brave, hardy, and resourceful.

Soon great wealth was flowing to Lisbon, and the Royal coffers were expanding from the raw materials the Portuguese traded with the rest of Europe. So envious were the other land-hungry nations of the era that the Dutch, French, and Spanish all tried to encroach on Portugal's claim. Much of her new wealth was spent in keeping the intruders at bay.

While riches were being reaped from the soil in the northeast, other riches were being dug up in the mountains to the south. No sooner had the present site of Rio de Janeiro been put on the map than thousands of fortune hunters poured through it on the way to the mines of Minas Gerais. Here were what seemed like entire mountains of amethysts, aquamarines, and diamonds waiting to be scooped up. A procession of miners and trouble-makers took over an area many times bigger than Alaska. Wealth made them remember how the nobility had lived back home, and as soon as a miner had enough to live, he wanted to live well. By the boat loads from Portugal came carpenters, stonemasons, sculptors, and painters to build churches, palaces, and cities in the Brazilian wilderness. Up went such architectural treasures as Ouro Petro and Diamantina. There were gas lights and golden horse-drawn coaches in the streets and gem-studded, silver ornaments in the churches. Lace came from Europe to adorn milord's cuffs, and actors and musicians brave enough to make the trip from Portugal had diamonds tossed to them after their performances.

Other men were busy too. A hardy group of adventurous, bloodthirsty crusaders banded together near what is now São Paulo and set out to find more diamond mines and more riches. Carrying the flag of the new colony, these "Bandeirantes" (Flag Bearers) pushed out in all directions, claiming each new step for Portugal. There had been a

BRAZIL

Treaty of Tordesillas signed between Portugal and Spain in the year 1494. It was the idea of Pope Alexander VI, who wanted as little blood spilled in the New World as possible. Both sides agreed to the dividing of the southern continent in a straight line from what is now Belem on the Amazon River to a little east of Porto Alegre. Everything to the west belonged to Spain, everything to the east to Portugal.

Fortunately for modern Brazil the Bandeirantes knew nothing of this treaty, didn't care, or didn't have a compass. For they spread out over thousands of miles, planting their banner on the banks of the Amazon to the north, Paraná to the south, and on the Paraguayan and Bolivian frontiers to the west. Spaniards, so busy with wars with the Indians, hadn't any idea what was going on in the heart of their lands. When they finally woke up it was too late, for the Bandeirantes had claimed it all for Portugal.

Brazil was ruled from afar by Portugal for many years. When Napoleon captured Portugal, the royal family fled to the new colony. It was like a shot in the arm for the New World. At once the exiled royal family opened the ports of Brazil to trade with some European nations, especially with Napoleon's enemy, England. When the French were defeated, the king, Dom João VI, went back to Portugal and left his young son Pedro I to govern. But Pedro had ideas of his own and did away with a number of reforms his father had set up. He proclaimed Brazil's independence on Sept. 7, 1822. As a new nation, Brazil had a long way to go and a lot to learn. So unsure was the nation and so ineptly governed, that after a series of costly wars with Argentina and Uruguay, Dom Pedro I stepped aside in favor of his son Pedro II, who was only five years old. A series of regents then came into power that managed so badly parliament finally decreed Dom Pedro II "of age" when he was just 14.

Then came almost a half century of peaceful and fruitful ruling on the part of the Western Hemisphere's only Emperor (if you don't count the short reign of Maximilian in Mexico), who mingled with his subjects, made a trip to the United States, and declared that he would rather have been a school teacher than an emperor. Under his constant vigilance the nation prospered, trade agreements were signed, an attempt by Argentina to take control was put down. Princesa Isabel freed the slaves on May 13, 1888 by signing the "Lei Auréa," Brazil's Emancipation Proclamation. But a democratic movement was brewing in the military, and in spite of progress and prosperity the army took over and banished Pedro and his royal family back to Portugal. On November 15, 1889, the Republic was born.

Thereafter Brazilian history grows dull with the parade of easily forgettable presidents and minor revolutionaries. There were all sorts of problems that needed to be solved, and very few able men around to solve them. Brazil stuck mostly to what the U.S. was doing politically, while staying close to France for its cultural instruction. Politicians made a number of efforts to gain power at the expense of the nation but the proud giant, in spite of them, kept growing.

Brazil has had very few actual internal wars and has never had a real, bloody revolution à la Spanish-American style. There have been some

INTRODUCTION 5

skirmishes among the gauchos in the south, and once in 1932 the state of São Paulo took on the rest of the nation. It lost.

Getulio Vargas was a strongman who took over in a military coup in 1930. The country was horrified, but soon liked the idea of having one man in charge and did very little except grumble against him. When he was deposed by another military coup in 1945 he sat out his exile on his home ranch in Rio Grande do Sul and prepared for the elections. In 1951 he was elected—legally this time—president of the Republic and right beside him rode his protegé Joao "Jango" Goulart, later to govern the nation. Vargas tried to be more democratic this second time around and supported labor unions and the like, but still that old obstacle, the Latin military, was against him. After a long period of interoffice fights and counter charges, the tired old man put a pistol to his heart and pulled the trigger.

After him came President Café Filho, and then the dynamic spend-thrift Juscelino Kubitschek. Kubitschek built Brasilia from a dream into a multimillion dollar reality and put industry and commerce on a fast pace to compete with the rest of the world.

His immediate successor was Janio Quadros, a thin man with a thick moustache who insisted that everything be done exactly his way. He wrote little notes that became law, and tried to squeeze the growing giant of a nation into a special form that he never quite defined. Under some pressure, he suddenly resigned one day in August 1961 and threw the nation as close to a civil war as it has ever come. (Quadros is currently the mayor of the city of São Paulo.)

The successor to Quadros was leftist-leaning, rabble-rousing Jango Goulart, the old pupil and confidant of Dictator Vargas. The military wanted little of Jango and his friends, and above all did not want the plans and mass platitudes of Vargas back again. In a dramatic ten days, the military kept Jango—on his way home from a trip to Red China when Quadros resigned—out of the capital and virtually a prisoner in his home state of Rio Grande do Sul. Congress hastily voted in a Parliamentary system, drastically curtailing the President's powers, and Jango finally took office, managing to persuade the people to vote the old presidential system back the following year.

Under Goulart the country seethed with strikes and instability. Prices soared to an all-time high and red-tinged politicians were appointed to key positions all over the nation. Goulart himself became swayed by ambitious leftists and many Brazilians feared for their country as never before. Then on March 31, 1964, Goulart was overthrown by the military. As before, the revolt was virtually bloodless, and while Goulart and his family fled into exile in Uruguay, where he died in 1977, the army clamped down and installed one of their own men, General Humberto de Alencar Castello Branco, as president. Again, Brazil had a military government, but this one was different. The Army seized Brazil by the scruff of its neck and shook it—hard. Sweeping reforms paid dividends as inflation began to drop, exports to rise, and overall growth to move out of the red where Jango had left it to a steady 10 percent within 5 years. Hundreds of old-time politicians lost their political rights, and two new parties replaced the countless former ones. In 1967, Castello Branco handed over the presidency to Marshal Costa

BRAZIL

e Silva, who closed Congress and made things difficult for dissident students and labor leaders. Upon his death in 1969 he was replaced by General Emilio Garrastazu Médici, who continued the Army's reform policy, strengthened the economy, waged war on illiteracy, and initiated bold development plans for the Northeast and Amazon regions.

Médici was succeeded in 1975 by retired General Ernesto Geisel, son of German immigrants and Brazil's first Protestant president. Geisel, who was previously head of the state petroleum enterprise, Petrobrás, maintained most of the policies that brought about Brazil's "economic miracle" and at the same time tried to bring more political liberty and an equitable distribution of wealth. But the petroleum crisis caused problems, and the country's growth slowed from 9.2 percent in 1976 to about 6 percent in 1977 as his government took anti-inflationary measures. Inflation, however, soared again in 1980, hitting 110 percent. This sudden upward surge forced the Brazilian government to take strong anti-inflationary measures in 1981, which, together with the general economic recession in the western world, produced the country's first negative growth since World War II. In 1983 growth was 3.9 percent negative. Trade problems forced a devaluation of the cruzeiro by 30 percent in February, 1983—over 200 percent inflation.

The next president of Brazil, João Figueiredo, a former army general chosen by the military to succeed Geisel, vowed to return the nation to democracy. After taking office in 1979, Figueiredo took the country a long way toward realizing that goal. Press censorship ended, political prisoners were released, and exiles living abroad were able to return without facing arrest or harassment. General elections for all offices except president were held in November, 1982.

In January, 1985, Tancredo Neves was chosen to be President by the Electoral College, made up of Congress and representatives from state legislatures. Although this was not a direct election by the public, Neves is generally regarded as having been the first popularly elected president in Brazil's history because he took his campaign to the people and conducted it as if it *were* a direct election. This tactic created so much popular momentum in his favor that the Electoral College was under considerable pressure to vote for Neves.

A man of advanced age and failing health, Neves fell ill and died before he could take office. After a great outpouring of grief, the nation consolidated behind José Sarney, who assumed the presidency in Neve's stead. In February, 1986, Sarney launched an economic package which established the cruzado as the new currency of Brazil and, in its first phase, lowered the inflation rate from 16 percent to 1 percent a month. Sarney has already changed the constitution to set up direct elections and supported the fourth rewriting of Brazil's constitution, which occurred in 1987. In addition, Sarney is attempting to address issues of social justice, such as the status of women and agrarian reform.

The Brazilian Heritage

The people of Brazil are a symphony in colors. There are few other nations on earth where such a wide spread of skin tones from whitest

INTRODUCTION 7

white to yellow to tan to deepest black are all grouped under one nationality.

Brazil has long been praised for its alleged lack of discrimination and overt racial prejudice. Although a "black revolution" like that in the United States is unlikely to occur in Brazil, the surface calm is deceptive. There is no discernible feeling of unity among Brazilian blacks or between blacks and mulattoes similar to the organizations of Afro-Americans that brought about the far-reaching social reforms in the U.S. over the past 20 years. There are few, if any, black or mulatto diplomats, judges, or ranking government officials, very few physicians, dentists, college professors, lawyers, or ranking officers in the armed services. In the latter case, a large proportion of enlisted men are black or mulatto but they are commanded by whites.

The mixture that makes up Brazilians began way back in the colonial days when the first Portuguese sailors were left to manage the new land. From the beginning, Portuguese migration to Brazil was almost entirely male. Unlike the British, who migrated to the new world in families, the Portuguese colonizers were men who arrived alone, a situation which encouraged unbridled sexual license, ranging from seduction to rape, first of Indian women and later of African women brought to Brazil as slaves. Miscegenation and cohabitation between white men and women of other races was always practiced openly, and such unions naturally produced children, who, in turn, mated and produced their own offspring. Eventually, both the Catholic Church and the Crown urged such couples to marry. Thus were born the Brazilian people.

In the old plantation houses, it was quite common for the master of the house to have a white wife and a series of slave concubines. All sets of children would be raised together, until the arrival of adolescence and the assumption of adult roles put everyone in their proper places.

Under a benevolent master, a baby of color might be looked upon as an heir by his white father, who might free the mother and allow the son to learn and practice a trade. The father knew that the mother would stay on and work for him and that she needed a place to rear her child, there being no other real alternative for her. After a certain point in the movement toward Abolition, the wombs of slave women were freed (that is, children born to them were free), but the mothers themselves were still considered slaves. There were times when a mulatto son turned out to be smarter, more gifted, or better loved than the master's white sons, and might even be allowed to inherit a share of the plantation upon his father's death. But while acts of munificence like this were thinkable and doable, they should not be wrongly construed. Slavery in Brazil was still a cruel institution, and its legacy continues.

So does the old pattern of interracial and sexual relations. Today, women are still relatively powerless within the society. White men are frequently paired with women of color, but interracial marriages are rare. Open liaisons between white women and blacks or mulattoes are rarer and meet with considerable disapproval due to the class differential correlating with race.

BRAZIL

Slavery in Brazil

Slavery as an economic and social institution was as fundamental to Brazil's history as it was to the history of the United States, with significant similarities and differences. The first African slaves arrived in 1532, along with the Portuguese colonizers, who continued to buy them systematically from English, Spanish, and Portuguese slave traders until 1855. All records pertaining to the slave-trading period were destroyed in 1890, making it impossible to know exactly how many slaves were brought to Brazil, but it is estimated that about 3.3 million were captured and shipped from the Sudan, Gambia, Sierra Leone, Liberia, Senegal, Nigeria, Angola, Mozambique, and Guinea. Many were literate Moslems who were better educated than their white overseers and owners.

The slaves were put to work on the sugar plantations, which depended for their existence on black workers. When the sugar boom came to an end, the days of slavery were numbered: It became too expensive for slaveholders to support their "free" labor force. Abolition in Brazil occurred without a cataclysmic American-style civil war and was a gradual process, beginning around 1871 with the passage of the Law of the Free Womb, which liberated all Brazilians born of slave mothers. In 1885, another law was passed freeing slaves over age 60. Finally, on May 13, 1888, Princesa Isabel signed the law freeing all slaves.

As in the United States, sudden freedom for the slaves was a mixed blessing. Uneducated, unskilled, unaccustomed to conducting their affairs or organizing their lives, the former slaves entered a permanent unemployed, underprivileged underclass. Considered racially inferior by their owners during slave times, Afro-Brazilians are still the lowest on the economic and social ladder, with an average of 2.1 years of schooling compared with 4.8 years for whites. No matter what their occupation, blacks do not receive equal pay for equal work, and the work they do is undervalued. The implications of this situation for women of color, who also face sexual discrimination, are obvious.

The legendary Xica da Silva, a slave concubine elevated to the status of mistress of the manor by her wealthy master, then consigned to oblivion and abandonment when he was ordered back to Portugal by the Crown, vividly demonstrates the nexus of Brazilian sexual and racial politics. Xica's story was dramatized by Carlos Diegues, a white Brazilian filmmaker, in a movie named after her which is both entertaining and illuminating. Diegues also made a film called *Quilombo*, based on the Quilombo dos Palmares, a kingdom of unsubdued slaves who formed a community of refugees that lasted over 100 years until it was destroyed in a desperate fight for freedom. November 20, the anniversary of the death of Zumbi, the leader of Palmares, has been named National Black Consciousness Day.

The Vanishing Indians

In the center of Mato Grosso and in the Amazonian states, tribes still roam along the watersheds and the deep jungles exactly as they did

INTRODUCTION

thousands of years ago. Very little is known of their origins. They seem to have none of the ability that the Indians of Peru or Mexico had in pottery or painting but bear remarkable resemblance to the tall proud Polynesians. Theories abound as to their origin, many people having the idea that they drifted over the Andes from Peru about the same time that other Peruvian Indians were taking boats for the South Seas. Others say they were always in the heart of the jungle and have been flushed out because of the scientific light of the 20th century. Still others hold them as remnants of the original peoples from the lost continent of Atlantis. Whoever they are, and wherever they came from, they make up one of the most interesting segments of the Brazilian population.

Unfortunately, the Brazilian Indian has suffered largely the same fate as has his U.S. and Canadian cousin in being pushed back constantly and falling ready victim to European avarice and disease. Like an endangered species, the natives have been driven from their natural habitat by the encroachment of "civilization." Some die, some opt to enter the mainstream of Brazilian culture, but either way, experts predict their time is limited and they will soon be extinct.

There are over 170 Indian cultural groups speaking as many languages in Brazil today, each tribe with its own well-developed system of religious beliefs, social customs, economic activities, and relationship to the majority culture of Brazil. Between 2 million and 5 million Indians are thought to have lived on the land that constitutes modern Brazil when the Portuguese discovered it in 1500. Contact with the colonizers proved fatal for most of them, and the number of Indians is estimated to be between 187,000 and 227,000 today.

From the beginning, the Portuguese fell into two camps in terms of their attitudes toward the natives: the missionaries, who wanted to tame them and convert them to Catholicism, and the colonizers, who wished to enslave them. The missionaries lost, and the Portuguese Bandeirantes proceeded to carry on a relentless persecution of the Indians designed to "liberate" the lands they occupied. When it became obvious that the Indians could not be enslaved, the men were slaughtered and the women were taken captive.

In 1831, an attitude of protectionism surfaced, but it was too weak to put a stop to the never-ending Indian wars. In 1850, all property in Brazil was divided into public and private lands, which technically entitled the Indians to possession of their territories. However, since the Indians had no Western notion of land ownership and could not manipulate the colonial legal system in their favor, they wound up being driven off or cheated of their land.

Efforts to protect the Indians achieved some success under Coronel Rondon, who directed the first Service for the Protection of the Indians, founded in 1910. Rondon, an intrepid explorer and a great friend of Theodore Roosevelt, had already come into contact with many native tribes in the process of constructing telegraph lines through the interior of the country. Initially under the aegis of the Ministry of Agriculture, the agency under Rondon's direction adopted a new posture toward the Indians. They were to be allowed to practice their own traditions and were guaranteed possession of their lands, which were

BRAZIL

now to be regarded as inalienable rights. They were also granted the rights of Brazilian citizenship. Funds and qualified personnel to institute these measures were exhausted, however, and by 1930, well after Rondon had left as bureau chief, the protective service for the Indians fell into administrative corruption so serious that it was eventually abolished and replaced by a new agency under the Minister of the Interior, the Fundação Nacional do Indio (FUNAI).

FUNAI, founded in 1967, still exists and is responsible for mediating between the conflicting interests of the Indians and those of developers building roads and communities within Indian territories. FUNAI operates over 150 stations throughout Brazil, supposedly to serve Indians, and also administers the parks and Indian reservations that have been established. Not surprisingly, few are satisfied with the job FUNAI is doing, and it is increasingly falling to a new group of Indian leaders, sophisticated in the art of straddling cultures, to speak up for the interests of Indians and defend them in the mainstream culture.

A Nation of Immigrants

For many Europeans and Asians, Brazil, not America, was the land of opportunity, and like the United States, Brazil owes a great deal to the waves of immigrants who built their lives there.

After the initial bands of colonizers and the massive involuntary immigration of Africans came others, first Europeans, then Japanese, and most recently, Latin Americans from neighboring countries.

Immigration to Brazil did not begin in earnest until the abolition of slavery. The greatest wave of immigrants arrived between 1884 and 1914, and the overwhelming majority of these were Italians. In 1908 the Japanese began to arrive. These two groups permanently transformed Brazilian agriculture. Many entered under a program of modified indentured servitude in which they were required to work for a large farm, then buy their way out of poverty with savings and the benevolence of the boss. (*Gaijin,* a film portraying the first Japanese immigrants, dramatizes this struggle.)

Immigration came to a virtual standstill during World War II, then picked up again as refugees from both sides of the European conflict sought sanctuary. Between 1974 and 1975, Brazil welcomed 50,000 Portuguese, mostly ex-colonials from Angola and Mozambique.

Immigrants make up a large percentage of Brazil's populace. And once they have become established they are considered Brazilian and no longer as "foreigners." Of all countries, Portugal still sends the most immigrants per year. There are a great number of Italians (especially in the industrial São Paulo area) and many Germans and Poles in the rich agricultural south. A very important group of immigrants to Brazil are the Japanese. Many of them came before World War II, and a great many more followed. Because of special treaties signed between Brazil and Japan, they were given land, special farming equipment, and special considerations. What they have managed to do with the land, especially in the Amazon area where they've filled local markets with fruits and vegetables hitherto unknown, is truly impressive.

INTRODUCTION 11

All of these races and nationalities have managed to get mixed together in Brazil's melting pot, and there is a beneficial national trait of "live and let live" that is commendable. You are unlikely to find people attacking or killing others for purely racial motives. Racial hatred, per se, is difficult to maintain in a nation of mixed genetic inheritance. At the same time, wealth correlates positively with whiteness, resulting in resentments born of economic causes. Although Brazilians do not call this de facto discrimination "racism," there is much tension beneath the friendly surface.

Brazil Today

When you stop and remember that most Brazilians in the cities have an education that goes only to the eighth grade and that many in the interior who have but three or four years of schooling are considered "educated," you will marvel that anything has been done to improve the country at all.

In spite of these problems, Brazil is making giant strides into the industrialized world. Already its economy ranks as the eighth largest in the free world, its gross national product is twice that of Mexico, and Brazilian exports sell so well abroad that they now bring an annual positive trade balance to the country.

Brazil has shown more gains in manufacturing, exports, agricultural, and educational improvements than any other nation in Latin America. Although the desire to put everything off until tomorrow and go to the beach today is always strong, there are many who are doing things for their country.

The population of greater São Paulo is now over 14 million and Rio has around 8 million inhabitants. Industrially speaking, São Paulo is now the heartbeat of Latin America economy. It has few unemployed, and an intelligent system of social services and public improvements. Across the nation highways are being cut through jungles and over mountains. Twenty-five years ago the road between the two cities was unpaved and impassable during the rainy season. Today there is a double-lane toll freeway, partly financed by U.S. aid. But although highway construction has been a top priority of all post-1964 governments, there are still only about 50,000 miles of paved highway in the whole country, little more than the U.S. had in 1840.

For its manufacturing, Brazil needs power and lots of it. In the past few years the country has been building huge plants in the Paraná River area to service São Paulo, one in the interior of Minas Gerais and two others in the northeast. The mighty Itaipu project, built in partnership with Paraguay, was inaugurated in 1982 and is the largest hydroelectric power plant in the world. Brazil also has its first nuclear power plant operating near Angra dos Reis between São Paulo and Rio. With this energy, Brazil manufactures enough plastics, textiles, automobiles, toys, canned foods, cement, and chemicals to satisfy the home consumer without importing. But some wheat, rubber, petroleum, paper, and machinery for both light and heavy industry must be imported. Economists predict, however, a likelihood of the country becoming self-sufficient in food and many other critical resources in the near future.

12 BRAZIL

Brazil hopes enough oil will be discovered offshore to bring self-sufficiency in that area too. Recent discoveries indicate that this once-distant goal may be reached by the end of the century, freeing Brazil from its costly dependency on imported oil.

With respect to health, the government has been busy with the eradication of malaria, yellow fever, denguê, and other mosquito-borne diseases. Efforts have been concentrated in Belem and Manaus to stamp out the dreaded Chagas disease that comes from the bite of little beetles. The Butantan Snake Farm in São Paulo has been doing great work with venoms from snakes, spiders, and scorpions making antidotes for the bites and supplying them free of charge to doctors and interior clinics. Hospitals are being built all over the nation, but the problem of persuading doctors and nurses to leave the big cities to staff them remains. Almost every town has a free clinic that is open day and night for anyone who needs attention; they do everything from setting broken legs to delivering babies.

Many efforts have been made in recent years to update the country's education system on all levels, starting with a nationwide literacy campaign and ending with university reforms. Secondary education has been restructured to stress the practical arts and sciences more heavily than preparation for university; previously, the system turned out a huge surplus of poets and politicians, but too few plumbers, scientists, and computer programmers.

Geographically Speaking

People get set ideas of Brazil's geography either from seeing too many picture postcards or remembering too many Hollywood films. Actually a great part of this enormous nation consists of hilly uplands, plateaus, and low mountains. There is a vast plain that stretches far into the Amazon region and another that spreads out through Mato Grosso and into Bolivia and Paraguay. The Brazilian highlands are some of the oldest geological formations anywhere on earth. These hills are granite and other tough stones that are heavily veined with gold, diamonds, and a variety of semiprecious stones. The Serra do Espinhaço (Spiny Mountains) that run from northern Minas Gerais to Bahia also contain iron ore, gold, and manganese. Here the highest mountain in central Brazil can be found, old Pico da Bandeira (Flag Top), which stands 9,482 feet. Another recently discovered peak in the state of Amazonas is even higher—Neblina (Haze) reaching 9,889 feet. One of the world's largest lava plateaus is to be found in the south of Brazil; termed the Paraná plateau, it is covered with dark, purple-colored soil that is excellent for raising coffee. Along the coast rich deposits of oil have been found.

The eastern side of the Brazilian highland descends abruptly into the sea and has been given the name "The Great Escarpment." There is no coastal plain but a sloping series of steppes that continues far out into the water. All along this there is a series of small rivers and sandy beaches. Wide expanses of white sand reach from way above Recife down past the Uruguayan border. Some beautiful, unspoiled beaches can be found in the far north and the far south. The sands in the states

INTRODUCTION

13

of Paraná and Santa Catarina, for example, are solid and pure. The lack of tourists and year-round dwellers keeps them that way. This combination of sand and escarpment has given Brazil some of the finest natural harbors in the world. Rio is perhaps the best known, but the harbors at Santos, Bahia, Recife, São Luiz, Vitória, and Ilhéus have contributed greatly to the wealth of the nation.

Brazil's rivers are some of the longest and deepest in the world. For scientific study, they've been broken into the three major systems that drain the country's highlands. The first, in the north, is the mighty, almost unbelievable Amazon River, fed by the waters that pour down through jagged peaks, lush jungles, and rich plateaus. Its tributaries sound and look exotic and offer the visitor who is not afraid of discomfort some of the most unforgettable experiences in Latin America. There the great Tocantins and the Araguaia flow. There are the mysterious and unexplored Xingú, the rubber-laden Tapajós and the Madeira. To the far west runs the impressive, and almost unknown, Rio Negro.

The second river system gathers the waters from southwestern Minas Gerais and empties them into the placid yet treacherous Paraná. The water on the western slope of the São Paulo Escarpment flows until it reaches the sea by joining the Rio de la Plata near Buenos Aires.

The almost legendary São Francisco, the largest river wholly within Brazil, is the third system. Beginning in the plateau near Brasília it flows northward for over a thousand miles until it pours into the sea between the states of Sergipe and Alagoas. Navigable and studded with power plants, the São Francisco has been the main artery to the heart of Brazil for generations.

The vegetation in Brazil varies according to climate and geological conditions. In the Amazon Basin and places along the coast where the rainfall is very heavy, there is a tropical rain forest where broadleafed trees and shrubs grow to gigantic proportions and as many as 3,000 different species of trees have been catalogued within a single square mile. Through these tall shady trees very little sunlight manages to filter down, and consequently the ground is rich in decaying foliage, industrious bugs, and small animals. In the northeast, lack of rain has produced a parched desert of hundreds of square miles, where cattle and humans die together in their search for water. In the south huge stands of pine trees grow wild and are used in the manufacture of paper. There are open prairies that start in São Paulo state and run down into Argentina to form the Brazilian pampas. In the northeast rain forests stand the huge Jacaranda trees and the very wood that gave the nation its name, the Brazil tree. The Jacaranda is a hard, beautifully grained dark wood almost like mahogany. Most of the fine colonial furniture in the antique shops was made from this wood. Durable yet attractive, it is one of the most sought-after materials in use today.

Sugar, Rubber, and Coffee

That a country as big as Brazil used to be a "one crop" country has always amazed outsiders. "Banana Republics" are usually small islands, not nations as large as the continental United States. Yet until

BRAZIL

recently, when industrialization diversified the country's economic base, Brazil's entire economy rested on a series of agricultural products the way the American South relied on "King Cotton" before the Civil War.

First there was sugar. It was the earliest crop established on the new lands. The Portuguese crown eagerly awaited the money that sugar gave to the Royal coffers. The climate along the coast, from far below Bahia to way above Recife, was perfect for its growth. It was hot and muggy with abundant rainfall. It added to the nation's prosperity, population, and culture. Then other empire builders like Great Britain and France began to plant and sell sugar on the world market. The Brazilians had to lower their prices and improve their quality to meet the competition. But the English-speaking and the French-speaking peoples preferred their own sugar, put high tariffs on the Brazilian product and almost drove it completely out of competition.

Fortunately rubber was just coming into its own in the Amazon. There were all sorts of uses for rubber in the United States and in Europe. Once it had been discovered that rubber could be vulcanized for longer lasting and more efficient service, there was almost no industry that didn't want and need Brazil's crop. The town of Manaus in the heart of the Amazonian jungle grew to international importance. Jenny Lind came to sing there in a lavish opera house, one of several monumental buildings constructed during the boom years. Supporting all this luxury were thousands of Indian, black, and white day laborers, working deep in the malarial jungles under slavelike conditions. The rubber trees grew wild and had to be worked where they were found. Planting them according to then-popular agricultural precepts produced no rubber at all. Then an Englishman visited the interior and smuggled out a few hundred rubber seeds which he took to Indonesia and cultivated. There the trees flourished, and in seven years Indonesia was competing with Brazil. The Brazilians, proud and overly sure of themselves, refused to lower their prices to meet the new competition. Buyers flocked to Indonesia and almost overnight Brazil was driven out of the rubber market.

The next crop to rise to importance was coffee, first in the State of Rio de Janeiro, then in São Paulo. Coffee had become an important cash crop in southern Brazil, and with rubber out of the way, all energy was devoted to increasing coffee production. São Paulo had the ideal climate of chilly weather followed by warm and rainy days. There was fertile land that was more European in makeup than in Bahia or other places. There was also the added advantage of Italian and German immigrants who wanted to be farmers and raise a cash crop. With everything working smoothly, coffee soon became the most important national product and Brazil depended heavily on it.

Coffee actually built the gigantic industrial city of São Paulo. With the money the growers got from the exports and the taxes the state got from the growers, new industries were started and new ideas tried. There were even many small industries that sprang from the by-products of coffee. The protein in coffee is used to modify certain oils and tars. The carbohydrates are used in the making of cellulose, dyestuffs, and plastics. The coffee bean oil is used in dozens of varied industries.

INTRODUCTION 15

While production has increased elsewhere, particularly in Africa, Brazil remains the world's biggest coffee grower. Surpluses have disappeared, due in part to controls imposed by the International Coffee Agreement.

Catholicism and the Church of the Spirits

Brazil is officially a Roman Catholic country. The Holy See in the Vatican likes to boast that it is the "largest Catholic country in the world," and at first glance it may appear to be, for there are beautiful churches and cathedrals ranging from the colonial to the baroque and modern all over the nation. The church owns huge parcels of choice lands in Rio and São Paulo; and in interior towns long-robed fathers and nuns can be seen everywhere. When a president takes the oath of office there is always a priest and a Bible close at hand. Children study catechism, are baptized with the names of saints, and attend Catholic schools. Everybody wears a religious medal or two. Taxi and bus drivers have prints of St. Christopher prominently placed, and in June the two biggest winter celebrations are reserved for St. John and St. Peter. To the tourist, overcome with the gold and gems of Bahia's São Francisco church or the impressive concrete modernism of the cathedral designed by Oscar Niemeyer in Brasilia, Catholicism and allegiance to Rome seem to be everywhere. Actually, much of this is on the surface. The real church for masses of Brazilians is the church of the spirits.

The Portuguese brought their religion all ready made to the new colony and planted it right along with the rows of cotton and sugar cane. The Indians had their own gods whom they worshipped and, even when driven into slavery, refused to relinquish. When the African blacks were beaten and chained aboard stinking slave ships bound for the new world, they may have been forced to leave their families and their possessions behind, but they brought along their gods. And what an impressive array they were.

Foremost among them was Iemanjá who was the goddess of the rivers and water. There was also Oxalá who was the god of procreation and harvest. Exú was a wicked spirit who could cause mischief or death. There were others of lesser rank, but all powerful, like Ogun, Oxôssi, Xangó, and Yansan. They arrived in Brazil together with the slaves who, when things were going badly, turned to the gods of their homeland.

The Catholic Church was naturally against this, threatened excommunication to the whites who did not control their slaves' religious practices, and threatened corporal punishment to the slaves themselves if they continued to believe in their old gods. The slaves, most of whom came from the very best and aristocratic native tribes, were smart enough to realize they couldn't fight the priests but would have to compromise. So they took on all the ritual of Rome but didn't take their old gods from the high places.

Many times all they did was give the African god a new Christian name. Thus Iemanjá became the Virgin Mary and was queen of the heavens as well as queen of the seas. Oxalá, already most powerful in

BRAZIL

Africa, became the most powerful in Rome, Jesus Christ. Exú, full of evil to begin with, became Satan. Ogun became St. Anthony, Obaluayê became St. Francis, Yansan, St. Barbara, and Oxôssi was turned into St. George. On their altars, along with the sacred white feathers, the magical beads and the bowls of cooked rice and cornmeal, were placed plaster statues of the Virgin, Christ, and gleaming crosses. The Roman Church was content to let matters lie, hoping for an eventual dying off of African tradition over the years and a strengthening of Christian beliefs—which hasn't been the case.

Bahia is still the stronghold of the voodoo religion, which they prefer to call "Candomblé." Rio holds second place with its powerful "Macumba" and Recife is third with its spiritist doctrine called "Xangô." Visitors to all three places—as well as almost any small town across the nation—can witness a voodoo ceremony. All it takes is an arrangement with someone who knows the right time and place, and the patience and good manners to sit through the ceremony once you get there.

Rites on the Beach

There is no stranger or more pagan sight in all Latin America than that which takes place on the sands of Copacabana Beach each new Year's Eve, a ceremony that is enacted on every beach along Brazil's extensive coastline. Travelers who have seen things all over the world still stare at this with fascination and disbelief. For under the warm, tropical sky and with the tall modern apartment buildings for a background, literally thousands of voodoo worshippers meet to pay homage to Iemanjá, the goddess of the sea.

The end of the old year is a time for thanksgiving and the beginning of a new year is the time to ask for the things that will make you happy for the next twelve months. From all over the city stream the faithful, determined to start the new year off right. They are of all ages, both sexes, and all colors and economic brackets. Armed with fresh flowers, candles, and cachaça (sugarcane alcohol), they invade the beach around 10 P.M. and get ready for the stroke of midnight. Some draw mystic signs in the sand. Others lay out a white tablecloth loaded with the gifts that a proud, beautiful woman would like to receive. There are combs, mirrors, lipsticks, hair ribbons, perfumes, and wines. Around this offering they set a chain of lit candles and chant and sing over it. Some of them bring bouquets of flowers with notes asking for special favors tucked in among the blossoms. Even whole spiritist temples show up in full force, with their white costumes, drummers, and altars. They rope off a section of the beach, light candles, and begin to dance. Others bring a live chicken or goat that will be sacrificed to the goddess.

By 11:20 P.M. the six-kilometer-long beach is a mass of white-dressed bodies and flickering candles. From a distance it looks as if it has been invaded by millions of fireflies. Amid the worshippers, the curious and the tourist may freely wander, if careful not to step on an offering or to offend the goddess in any way.

At exactly midnight, fireworks, sirens, and bells can be heard from all parts of Copacabana, Ipanema, and Leblon beaches. Now the fes-

INTRODUCTION   17

tivity reaches its maximum. Shrieking, sobbing, and singing, the mass of humanity rushes into the water carrying the flowers and gifts for the goddess. Others stay patiently on the shore waiting for the third wave after the stroke of midnight to come up and claim their offering. Be it hypnotic suggestion or whatever, the waves suddenly seem to grow in size and come slapping onto the sand with a new fury. Once the water has carried the gift into the sea, the giver relaxes and goes home, for this means that the goddess was satisfied with the gift and has promised to grant all wishes. If the ocean should throw the offerings back, this is considered an ill omen.

Many are the aristrocratic white Carioca women who decline to attend the festivities but, nevertheless, excuse themselves to place bare feet in water on the stroke of midnight!

Music

Brazil is one of the world's most musical countries, and talent flourishes in the tropical climate as exuberantly as the exotic creepers that grow two inches a day. Brazil is well known for having invented the samba and bossa nova, but just take a look at the list of "serious" musicians Brazil has also given the world in this century: composers Heitor Villa-Lobos, Claudio Santoro, Camargo Guarnieri, and Marlos Nobre; pianists Guiomar Novaes, Ophelia de Nascimento, Jacques Klein, Roberto Szidon, Joao Carlos Martins, and Nelson Freire; singers Bidu Sayao, Maura Moreira, Maria d'Apparecida, Joao Gibin, and Maria Lucia Godoy; guitarists Eduardo and Sergio Abreu; conductors Eleazar de Carvalho and Isaac Karabtschevsky; early music specialist Roberto de Regina and ballerina Marcia Haydée, to mention only a few.

The four musical centers of Brazil are Rio, São Paulo, Salvador, and Curitiba. Salvador has the best music school, where many rising young composers have learned their trade from a German-influenced faculty; Curitiba presents an annual music festival that puts anything similar in the rest of South America to shame, while both Rio and São Paulo offer a musical season that can match that of many a European capital in quality.

Rio's musical life, like the city itself, is essentially cosmopolitan, with fine musical performances. You never know whom you might discover for yourself at Rio's Teatro Municipal or Sala Cecilia Meireles (a rare example nowadays of a cinema's being converted into a concert hall). One advantage is that you can usually get a ticket if you show up half an hour before the concert, unless a major international star is appearing, in which case book a few days in advance.

There is also the popular music of Brazil, "musica popular brasileira" (MPB), which, in the form of bossa nova and samba, has reached out and embraced the entire world with its happy, vibrant rhythms. Brazilians are equally in love with their music and every city has dozens of bars and restaurants where drums and guitars blend into the hypnotic sounds of MPB. For tourists wishing to buy records, there are plenty from which to choose: Tom Jobim, João Gilberto, Chico Buarque de Holanda, Milton Nascimento, Ney Matagrosso, Gilberto Gil, Gaetano

BRAZIL

Veloso, and Roberto Carlos. Among female singers, Gal Costa, Maria Bethania, Elba Remalho, Alcione, Tetê Espindola, and Simone are the best-known. Record stores can be found along virtually any commercial district and in all shopping centers. If you see a record you like, ask to hear it first. Records, unfortunately, are also expensive in Brazil, running up to $10 for a popular LP. But nowhere else will you find the variety or quality of this exciting music.

Architecture

Brazilian architecture, though it has not fulfilled the bright promise of the thirties, has much to offer both the architectural student and the amateur photographer. The most striking modern building in Rio, the Palace of Culture, completed in 1945, is now protected as a national monument. When started, it was one of the most revolutionary buildings anywhere in the world, being one of the first to be built on *pilotis*—huge concrete pillars that leave almost all the ground level of the site free for patios, plants, and parking areas.

Le Corbusier, a long-time friend of Brazil, was largely responsible for the design, ably assisted by the brilliant Brazilian Lucio Costa, the man who planned Brasilia and the Barra de Tijuca suburb of Rio. Take a stroll among the pillars and gardens of the Ministry for a glimpse of what 20th-century city planning could be like if visionaries like Le Corbusier and Costa had their way. The block it occupies is an oasis of civilized urban delight in one of the world's most overcrowded and underplanned cities. (Students of population explosion may like to study the average Copacabana residential street, where the cars park on the sidewalks and the children play ball in the street, and draw their own conclusions.)

Equally delightful is a stroll around the Rio Museum of Modern Art, designed by the late Affonso Reidy, whose exuberant use of concrete is matched by his structural daring; the whole floor of the Museum's main wing is one single slab without divisions or central supports, and all around are the splendid gardens laid out by Roberto Burle Marx, one of the outstanding landscape gardeners of our time. A disastrous fire swept this building in 1978, but it is being restored. Its artistic holdings, however, can never be replaced and it will take years to find and acquire new ones.

For architects, though, Brasilia is the real thing. Despite its many problems it is here to stay and is a truly great place to visit, wander around, and photograph. The air is fresh and unpolluted, the traffic well organized by Brazilian standards, and many of its buildings, like the new Foreign Ministry, are outstanding.

Brazilian Ways

Manners change from place to place, and behavior that English speakers may find impolite constitutes the normal way of doing things in Brazil. For example, it is common to snap one's fingers, hiss, or make a sshhing sound (as if one were trying to tell someone to be quiet) to get a person's attention, especially in stores and restaurants. You'll feel

INTRODUCTION   19

odd doing this at first, but it's the only way the waiter will recognize that you want service. Also, it is considered bad form in restaurants to bring the check before the customer asks for it. What is deemed efficient service in the United States is viewed as a lack of courtesy in Brazil. If you want to pay and leave, request your bill by saying, "A conta, por favor." Toothpicks are provided on every table, and no one feels embarrassed about performing acts of dental hygiene in public.

Attitudes toward smoking reflect another cultural difference. Without the benefit of the American Cancer Society's antismoking campaign, Brazilians remain rabid smokers who see no offense in lighting up in elevators or next to you in a restaurant while you are still eating. There are no "no smoking" sections in Brazilian restaurants or public places. Requests to put out that cigarette are not well received.

Be aware of cultural differences when interpreting Brazilian body language, which is as far from what you are used to as Portuguese is from English. When a Brazilian snaps his fingers several times in succession, he does not mean something was easy or instantaneous—he means that it happened a long time ago. Tugging the earlobe is a sign of approbation and approval. To signal "come here," open and close the hand, palm down, as if waving good-bye to the ground, without fluttering the fingers. Of course, the thumbs-up sign, widely used to mean "everything's OK" or "thanks," is universally understood. The American "A–OK" sign, formed by making a circle with the thumb and forefinger, is an obscene gesture in Brazil.

In general, Brazilians are much more openly affectionate and physical than Americans or British, even with people they don't know well. The women greet each other and male friends with kisses to both cheeks, and men also embrace.

It will save you a lot of aggravation to realize that time does not have the same cultural weight for Brazilians as it does for Americans and Europeans. Punctuality is definitely not a Brazilian strong point. While the business-minded Paulistano can usually be counted on to show up more or less at the appointed hour, the Carioca cannot, and people get slower the farther north you go. In fact, it is common for a Brazilian to appear two or three hours later than planned—if at all—and think that nothing is amiss. You will consider this rude and infuriating; the Brazilian will find it inconsequential and wonder at your compulsiveness. Get used to it. In Brazil, everything is slower and takes longer than you think it's going to, and events often start later than scheduled. Free yourself from the constraints of time; leave your watch at home.

Finally, a well-placed "gorgetinha" ("little tip") can go a long way in Brazil and falls under the heading of what we might call petty bribery. Brazilians call this familiar practice "finding a way" ("dar um jeito"), and it is standard operating procedure everywhere, among all social classes. If you find your path inexplicably obstructed, a discrete "gorjetinha" may very well open doors for you. Remember that what appears to you to be a minor sum—a couple of dollars to the skycap to move you through the airport lines quickly, a few more to the baggage handler so that he won't charge you for excess weight—is a small windfall to the people receiving it, whereas the total to you is less than it would have cost to handle the matter through "proper" chan-

BRAZIL

nels. They're happy because they think they've gotten the better of you, and you're happy because you've avoided bureaucratic hassles. Avoiding entanglement with the Brazilian bureaucracy is always the path of greater wisdom. Bureaucratic red tape has become so great a problem in Brazil that the federal government has created the Office of Debureaucratization, a hopeful if ironic measure.

PLANNING YOUR TRIP

PLANNING YOUR TRIP

Before You Go

WHAT IT WILL COST. In Brazil this comes down to a question of how comfortably you want to travel. It is possible to travel on an extremely low budget. By American standards, Brazil is a travel bargain. With the exception of super deluxe hotels, which cost between $100 and $150 a night for two, comfortable, clean accommodations are available for $17 to $75. However, first class travel is expensive due to the high costs of quality hotels and air travel. In all areas of the country, though, you will find that top restaurants are significantly cheaper than their counterparts in the U.S. or Europe and for the most part the food is excellent, and except in nouvelle cuisine restaurants, a single order of an entree is usually enough for two people.

Even in the most elegant restaurants in Rio and São Paulo, you'll have a hard time spending more than $50 for two and you can eat well for much less. Simple meals run from $3 to $5, fancier ones cost about $15 a person. Entertainment expenses are low, too. You can hear a great concert for $10 or less in a large hall; clubs rarely charge more than a few dollars to get in. Shows sponsored by Funarte, Funarj, Fundação Roberto Marinho, and other arts organizations offer tickets for a dollar or two. If you have a student I.D., further reductions are sometimes available. Bus travel is a fine alternative to the expensive air flights. Brazil has top quality regional bus companies with modern air-conditioned vehicles that crisscross the country on regular and on-time schedules. One warning though: be aware of the distances. Brazil is larger than the continental U.S.

SOURCES OF INFORMATION. Embratur, Brazil's National Tourism Authority, came under the dynamic leadership of João Dória, Jr., in April, 1986. Prior to that, the agency had closed its doors in New York and had discontinued service in European capitals as well. At press time, Embratur's headquarters were located in Rio at Rua Mariz e Barros, 13, near Praça de Bandeira (273–2212). It is likely that the agency will relocate to the Zona Sul, where it will be better able to serve tourists, but for the moment, inquiries should be addressed to the existing address. Meanwhile Embratur's New York bureau has reopened at 551 5th Ave., Suite 421, New York, NY 10176 (916–3206). In Rio, **Pan American Airlines,** Avenida President Wilson, 165 A, Centro (240–6662) and **Varig Airlines,** Brazil's national carrier, at Avenida Rio Branco 128 (222–2535), can both provide information on travel in Brazil.

TRAVEL DOCUMENTS AND CUSTOMS. Brazil requires tourist visas of all citizens of countries demanding visas of Brazilians. This includes the United States, but not Canada and Great Britain.

Americans: Passports and visas—the latter available from the nearest Brazilian Consulate—are required for travel to or in Brazil. A tourist visa, valid for 90 days, is easily obtainable and free. A 2-by-3-inch passport photo, passport, and a round-trip ticket will secure your visa.

Passports must be valid for at least six months from the intended date of arrival in Brazil. Adult passports are valid for 10 years, others for five years.

23

24 BRAZIL

When you receive your passport, write down its number, date and place of issue separately. If it is lost or stolen, notify either the nearest American Consul or the Passport Office, Department of State, Washington, D.C. 20524, as well as the local police.

If a resident alien, you need a Treasury Sailing Permit, Form 1040 C, certifying that federal taxes have been paid; if a non resident alien, Form 1040 NR; apply to your District Director of Internal Revenue for these. You will have to present various documents: (1) blue or green alien registration card; (2) passport; (3) travel tickets; (4) most recently filed Form 1040; (5) W-2 forms for the most recent full year; (6) most recent current payroll stubs or letter; (7) check to be sure this is all! There is an IRS office in the U.S. Embassy in São Paulo. To return to the U.S. you need a reentry permit if you plan to stay abroad more than one year. Apply for it in person at least six weeks before departure at the nearest office of the Immigration and Naturalization Service or by mail to the service, Washington, D.C.

Canadian citizens may obtain application passport forms at any post office; these are to be sent to the Central Passport Office, 125 Sussex Street, Lester B. Pearson Building, Ottawa, Ontario. You may apply in person to the province in which you reside. However, a mailed application must be handled by the central office. A remittance of $20 Canadian, three photographs, and a birth certificate or certificate of Canadian citizenship (naturalization papers) are required. Canadian passports are valid for five years and are nonrenewable.

British citizens may apply for a passport at any U.K. passport office or British consulate, either by mail or in person. Two photographs, a birth certificate or proof of citizenship (naturalization papers), and £5.50 are required.

Customs Entering Brazil. Travelers from abroad may bring duty free to Brazil the following items: clothing, jewelry for personal use, personal books and magazines, cosmetics, and toilet articles; 400 cigarettes and 250 gr. tobacco, and 25 cigars; 2 bottles of any liquor if bought before arriving in Brazil. In addition visitors are allowed to bring one camera, hair dryer, electric razor, video camera, cassette player, tape deck, tape recorder, portable radio, and other electronic devices obviously for personal use. Carrying tools or machines obviously intended for work use or electronic items that are out of the ordinary for personal use (e.g. can openers, typewriters, toasters, microwave ovens) will require justification. You must register such items at the Brazilian Consulate before you leave your country of origin, since you must have permission to enter with them and you will be checked as you leave to make sure you haven't sold them. Get everything in writing, and carry receipts with you, especially if the articles are in their original packaging. It is difficult to get personal computers approved. You are, however, allowed to bring in up to $300 worth of presents over and above those items you intend to use personally. Electronic items may be given as gifts up to this monetary limit. Whatever you buy at the duty free shop between deplaning and passing through customs is to be included as part of the $300. (You are allowed to buy up to $300 worth of liquor, perfumes, and other goods in the duty free shops.) Once you pass customs, you may not reenter the duty free shop, so make all purchases beforehand. Regulations are constantly changing, so make sure to ask and hang on to all paperwork. If you are traveling on business, it is the responsibility of your company to arrange the proper documentation. Otherwise, be prepared for a lot of red tape and/or heavy duties.

Health certificates. No vaccinations are required to enter Brazil unless coming from an infected area.

Pets need to be vaccinated—inquire at the Brazilian embassy as to what is required for your pet, and do so well in advance.

PLANNING YOUR TRIP

WHEN TO GO. Tropical rains are usually intermittent and allow time for outdoor activities. In some towns the rain comes at a certain time during the day and thus seldom interrupts activities because they are planned around it.

There are festivals, special events, and sporting attractions year round.

Seasons below the Equator are the reverse of the north—summer, December 21 to March 20; winter from June 21 to September 20. Temperatures vary with altitudes—warm along the coast, colder in the highlands.

Rio de Janeiro is located on the Tropic of Capricorn and the climate is just that—tropical. In summer, temperatures can rise to 105°F., although the average ranges between 84–95°F. In winter, temperatures stay in the 70s. Occasionally dipping into the 60s. São Paulo, due to its higher altitude, is always cooler than Rio, and the weather fluctuates frequently, even within the same day. Further north where the equator crosses the country, the weather is always hot.

High season in Brazil begins in November and lasts through April, with Carnival as the peak tourist attraction.

AVERAGE TEMPERATURE CHART IN ° FAHRENHEIT

Rio de Janeiro

	Jan.	Feb.	Mar.	Apr.	May	Jun.	Jul.	Aug.	Sept.	Oct.	Nov.	Dec.
Max.	84	85	83	80	77	76	75	76	75	77	79	82
Min.	73	73	72	69	66	64	63	64	65	66	68	71

Carnival Week. Brazil starts Carnival on the weekend preceding Ash Wednesday. A word of caution about "carnival-time" visits. Tourists have complained about minimal hotel services resulting in their rooms being left uncleaned, the beds unmade for days, and late or no breakfasts. Gas pumps and garage services often closed down. Be prepared for the otherwise orderly system to take a holiday during Carnival.

PACKING. Informality is the rule in Rio—fortunately, considering summer (December-March) temperatures occasionally reach a humid 40°C. (104°F.). One seldom sees a tie at Copacabana restaurants or nightclubs. Ironically, jackets and ties are needed in the daytime at some of the better downtown luncheon clubs where bankers and businessmen gather. A hat is needed only on the beach or golf course.

Slacks are acceptable for women. Shorts are worn in beach neighborhoods but not in downtown areas, and bathing suits are about the skimpiest you'll ever see. You will surely see the Brazilian "tanga" (the "string" originated in Rio). In wintertime (summer in the Northern hemisphere), there can be chilly days (in the lower 50s, F.), so a sweater or wrap is a necessity. As a general rule, dress in Rio as you would in Miami, but with seasons reversed.

In São Paulo, weather is cooler and dress is more formal. Temperatures can change rapidly and drastically within a single day, so it's wise to take a jacket or sweater with you wherever you go. Always carry an umbrella in São Paulo. Businessmen often wear suits and ties but not always. Sportswear is enough for a Brasilia sight-seeing trip of a day or two; if you stay longer or have diplomatic contacts, more formal clothing will be needed. But a man will rarely need a dinner jacket in Brazil—unless he wants to swelter at one of Rio's gala Carnival

BRAZIL

balls rather than wear a costume (a common, simple one consists of bright shirt, Hawaiian leis, captain's cap and shorts).

During winter (May to October), you will need warmer clothing in the South, whereas in Bahia, the North, and Northeast, the climate is humid and tropical year-round. Sun glasses and a light raincoat or umbrella are good items to have along when visiting anyplace in Brazil. Outside Rio and São Paulo, an insect repellant will be needed. Local druggists have preparations for local problems, but you might carry some antidiarrhea capsules and whatever prescription medicines you require.

Dry Cleaning and Laundry. Good service is available in the better hotels. Usually the best dry cleaning and laundry service in Brazil is done in the private plants of such leading hotels as those of the Intercontinental chain. Prices for dry cleaning can be expensive. You might object to the strong odor of the cleaning fluids used. It is better to take clothing that is washable.

SPECIAL EVENTS. January: In Salvador, Bahia, *Festival of the "Boa Viagem"* or the Good Lord Jesus of the Seafarers (1st). A procession of hundreds of small vessels led by a decorated galley to the end of Boa Viagem beach. Lasts four days with samba, capoeira, and dancing, plus feasts of Bahian food. In Salvador, Bahia, *Feast of Bonfim,* the highpoint of which is beautifully dressed Bahian women cleaning the steps of the Basilica of Bonfim (3rd Sun.). **February:** In Salvador, Bahia, *Festival of Iemanjá.* The holy mothers and daughters begin singing the goddess's praises at the crack of dawn. (2nd). **Feb-March:** *Carnaval.* In Rio, the year's biggest tourist attraction, but also spectacular in Bahia, Recife, and Olinda. Always 4 days before Ash Wednesday, extending to the next Saturday. **March:** *Formula I Grand Prix,* Rio de Janeiro. *Holy Week,* Ouro Preto, Minas Gerais. Solemn celebrations in the biggest urban complex of the 18th century considered by UNESCO to be part of the World Cultural Heritage. Religious rites from the baroque and Gold Rush eras. **April:** Ouro Preto, Minas Gerais, *Tiradentes Day* is the centerpiece of the national holiday weekend celebrating the Father of Brazilian Independence, Joaquim José da Silva Xavier, known as Tiradentes because he was a dentist (17th–21st) **June:** *Festas Juninas,* a cycle of celebrations honoring various saints throughout the month. Particularly noteworthy in Paraty, Rio de Janeiro state. *Bumba-Meu-Boi,* São Luis, Maranhão. A festival occurring here and in other cattle-raising areas of Brazil celebrating the religious legend of the slave who kills his master's ox and must resurrect it or be put to death himself. Festivities include street processionals and dancing, begin June 24 and last well into July. *Amazon Folklore Festival,* Manaus, Amazonia. **July:** *Bahian Independence Day.* (2nd). **August:** *Brazilian Grand Prix Sweepstakes,* Jockey Club, Rio de Janeiro (1st Sun.) **September:** *Biennial Art Exposition,* São Paulo, S.P. Held every other year in odd years, this is the largest art show in Latin America. Lasts several months. **October:** *Oktoberfest,* Blumenau, Santa Catarina. A celebration by Southern Brazil's large German colony. **November:** *Aleijadinho Week,* Ouro Preto, Minas Gerais. Honoring the great 18th century sculptor whose work has made this area a living art treasure. **December:** New Year's Eve celebration, Rio de Janeiro.

TOURS. When it comes to choosing among an all-inclusive, fully escorted tour, a loose, plan-your-own-itinerary package tour, or totally independent travel, the factors to be considered are time, convenience, and cost.

PLANNING YOUR TRIP

Package tours are the easiest to arrange and are probably the most economical and efficient way to get an overview of the most famous sights. If you have only a limited amount of time, a well-constructed package tour will focus your travel time and minimize costs by arranging for all transportation, transfers wherever needed, well-versed tour guides, and generally comfortable accommodations.

Package tour operators have the advantage of booking great numbers of people at what might be considered wholesale prices. In addition, as a client of a tour operator you can pretty well rest assured that all your reservations will be honored: Airline and hotel managers are reluctant to "bump" tour members for fear of alienating the operator, who virtually guarantees full flights and fully booked rooms for extended periods, as one tour group moves out and another moves in. (And if by chance your room isn't what you'd anticipated, voice your displeasure in a friendly manner at the tour operator's desk and/or to the concierge; even if a change isn't possible that day, the hotel will usually make every effort to improve your situation as soon as another room becomes available.)

A good travel agent can make all reservations in advance for "GIT" (Group Inclusive Travel plans, which are built around transportation and lodging only) and "FIT" (Foreign Independent Travel, as it is known in the U.K.) travelers. In Europe a fee is sometimes charged for these services; in the U.S. the fees— except the cost of any necessary long-distance telephone calls or other out-of-the-ordinary expenses—are almost always paid by the airlines, the hotels, and other businesses.

In America, if you cannot locate a travel agent near your home, write to the *America Society of Travel Agents,* 4400 MacArthur Blvd. N.W., Washington, D.C. 20007, or *A.S.T.A.-West Coast,* 4420 Hotel Circle Court, Suite 230, San Diego, CA 92108. In Canada, write to *A.S.T.A.-Canada,* Barbara Watts Travel, Inc. 117 W. Pender St., Vancouver BC V6B 1S4. Any agency affiliated with these organizations is likely to be reliable. The *United States Tour Operators Association* (U.S.T.O.A.), 211 E. 51 St., Suite 4B, New York, NY 10022 will send you a list of its members, all of whom are bonded for your protection. (In the last few years, the upheavals in airfares particularly have caused the failure of a number of smaller tour operators, leaving their customers stranded and with no recourse, This cannot happen with U.S.T.O.A. members.)

Following is a *partial* list of wholesale tour operators. Although your travel agent probably is familiar with these options and can make reservations, you may want to contact some in advance for brochures.

Abreu Tours
60 East 42nd Street
New York, NY 10165
(212) 661–0555

**Amazon/African
Explorers Inc.**
Rte. 9
Parlin, NJ 08859
(800) 631–5650; (201) 721–2929

American Express
Travel Division
American Express Plaza
New York, NY 10004
(212) 323–2000

Brazil Vacation Center
55 West 46th Street
New York, NY 10036
(212) 840–3730, 730–0515

Hotur
20 East 53rd Street
New York, NY 10022
(212) 371–8885

Ipanema Tours
9911 West Pico Boulevard, Suite 580
Los Angeles, CA 90035
(213) 278–4656

Ladatco Tours
2220 Coral Way
Miami, Florida 33145
(305) 854–8422; (800) 327–6162

BRAZIL

Melia International
1501 Broadway, Suite 1401
New York, New York 10030
(212) 719–3604

Portuguese Tours
321 Rahway Avenue
Elizabeth, New Jersey 07202
(201) 352–6112

R.N. Tours Inc.
666 Old Country Road
Garden City, New York 11530
(516) 222–9090

Unique Adventures
140 Geary Street
Suite 900
San Francisco, California 94108
(800) 227–3026; (415) 986–5876

Wilderness Travel
801 AllstonWay
Berkeley, CA 94710
(415) 548–0420

**Wrightway Tours
International**
16030 Ventura Boulevard,
Suite 250
Encino, California 91436
(818) 906–1141

Special-Interest Tours. In the past few years several special-interest tours have been organized to visit Brazil. Amazon River cruises and hunting tours and special package tours to Carnival in Rio are all available. Your travel agent will have information on camera tours, horticultural tours, agricultural tours, and many others.

There is also an excellent publication devoted entirely to the subject of special-interest travel: *The Specialty Travel Index*, #9 Mono Avenue, Fairfax, CA 94930, phone (415) 459–4900. One of their biannual issues (costing $3) will give you an exhaustive list of special-interest travel operators worldwide.

In Rio, the following agencies specialize in adventure travel or will tailor a tour according to the customer's desires:

Abreutur, Rua México 21, Centro, Tel: 231–3394.
Expeditours, Rua Visconde de Pirajá 414, Ipanema, Suite 1005, Tel: 287–9697.
GB Internacional, Ar. Princesa Isabel, 7, Copacabana, Suites 3 and 4, Tel: 275–5148
Soletur, Rua Visconde de Pirajá 550, 17th floor, Ipanema, Tel.: 239–7145.

Plan-As-You-Go Travel. Wandering in Brazil on a plan-as-you-go basis can be the most rewarding way of all, or it can be a disaster, depending on the individual. To do it successfully you need a knowledge of Portuguese, some experience in foreign travel, an open schedule, and a good deal of willingness to take things and people as they are.

To the stranger there is no friendlier country than Brazil. Nevertheless, the novice international traveler is advised to make some definite plans and reservations before leaving.

A formula that provides experienced planning and guidance, avoids the sterility of standardized international hotels and airports, and gets you much closer to the real life of the countries you visit is touring by motorcoach and either staying in small hotels or camping out. This kind of travel is not only more colorful, but it is also obviously less expensive.

Handicapped Travel. One of the newest, and largest, groups to enter the travel scene is the handicapped, literally millions of people who are in fact physically able to travel and who do so enthusiastically when they know that they can move about with safety and comfort. Generally these tours parallel

PLANNING YOUR TRIP

those of the non-handicapped traveler, but at a more leisurely pace, with everything checked out in advance to eliminate all inconvenience, whether the traveler happens to be deaf, blind or in a wheelchair.

For a complete list of tour operators who arrange such travel, write to the *Society for the Advancement of Travel for the Handicapped,* 26 Court St., Brooklyn, NY 11242. An excellent source of information in this field is the book, *Access to the World: A Travel Guide for the Handicapped,* by Louise Weiss, available from *Facts on File,* 460 Park Ave. South, New York, NY 10016. This book covers travel by air, ship, train, bus, car, recreational vehicle; hotels and motels; travel agents and tour operators; destinations; access guides; health and medical problems; and travel organizations. Another major source of help is the *Travel Information Center,* Moss Rehabilitation Hospital, 12th St. and Tabor Rd. Philadelphia, PA 19141. And for an international directory of access guides, write to *Rehabilitation International,* 1123 Broadway, New York, NY 10010, for their listing of sources of information on facilities for the handicapped all over the world. *LTD Travel,* a newsletter packed with helpful tips and travel notes, is available from 116 Harbor Seal Court, San Mateo, CA 94404.

From the U.K.: The *Air Transport Users Committee,* 129 Kingsway, London W.C.2 (01–242–3882), publishes a very useful booklet for handicapped passengers entitled *Care in the Air,* available free of charge.

TIPS FOR BRITISH VISITORS. The *Brazilian Consulate,* 6 Deanery St., London W1, can provide you with **information** you'll need to plan your trip. Be sure, too, to confirm what travel documents are necessary before leaving. Another source of information is the *London Chamber of Commerce, Latin American Section,* 69 Cannon St., E.C.4, and *The Hispanic Council,* Canning House, 2. Belgrave Square, London, S.W. 1.

The following **tour operators** specialize in South America and offer both multi-center tours and single destination holidays.

Bales Tours Ltd, Bales House, Barrington Rd., Dorking, Surrey RH4 3EJ (0306–885 991).

Dellstar Travel (South)Ltd, 98 Field End Rd., Estcote, Pinner, Middx. HA15 1RL (01–868 2968).

Encounter Overland Ltd., 267 Old Brompton Rd., London SW5 (01–370 6845).

Exodus Expeditions, All Saints' Passage, 100 Wandsworth High St., London SW18 4LE (01–870 0151).

Hallmark International, Sandbourne House, 302 Charminster Rd., Bournemouth, Dorset BH8 9RU (0202–525 167).

South American Travel Ltd., South America House, 31 Exmouth Market, London ED1R 4TE (01–833 2641).

Windotel, Suite 19, College House, 29–31 Wrights Lane, Kensington, London W8 5SH (01–730 7144).

Getting to Brazil

BY AIR. In general, the cheapest fares are going to be those available on charters or through package tour operators. Unfortunately, there are no standby fares to Brazil. Package and charter bookings will definitely save you money on the routes they cover, but they lock you into their schedules and itineraries.

BRAZIL

Airfares to South America are constantly changing. Unfortunately, there is no inexpensive "no frills" type of air service to South America, such as that offered by People Express to Europe. Following is an attempt to outline the complex airfare situation to help you narrow your choices:

Charters. This is the cheapest but least flexible way to travel. There are a couple of charter operators to Rio de Janeiro. The charters are strictly to a single destination, do not offer stopovers en route, and are for a fixed, limited length of time. The charters can, however, usually offer an air and land package tour for about the same price as the lowest available airfare alone via scheduled airlines. The charters are not operated via regularly scheduled airlines, therefore, service is limited, legroom cramped, and schedules changeable.

"APEX" Fares. The advantage to these fares is that they do permit long stays (usually 60–90 days) but do not permit stops anywhere else. The fares also require a minimum stay, usually about 21 days.

Group Airfares. The group airfares to South America are just about all gone, with the one notable exception of the GROUP 10 (GV10) airfares to Rio and Buenos Aires. These fares are offered by Varig and Pan Am out of New York, Miami, and Los Angeles and anyone can book into them. The airlines "consolidate"; that is, they block 10 seats on every flight that the tour wholesalers can sell into, so that the group departure is guaranteed. The airfare does require that it be sold in conjunction with a minimum land package of $18 per day, but you have a choice of many different tour wholesalers' packages to choose from. The fares permit a maximum stay of 14 days, plus one day of travel, and permit two stopovers on the way. Sample Group 10 airfares: Miami/Rio—high season $899, low season $660; New York/Rio—high $999, low $799; Los Angeles/Rio —high $1099, low $927.

(High season is June 1-Aug. 15, and Dec. 1–31. The fares are not valid during Carnaval.)

Varig Brasilian Airlines has the most flexible packages for these fares, primarily because it has the best route structure to Brazil. Besides a simple round trip to Rio and/or Buenos Aires (with a stopover in Iguassu Falls permitted at no extra charge), Varig also has the following tours available for the same Rio GV10 airfare: Miami/Salvador (Bahia)/Rio Miami; Miami/Manaus/Rio/Miami; Miami/Salvador/Rio/Manaus/Miami.

For more information on these tours, contact Varig or Pan Am tour desks or local sales offices.

Individual Tour Basing Fares (ITX): This is a very economical fare system, considering the amount of flexibility allowed. It usually permits a maximum of 21 days' travel with a maximum of five stopovers on the airlines' routing, plus your final destination, at no additional charge. The fare does require that you purchase a minimum specified amount of land arrangements (i.e. either a packaged tour or a prearranged independent tour). The fare requires travel all on one airline.

30-Day Excursion Fares. These fares are more expensive than the ITX fares, but they have two important advantages. First, they permit a maximum stay of 30 days (versus 21) and permit 4 stopovers (two in each direction to and from your furthest point, with each additional stopover costing $30.00). Second, they permit you to fly on as many different airlines as necessary to complete the trip.

There is a host of other fare groupings, ranging from full-fare economy (generally used by business travelers), to business class, first class, and "sleeper class." All of these fares, and the restrictions that govern them, are constantly changing, depending on the time of year (peak, low, or "shoulder" periods), on how heavy the competition is at any given moment, and on how well-traveled a particular route is. The advantage of an independent booking at a full economy

PLANNING YOUR TRIP

rate is that you may be able to add additional stopovers at no extra charge. Here, again, the rules vary and change frequently. Similarly, you are more likely to be able to change your reservations as you go when flying regularly scheduled major airlines. Be sure to check with airlines and travel agents for the restrictions on fares.

The majority of flights terminate in Rio, though the national *Varig Airlines* also services São Paulo, Manaus, Brasilia, and other destinations, primarily from Los Angeles, Miami, and New York. *Pan American Airlines* runs daily flights to Rio and São Paulo from these major American cities, plus you get the convenience of Pan Am's network of connecting flights within the U.S. Among the airlines serving Brazil from Europe are *Varig, Aerolineas Argentinas, Air France, British Airways, Iberia, Lufthansa, Pan Am, SAS, Swissair,* and *TAP. Pan Am, Varig,* and *South African Airways* fly to Rio from points in the Pacific and Africa. From the U.S. to Rio and São Paulo there are smooth jet flights on six airlines: from New York, Miami, Los Angeles on *Avianca, Argentine Airlines, Pan American,* and *Varig;* from Dallas-Houston on *Pan American.* From Miami to Brasilia on *Pan American* and *Varig,* to Manaus and Belem on *Varig.*

From London to Rio and São Paulo: *British Airways, Varig* (some flights stop in Bahia), and main European and South American airlines from other principal capitals on the Continent.

From South Africa: *South African Airways* and *Varig* have flights from Johannesburg and/or Cape Town.

From the Pacific, Australia, and New Zealand: *Qantas* through Tahiti to Acapulco and Mexico City, changing for South American desinations, or *LAN-Chile* from Fiji, Tahiti, or Easter Island through Santiago.

From the Orient: *Varig* or *Japan Air Lines* from Tokyo, or other airlines, changing for South America on the U.S. West Coast.

BY SEA. By and large there is very little ocean-going passenger service left to any part of the world these days, and South America is no exception. What there is has largely polarized between passenger-carrying freighters on the one hand and cruise liners on the other. The steady progress of containerization has cut into the freighter facilities available.

On a cruise you get a very pleasant vacation in a floating luxury hotel, and brief tastes of several countries by way of their major port cities. Below is a list of some cruise services available to Brazil, followed by sources of information on freighter travel. However, in view of the constant changes in cruise itineraries, it is recommended that you contact your local travel agent, who can provide you with the most up-to-date information and make all arrangements—for the same price you would pay if you made the arrangements yourself.

Cunard, Ltd., 555 Fifth Ave., New York, NY 10017, has the *Cunard Countess* sailing year-round from San Juan with a stop at La Guaira, Venezuela. Now operating the *Sagafjord,* she has one world cruise in 1987 which calls at Buenos Aires, Montevideo, Rio de Janeiro, Salvador, and Belem before returning through the Caribbean to Ft. Lauderdale; this 15-day cruise may be booked as a segment of the world cruise. The *Sagafjord* also offers two Amazon River cruises a year, one from Ft. Lauderdale to Belem and up the Amazon to Manaus (14 days) and a second returning from Manaus to Ft. Lauderdale (13 days). In Britain: 35 Pall Mall, London SW1; in Canada: One Dundee Street, Toronto, Ont. M5G 2B2.

Holland America Cruises, 300 Elliott Ave. W., Seattle, WA 98119, has a world cruise in January that sails for 31 days from Ft. Lauderdale around South America and can be booked in certain segments. Ports of call are Fortaleza, Rio,

BRAZIL

Sao Paulo, Montevideo, the Falkland Islands, Punta Arenas, the Strait of Magellan, Valparaiso (Chile), and Callao (Lima).

Sunline Cruises, One Rockefeller Plaza, Suite 315, New York, NY 10020 has its *Stella Solaris* sail in winter and early spring from Galveston, TX, on 21-day trips to the Caribbean and South American ports of La Guaira and Cartagena. The *Stella Solaris* will also operate special Amazon River cruises in December and January of 15 days from Ft. Lauderdale to Manaus or vice-versa, and a Rio Carnaval cruise in February of 15 days from Ft. Lauderdale. The *Stella Oceanis* has special cruises in December and January from San Juan up either the Orinoco River in Venezuela or the Suriname River in Suriname.

Passenger accommodation on freighters from the U.S. is offered by *Columbus Lines, Torm Lines Holland-America, Ivaran Lines, Moore-McCormack Lines,* one-way or round-trip cruises. *Lloyd Brasileiro, Brodin Line* call at Rio, Santos, and Paranagua.

BY CAR. Roadbuilding in Central and South America has progressed to the point that one can drive all the way from the United States to Brazil with just one short sea voyage. Political unrest in Central America makes driving a risky choice, however, as do natural disasters like earthquakes. There is no road yet from Panama to Colombia, but several shipping lines transport cars and passengers from Panama to Buenaventura or Cartagena in Colombia or La Guaira in Venezuela. About 85 percent of the principal highways and main roads are good to excellent and hard surfaced. The rest with few exceptions are adequate dirt roads, open year round, but there are still too many rough and hazardous areas to make driving pleasurable. Good hotels exist along the entire route; with careful planning, a room with bath or shower can be had every night.

A reliable, fairly new car, preferably of a well-known make, for which spare parts are available in South America, is a must. Good repair facilities are available; gasoline and oil can be obtained everywhere, but high-test premium gasoline is hard to come by except in the capitals. Use tires with tubes, and take extra tubes along. Consult your automobile dealer about what spare parts to carry, and be sure to take a towing cable, hand pump, pressure gauge, and tube repair kit.

For border crossings, besides car registration and license, you'll need about 25 passport size photos and a *Carnet de Passages en Douane.* The AAA, 8111 Gatehouse Rd., Falls Church, Va. 22042, will issue one for $85, plus a $200 deposit, which is refundable when you surrender the Carnet Letter of credit. A letter stating that your car value is 150 percent more than its list value is needed from the bank to secure a Carnet. No Carnet is needed for a tourist vehicle to enter Brazil for up to 60 days. Formalities are completed at the border. Also required are Inter-American driving permits and Inter-American registration papers plus a country identification plaque on the automobile. You cannot sell your car in Brazil; plan to drive or ship it.

Buy insurance in the U.S. beforehand. If you have an accident, pay the judgments against you and collect the amount afterward. Never leave your car unguarded or unlocked—there are organized gangs in every major city, expert at breaking into and stealing cars.

Shipping cars. There are ample facilities for shipping automobiles from the U.S., but unless the owner is planning to reside in Brazil for some time, it is advisable to rent a car.

Best suggestion for travelers wanting to see Brazil by car is to rent automobiles in the various cities.

Staying in Brazil

MONEY MATTERS. In February, 1986, the government of President José Sarney launched an economic package designed to stem Brazil's relentless inflation, which was averaging up to 250% a year. Prices on all goods and services were adjusted, tabulated, and frozen until the end of 1986. The "cruzado," abbreviated $CZ, replaced the "cruzeiro," abbreviated $CR, as the unit of currency.

Under the new monetary system, 1,000 cruzeiros became 1 cruzado, with 100 centavos to the cruzado. At press time, however, not all new bills were in circulation. Many cruzeiro notes were still in use. Cruzeiro notes come in denominations of 100,000, 50,000, 10,000, 1,000, 500, 200, and 100, and in small coins that look like dimes stamped 500, 200, and 100 cruzeiros. Most cruzeiro notes are marked with their equivalent value in cruzados, much like a cancelled postage stamp, and cruzado notes are gradually replacing the stamped cruzeiro bills.

To arrive at the cruzado value of cruzeiro notes, just move the decimal point three columns to the left, dividing by 1000. So 1,000 cruzeiros equals 1 cruzado, 10,000 cruzeiros equals 10 cruzados, 100,000 cruzeiros equals 100 cruzados, and so on.

The exchange rates, both "oficial" and "parallelo," are published daily in major newspapers under "cotação." You can obtain the black market rate at "cambios," which specialize in changing foreign currency. Banks and hotels are obliged to pay the official rate; stores usually change money at slightly below the black market rate. Some cambios accept only cash. At time of writing the official exchange rate was 17 cruzados to the U.S. dollar; the parallel or black market rate was 25–27 cruzados to the U.S. dollar.

In the Brazilian system of numerical notation, the role and position of the comma and period are exactly the opposite of what we are used to in the American system. If something is marked $CZ 1.600,00, you should read it to mean $CZ 1,600.00. Be careful not to be overcharged or shortchanged because of confusion over this convention.

Credit Cards. You will pay for the convenience of charging. All credit cards bill you in dollars back home at the official exchange rate on the day of the purchase or transaction. While this saves you the trouble of converting money, it also costs you more. Dollars can be changed on the "parallel" or "black" market for up to 35% higher rates. And this is altogether legal.

Traveler's checks are the best way to safeguard travel funds, although you will always receive slightly less for them in exchange than for greenbacks. Nevertheless, they are safer. Anyone can change dollar bills, no questions asked. But you must present a passport and sign in the presence of the clerk in order to change traveler's checks. It is advisable to carry the bulk of your money in traveler's checks, and a smaller quantity in bills. Outside of major cities it is more difficult to exchange your traveler's checks than cash.

BRAZIL

ACCOMMODATIONS. Although cost is as good an indicator as you're likely to find, the following price categories do not necessarily reflect the quality of every hotel accurately. *Super deluxe* hotels begin at $95 per night; *Deluxe* hotels charge from $70 to $95; *Expensive* hotels range from $45 to $70, *Moderate* hotels range from $15 to $45, and *Inexpensive* hotels are $15 or less. Continental breakfast is generally included in the room rate. While personal inspection of the premises is impossible if you are making reservations from afar, checking out the room in an inexpensive or moderate hotel before you take it is always a good policy. At the expensive and super deluxe establishments, reservations should always be made well in advance, especially during high season and when special events are occurring. Unless you are traveling with a tour during Carnival, you will need to reserve rooms in the best hotels at least a year ahead. Motels in Brazil are not hotels with free parking, as they are in the U.S. Motels are for couples engaging in amorous interludes and are rented out for short periods of time—hours, afternoons, overnight. These establishments are completely legitimate and are not designed to serve the prostitution trade. Many super deluxe hotels in Rio and São Paulo now offer American television programs via satellite dishes.

Roughing it. For a listing of hostels in Brazil, contact Casa do Estudante do Brasil, Praca Ana Amelia, ZC39, 2000.

DINING OUT. Our restaurant grading system has four categories: *Deluxe,* $15 and up; *Expensive,* $10 to $15; *Moderate,* $5 to $10; *Inexpensive,* under $5. These prices are for one person and do not include wine, beer, or other drinks, but do include the "coberto" or "couvert," an appetizer course including bread, butter, and, depending on the restaurant, cheese or pate spreads, olives, quail eggs, crudités, sausage, etc.

Remember that in Brazil, as in Portugal, the decor of the restaurant has very little to do with the quality of the food. Ambience is one thing; great eating is another. The only absolute criterion for your choice should be cleanliness and freshness. Otherwise, experimentation is definitely part of the adventure.

Brazilian Food and Drink. Indian, African, and Portuguese dietary traditions have simmered for centuries to produce Brazil's savory cuisine and eating habits, providing a sort of culinary profile of the nation's roots. Pre-Columbian cultures, a category which includes Brazil's aboriginal tribes, cultivated dozens of varieties of edible plants that have since become world staples,. including many that revolutionized global economies: potatoes, corn, manioc, bananas, tomatoes, cocoa, vanilla, pineapple, avocado, papaya, beans, pumpkin, and pepper. As in the United States, Brazil's natives taught their colonizers how to grow and use these vegetable products.

For their part, the Portuguese transplanted their national tastes and traditional recipes, introducing and adapting them to the foodstuffs found in the New World.

Many Brazilian dishes are adaptations of Portuguese specialties. Fish stews called *caldeiradas* and beef stews called *cozidos* are popular, as is *bacalhau,* salt cod cooked in sauces, or grilled. Dried salted meats form the basis for many dishes from the interior and northeast of Brazil, and pork is used heavily in dishes from Minas Gerais. You will find Brazilian cooking both sweeter and saltier than you are used to, and there are two categories of food called *salgados* (salties) and *doces* (sweets). The first are served as appetizers and snacks in

PLANNING YOUR TRIP

standup "lancheonetes," and the desserts are sold in sweet shops and restaurants. Many "doces" are direct descendents of the egg-based custards and puddings of Portugal and France.

It took the catalyst of African culture, however, to really turn out a national cuisine. When the slaves arrived, they carried their own knowledge of cooking, using tropical ingredients and spices. Coconut milk, dende oil, cashew nuts, the firey malagueta pepper, and other hot spices were insinuated into Portuguese and Indian dishes, transforming them through the addition or substitution of ingredients and cooking methods into something truly new. In actuality, Brazilian food, like that of any other heterogeneous country, is a collection of regional specialties and the national cuisines of the people who settled there.

In the big cities, it's as hard to find restaurants labeling their food "Brazilian" as it is to find "French" food in France, and most of the best restaurants in Rio and São Paulo are French and Italian. What you find in restaurants not specifically specializing in some other national cuisine is Brazilian food; a typical meal consists of beans, rice, french fries, and beef, chicken, or fish. Brazilians are not fond of vegetables and salads must be ordered separately.

Once you get out into the countryside, authentic regional foods are your best bet, since indigenous ingredients which may not travel well are fresh and readily available.

The national dish of Brazil is *feijoada,* traditionally served on Saturdays at lunch. Originally a slave dish, feijoada now consists of black beans, sausage, beef, and pork. It is always served with rice, finely shredded kale, orange slices, and farofa, manioc flour that has been fried with onion and egg.

The cuisine of Bahia is sometimes equated with Brazilian food as a whole, although it is actually best eaten in Salvador, where it originates. *Muqueca* is made out of many kinds of shellfish cooked quickly in a covered frying pan with dende oil, coconut milk, onions, and tomatoes. Dried shrimp, dende oil, coconut milk, and cashews are the basic ingredients of *vatapá,* and *xinxim de galinha,* which substitutes lime juice for coconut milk to make a sauce for chicken.

From Brazil's southeast comes *churrasco,* or barbecued meats marinated and grilled or roasted over charcoals. Restaurants specializing in meat are called *churrascurias,* which serve either á la carte or "rodizio" (all you can eat) style.

The national drink is the *"caipirinha,"* made of crushed lime, sugar, and *pinga* or *cachaça,* strong liquors made from sugar cane. When whipped with crushed ice and fruit juice, pinga becomes a *batida,* which sometimes includes condensed milk. Be sure to try *guaraná,* the Brazilian answer to Coca-Cola.

Coffee is served black and strong with sugar in demitasse cups and is called *cafezinho.* Coffee is only served with milk at breakfast.

TIPPING. At restaurants and nightclubs, when 10 or 15% is added to your bill, you usually add 5% more. In hotels, 10% is usually added to your bill as a service charge. However, you will find that porters, doormen, elevator operators, and chambermaids are accustomed to getting a small tip for their services, either at the time the service is performed, or when you check out. If a taxi driver helps you with your luggage, a per bag charge of about 5 cruzados is levied in addition to the fare. At the barber's or beauty parlor, a 10–20% tips is expected. Cinema and theater ushers do not expect tips. In general, tip washroom attendants, shoeshine boys, etc., about one-third what you would tip at home. At airports, tip the last porter who puts your bags into the cab; they work on a "pool" system and all earnings go into a general kitty.

THE LANGUAGE. A prime rule to remember for anyone visiting Brazil is that the national language is Portuguese and not Spanish. There is nothing that annoys a Brazilian more than to have a visitor make that mistake. They are extremely proud of their language and the literary and musical heritage that goes with it. It is not that Brazilians disdain the dominant language of their neighbors, it is just that they feel insulted that *norte americanos* are so ignorant of South American cultural differences.

Actually, Portuguese-speaking people readily understand Spanish, but Portuguese is not readily understood by Spanish-speaking people. Portuguese is a nasal and guttural language of Latin origin, heavily influenced by Arabic, and, like Spanish, has an extensive Arabic vocabulary.

Yet there exists a difference between the Portuguese of Brazil and the Portuguese of Portugal. It is a little like the differences between the English of the United States and the English of Great Britain.

But don't get discouraged right away. If you can speak Spanish you can get around in Brazil. You won't understand them but they will usually understand you. If you take the trouble to learn just a few Portuguese words to sprinkle in your conversation you will win your listeners over almost immediately. The statement that you read in many tourist folders, saying that everyone speaks English in Brazil and therefore you'll have no trouble, is pure fiction. Therefore a few minutes spent in brushing up on some Portuguese will pay big dividends. Besides, it's a beautiful tongue, spoken by more people around the world than French.

The accents and other curlicues you find above or below the letters of many words actually make pronunciation easier. For instance the word for coffee is café. When you see this acute accent at the end of a word you accent that syllable and it becomes ca-FAY. That strange word for saint as in Saint Paul (São Paulo) is pronounced SOWN (as in "down"). When there is a *cedilla* under a "c" in a word like braço (meaning arm), you pronounce it like a soft "s" and it comes out bras-so. If the "c" doesn't have the *cedilla* you usually pronounce it hard like a "k," as in buscar (bus-kar). Also "q" in a word is pronounced like "k" and most "x's" have a shhh sound. Because of this you will run into many English words that have been twisted around by the Brazilians. The gasoline company Texaco comes out tay-SHA-ko. Other words borrowed from English that you may (or may not) recognize in Brazil are *lanche* (a quick lunch), *time* (a soccer team but pronounced tea-me), *football* (pronounced foot-tea-ball) and *cinema* (here it is sea-NAY-mah).

See the *Tourist Vocabulary* at the end of the book for some useful words and phrases.

BUSINESS HOURS AND HOLIDAYS. Opening and closing hours naturally vary from city to city. Rio stores open 9 A.M.–6:30 P.M., Sat. to 1 P.M. Shopping malls open at 10 A.M. and close at 10 P.M. during the week and at 6 P.M. on Sat. The business day generally begins at 9 A.M. and ends at 6 P.M. although punctuality is not a Brazilian trait. Stores and offices may open later, and frequently stay open until the last customer leaves. Banks close at 4:30 P.M. Lunch is taken from noon to three, and while businesses in major cities do not close, you may not find who you're looking for.

National Holidays: Jan. 1, (New Year's Day); Jan. 6, Santos Reis (Three King's); Jan. 20, São Sebastian; Jan. 25, Anniversary of Founding of São Paulo; Carnival (always 4 days before Ash Weds.); Feb. 1, Anniversary of founding of Rio de Janeiro; Ash Wednesday; Paixão (Passion); Aleluia; 30 Páscoa (Easter);

PLANNING YOUR TRIP

May 1, Dia do Trabalho (May Day); Ascensão (Ascension); Corpus Christi; June 24–29, Festas Juninas; Aug. 15, Assunção da Nossa Senhora (Assumption); Sept. 7, Brazilian Independence Day; Oct. 12, Nossa Senhora Aparecida; Nov. 1, Todos os Santos (All Saints Day); Nov. 2, All Souls; Nov. 15, Proclamação da República (Declaration of the Republic); Nov. 19, Dia da Bandeira (Flag Day); Dec. 25, Natal (Christmas); Dec. 31, New Year's Eve and Festa da Iemanjá.

Note: People usually close up shop early the day before a holiday. Election days, when scheduled, are also considered holidays. Some holidays are celebrated on the nearest Monday to create a long weekend.

TELEPHONES. All parts of Brazil are connected by Embratel, the national telephone company. Public phones are everywhere and are called "orelhões," or "big ears." These are yellow with the blue phone company logo for local calls, or solid blue for calls between cities ("interurbana"). To use the public phones, you must buy tokens, called "fichas," at newspaper stands or Telerj stations, where you can make long distance calls. Local fichas cost 30 centavos, interurban fichas cost 3 cruzados. It is wise to buy several at a time so that you can insert them in the slot in advance and avoid getting cut off. Unused fichas will be returned when you hang up. To use the public phones, pick up the receiver and listen for a constant dial tone. Drop the ficha into the slot, listen again for a dial tone, then dial. For international telephone calls through an operator, dial "000111." For information on international calls, dial "000333." Operators who assist from these numbers speak English. To make an automated collect intercity phone call within Brazil, dial 9 plus the area code and number. The recipient of your call will hear a recorded message in Portuguese saying "you are receiving a collect call." After the tone, give your name and if the person on the other end does not wish to accept charges, he or she just hangs up to disconnect the call. Telephone numbers in Brazil do not always have an equal number of digits, nor do area codes. This irregularity does not indicate that you have a wrong number. The area code for Rio is 021, for São Paulo 011. Other area codes for all parts of the country are listed in the front of the phone directory.

MAIL. The post office is called "Correios" and is open from 8 A.M. to 6 P.M. weekdays, until noon on Sat. An airmail letter from Brazil to the U.S. costs 15 cruzados for 20 grams (17 cruzados to Europe, except Spain and Portugal) and takes at least 10 days to reach the U.S. from Brazil and vice versa. Brazil has both national and international rapid mail service, the price of which varies according to the weight of the package and the destination.

Major hotels will hold mail for arriving guests. Do not use general delivery to receive mail—have it forwarded to American Express. Telegraphic service is available everywhere from post offices, and many hotels have their own facilities.

NEWSPAPERS. English-language newspapers and magazines are for sale in all leading cities. With timely jet schedules to Brazil, there is little delay in receiving airmail editions of New York and Miami newspapers. International editions of news magazines are on sale in all leading hotels.

An English-language paper, the *Latin America Daily Post*, is published five days a week in Rio. Rio's two leading Portuguese newspapers are *Jornal do Brasil* and *O Globo*. In São Paulo, there are six major newspapers in Portuguese: *Folha de São Paulo, Folha da Tarde, Journal da Tarde, O Estado de São Paulo,*

CONVERTING METRIC TO U.S. MEASUREMENTS

Multiply:	by:	to find:
Length		
millimeters (mm)	.039	inches (in)
meters (m)	3.28	feet (ft)
meters	1.09	yards (yd)
kilometers (km)	.62	miles (mi)
Area		
hectare (ha)	2.47	acres
Capacity		
liters (L)	1.06	quarts (qt)
liters	.26	gallons (gal)
liters	2.11	pints (pt)
Weight		
gram (g)	.04	ounce (oz)
kilogram (kg)	2.20	pounds (lb)
metric ton (MT)	.98	tons (t)
Power		
kilowatt (kw)	1.34	horsepower (hp)
Temperature		
degrees Celsius	9/5 (then add 32)	degrees Fahrenheit

CONVERTING U.S. TO METRIC MEASUREMENTS

Multiply:	by:	to find:
Length		
inches (in)	25.40	millimeters (mm)
feet (ft)	.30	meters (m)
yards (yd)	.91	meters
miles (mi)	1.61	kilometers (km)
Area		
acres	.40	hectares (ha)
Capacity		
pints (pt)	.47	liters (L)
quarts (qt)	.95	liters
gallons (gal)	3.79	liters
Weight		
ounces (oz)	28.35	grams (g)
pounds (lb)	.45	kilograms (kg)
tons (t)	1.11	metric tons (MT)
Power		
horsepower (hp)	.75	kilowatts
Temperature		
degrees Fahrenheit	5/9 (after subtracting 32)	degrees Celsius

PLANNING YOUR TRIP 39

Diario Popular, and *Gazeta Mercantil.* Nightly news reports are broadcast on all major television networks in Portuguese.

ELECTRIC CURRENT. Most of the top hotels have transformers for current and adapters for plugs for guests with foreign electric razors, slide projectors, and so on. Usually 110 or 120 volts, AC 60 cycle in Rio and São Paulo.

PHOTOGRAPHY TIPS. Registration: We recommend that you have all your camera equipment registered with customs before your departure. At the very least, bring along your sales receipts as proof you bought the equipment before arriving in South America.

Film and Filters. After you think you have brought enough film, bring some more! Your unused film can always be kept fresh for a long time in the refrigerator, or sold at the end of your trip to some unfortunate tourist who did not bring enough film. A roll of film in South America will cost you double the price at home, and you cannot be sure it is fresh.

For you "SLR" enthusiasts, Kodachrome film, ASA 64 (for slides) or Kodacolor, ASA 100 (for prints) is recommended for the excellent color rendition. However, it is also a good idea to bring along some Ektachrome or some other "fast" file (with a higher ASA) for use when the sky is overcast. Whatever color film you use, a skylight or haze 2A filter will help cut down on the haze and color shift of high altitudes and the glare of the bright sun reflecting off white adobe buildings, sandy beaches, etc. For black and white photography, an orange or yellow filter will bring out the color contrasts in the sky.

X rays: When you fly, remember that in spite of official claims to the contrary, airport security X-ray machines do in fact damage your photographic films in about 17 percent of the cases. Have your camera and film inspected manually, or pack them in specially lead-lined protective bags available in photo supply stores.

Be Alert: It is important to remember that cameras, being an expensive item here, are worth even more in countries that have high import duties. Too many photographers, unfortunately, have been easy victims of robberies as they stroll through the streets, entranced and distracted. Buy camera insurance if your camera is valuable or if it is not covered under your homeowners insurance policy. Do not pack any valuables at all, especially camera equipment, in checked baggage. Leaving cameras and lenses in hotel rooms is not recommended.

USEFUL ADDRESSES. In Rio: *Riotur,* Rua da Assembléia 10, 8th and 9th floors, Centro (297–7117): information on tourist events in the city of Rio. Open Mon.-Fri., 9 A.M. to 6 P.M. Kiosk at Pão de Açucar. *Flumitur,* Rua da Assembléia 10, 7th and 8th floors, Centro (252–4512); tourist information on the state of Rio de Janeiro. Open Mon.-Fri. 9 A.M. to 10 P.M. *Embratur,* Rua Mariz e Barros, 13, 9th floor, Praça da Bandeira, (273–2212); Brazil's National Tourism Authority, information on all regions of the country. *American Consulate,* Av. President Wilson, 147 (292–7117). *British Consulate,* Praia do Flamengo, 284, 2nd fl. (522–1422). (The Canadian Consulate in Rio has closed.) English-speaking doctors can be contacted by calling the U.S. Consulate-General at 292–7117, or by calling the Rio Health Collective for a referral at 511–0940.

Addresses and telephone numbers of airlines serving North America: *Aerolineas Argentinas,* Rua São José, 40, Centro, 221–4255; *Air Canada,* Avenida Marechal Câmara, 106/suite 1016, Centro, 220–9888; *American Airlines,* Rua da Assembléia, 10/suite 3620, Centro, 221–9455; *Japan Airlines,* Avenida Rio Branco 108, Centro, 221–9454 and 221–9663; *Pan Am,* Av. Pres. Wilson, 165, Centro, 240–6662: *Varig,* main office Av. Rio Branco 277, Centro, 297–4400 and branches in Copacabana, Ipanema, and São Conrado.

In São Paulo: *Paulistur,* the city's Tourism Authority, was abolished. For information, contact the *Secretaria de Esportes e Turismo do Estado de São Paulo,* the state tourism authority, at Praça Antonio Prado, 9, Centro (229–3011) and at Av. São Luis 115, Centro (257–7248). Open Mon.-Fri. 9 A.M. to 6 P.M. Information is also available from the *São Paulo Convention Bureau,* Rua Columbia 582, Jardins (280–2979/4523). Open Mon.-Fri. 9 A.M. to 6 P.M.. *American Consulate,* Rua Padre João Manoel, 933 (881–6511). *British Consulate,* Av. Paulista 1938, 17th fl. (287–7722). *Canadian Consulate,* Av. Paulista 854, 5th fl. (287–2112).

HEALTH AND SAFETY. Rio and São Paulo are modern urban centers with good sanitary conditions, but once you get out of the major cities into rural areas, you will be subject to tropical diseases that periodically recur and sometimes reach epidemic proportions: yellow fever, denguê, malaria, and hepatitis are all recent outbreaks. Get inoculations before you go for those illnesses for which there are serums (e.g., yellow fever). Check with your local health authority, the travel clinic at your local hospital, the Department of Immigration, or some other public health outlet to see what you will need. Anyone planning adventure travel of any kind—including fishing expeditions in the Pantanal and trips to the Amazon—should take prophylactic malaria tablets before traveling in the affected area. Should you contract an illness while in Brazil, try to get it diagnosed and treated while still there, since doctors trained in tropical medicine and pharmaceuticals to treat various ailments are readily available. If this is not possible, be sure to tell your doctor at home where you have been. Most visitors who stay for a few weeks have no problems, but those that do occur are usually the result of overindulgence, unfamiliar foods, or trying to tan too fast. It is always safest to eat only peeled fruit and cooked vegetables, and to be selective with street food vendors and stands. Let overall cleanliness be your guide.

Drinking Water and Milk. The best general rule is to drink bottled water in Brazil. Many of the public water systems date almost to colonial times and are not 100 percent safe. Be sure to ask for bottled water (it is usually in your hotel room when you arrive).

Pasteurized milk is available in every major city. In the north and northeast, milk sold in plastic bags should be boiled before drinking. "Leite Longa Vida," processed milk that does not need refrigeration until it is opened, is sold in cardboard cartons and can be consumed as is.

Medical Treatment. In Brazil there is no shortage of competent, trained, English-speaking doctors. The International Association for Medical Assistance for Travelers (IAMAT), 736 Center St., Lewiston, N.Y. 14092, has participating doctors in every South American country. All speak English. They will send, on request, a booklet listing these physicians, which you can carry on your trip. The booklet takes from 6 to 8 weeks delivery time, so order it well in advance of your trip. English speaking doctors can be located in Rio through the Rio Health Collective, Av. das Americas 4430, Sala 303, Barra da Tijuca (325–9300, ext. 44). The RHC operates a free referral service for medical specialists of all

PLANNING YOUR TRIP 41

kinds, and can provide English-speaking nurse companions and translators if needed. Open from 9 A.M. to 2 P.M. weekdays. Elsewhere, consult the American Consulate.

British residents may rely on Europe Assistance, 252 High St., Croydon CRO 1NF, which operates an on-the-spot medical assistance service throughout the world. Note: This service involves a fee.

Pharmaceuticals pose no problem for the visitor. All major cities have excellent drugstores and many offer "round the clock" service.

Safety. Although Brazil has the eighth largest economy in the world, it is a country where 2 percent of the population are very, very rich and the rest are very, very poor. Poverty breeds crime. The tourist who can afford the trip is a millionaire by Brazilian standards, and thus a prime target for crime. Crime is a problem in large cities everywhere, and Rio and São Paulo are no exceptions. To lessen the risk of being assaulted, never wear gold or silver jewelry or watches; carry photographic equipment in a knapsack worn back-to-front; do not carry a bag at all, if possible; avoid trouble spots like the Jardim de Allah, the 553 bus, and the Santa Teresa trolley in Rio, and do not wander around the streets of downtown São Paulo alone at night. Be especially on the lookout for young boys working in groups or with prostitutes. In Rio, report crimes to *Poltur,* a police unit set up especially to aid foreigners located at Av. Humberto de Campos, 315, Leblon (259–7048). Poltur is open 24 hours a day. To minimize losses in case of assault, carry only as much money as you will need and leave all valuable documents (passports, airline tickets, traveler's checks, etc.) in the safe provided by your hotel.

SPORTS. Soccer, called "futebol" and pronounced fut-tea-ball, is as much a national heritage for Brazilians as wine is for the French and snow for the Eskimo.

The soccer the Brazilians play is a fast game, almost like a ballet, that begins when little boys take their first ball to the beach or into the middle of a vacant lot. You can see them bouncing the ball off their knees, giving a backward kick with a bare foot and sending it to a buddy who butts it with his head. In Brazil as well as the rest of the soccer-playing world, only the goalkeeper is allowed to touch the ball with his hands.

If you like sports at all and are in Rio on a Sunday when two of the major Rio teams are playing each other, you should visit the huge Maracanã soccer stadium. The four main Rio teams are Flamengo (Brazil's most popular team), Vasco (chiefly identified with the Portuguese colony in Rio), Fluminense (the high society team), and Botafogo (the least definable in personality). If you try to go, talk it all over ahead of time with someone at the hotel who can tell you how to get there, when to go, how to buy tickets, and so forth. Unlike baseball, U.S. or Canadian football, rugby, cricket, and the like, soccer is easy to understand even if you've never seen it before. But even if the game doesn't turn you on, the stadium is impressive, and the crowd itself is half the spectacle. Soccer crowds in the British Isles and northern Europe can be extremely surly; and in the Mediterranean and other Latin American countries (as well as most of Brazil), they can be dangerously passionate. But the Maracanã crowd is unswervingly good natured, and the stadium is exceptionally safely constructed, so don't worry about stories you may have read about soccer disasters. For one of the big games between two of the major local teams, large numbers of the rooters bring huge homemade flags, featuring the team's colors in a variety of homemade designs, and they wave these flags when their team comes on the field or scores a goal. Another feature you are not likely to encounter at the World Series or the Super Bowl is that drums start beating in various parts of the

BRAZIL

stadium well before the game and maintain their tom-tom rhythm without a break right through to the end. All in all, the crowd is one of the most colorful and exciting spectacles in sport. If you go, try to buy the highest-priced reserved seats. If you want to be with "the people" in the "arquibancada," be advised that it is plain concrete bleachers, so be sure to buy foam rubber pads to sit on before you go into the stadium.

Capoeira. A sport that is purely Brazilian, not to be found anywhere else in the world, is Capoeira. It is a fight, a dance, and a bit of judo all rolled into one. In the early slave days there were constant fights between the blacks, and when the owner caught them at it he had both sides punished. The blacks considered this unfair and developed a smoke screen of music and song to cover up the actual fighting. When a pre-arranged battle was to be fought, the natives brought their "berimbau," a bow-shaped piece of wood with a metal wire running from one end to the other, where there was a painted gourd. Using an old copper coin the player would shake the bow, and while the seeds in the gourd rattled he would strike the taut string. The effect is like background music for a Hollywood monster film. There would be a chorus chanting a fast song and the two fighters would get in the center and slug it out, primarily with their feet. Whenever the master came into view the fighters would do an elaborate pantomime of slashing the air with their fists and kicking out so as to miss their opponent. Over the years this was refined into a sport that is practiced in Bahia and Recife today. Both cities have their champion and there are many capoeira houses where the tourist can go to watch these dances. In Salvador (Bahia), they may be seen on any Saturday morning around the Modelo Market. The idea is to swing and kick to the mood of the music but without either man touching the other. The back-bending all the way to the floor, the agile foot movements to stay clear of a gleaming knife, and the strange African music make it a sport that needs great dexterity to play but is fascinating to watch.

There is also a **mountain climbing** society in Rio as well as a **spelunking** society that are happy to welcome experienced tourists on their weekend outings. If your meat is climbing up the pitted side of Sugar Loaf or delving deep into a grotto in Minas Gerais, any tourist agency can make the necessary introductions.

Rio has recently become a **hang-glider's** paradise. Taking off from a mountain peak, the colorful kites circle sometimes for hours before landing at the end of Gavea beach, beyond the Inter-Continental and Nacional hotels.

Water-skiing and **underwater diving** are also practiced by sportsmen in clubs all along the coastline. Brazilians are a very club-conscious people, and almost everyone you meet will be a member of something and will be able to take you to his particular club and introduce you around. They love to show off visitors and most clubs can only be entered with a member. Once you are inside you'll find the friendship and generosity for which the Brazilians are famous.

Horse racing is also immensely popular. The Grande Premio Brasil held first Sunday in August highlights the racing season. **Golf** and **tennis** are available in all leading cities. There are two golf clubs in Rio, where you can play by invitation only. **Yachting** is extremely popular in Rio. And there is **surfing** and **windsurfing** on the beaches.

For those who like to **fish**, Brazil can be a surprising wonderland. Many tourists try for some marlin fishing off the coast of Rio, and others go to the magnificent Foz do Iguaçu to try their hand at dorado. In the Amazon River there are monstrous fish called Pirarucú that reach up to 280 pounds each. The nation's rivers and streams are filled with a variety of game fish. No license is needed and no limit set.

PLANNING YOUR TRIP 43

If you have a taste for hunting; you're out of luck, because the government outlawed the hunting of big-spotted jaguars, wild boar, fleet-footed jungle deer, moss-backed turtles, and dozens of other animals which were once considered fair game. But a **camera safari** into the Mato Grosso or Amazon jungles can still be an adventure. Most travel agencies can tailor a program to suit you.

Traveling in Brazil

BY AIR. There are four major commercial airlines (Varig, Cruzeiro do Sul, Vasp, and Trans-Brasil), which together fly over 3 billion passenger-miles a year. The airline companies take good care of their planes, have top flight mechanics, and first-class pilots, and crews who refuse to let a plane go up unless they are absolutely certain it is ready to fly. The service is nothing short of excellent and full course meals are the rule rather than the exception, followed always by a cup of the ever-present black coffee.

Their plane scheduling is fairly imaginative and is designed to meet both passenger needs and the competition. One of the most successful and most used of all the airline services is the popular "air bridge" between Rio and São Paulo. In 1959, the four air companies pooled their forces to set up a system to keep both passengers and planes constantly flowing between the two major cities. The traveler does not even need to buy a ticket or make a reservation in advance, you just show up at the airport and get aboard the next plane. During the rush hours there is a plane leaving every 30 minutes, and every hour on the hour up to 10:30 P.M. The air bridge has been a success since its inauguration, carrying more than 2,000 passengers a day. If you want to leave on a specific flight, make a reservation. The cost is about $30 one way.

So successful was the Rio-São Paulo bridge that in 1962 air bridges were inaugurated to Belo Horizone and Brasilia. The flights are not so frequent, because the distances are greater, but the regular commuters seem more than satisfied. Planes tend to fill up on weekends; book well in advance if you plan to fly anywhere on a Friday, especially to or from Manaus or Brasilia.

If you're planning on doing a good deal of domestic flying in Brazil, check out the Brazil Air Pass, which must be purchased outside the country. There are two types: one costs $250 and allows you to fly to 4 cities within 14 days; the other costs $330 and gives you unlimited travel for 21 days. Both are well worth the money. Consult your travel agent before starting your trip.

BY RAIL. Train service between Rio and São Paulo is comfortable. An overnight trip for two in private cabin costs about $14; there is a dining car, and your porter can even provide "room service." There is excellent regional service from São Paulo on the Paulista and Sorocabana lines and 24-hour service from São Paulo to Brasilia, and also from Rio to Belo Horizonte. Most service to other areas of Brazil is inferior to air travel. Travelers save both time and often considerable trouble by avoiding long rail journeys in Brazil.

BY BUS. With its growing highway network, Brazil can offer comfortable bus travel over most of the country, and even internationally. Unless you're in a tour group, however, you can't book straight through from, say, Montevideo to Rio. Instead, you buy a ticket from one principal city to the next—Montevideo Porto Alegre, then Florianópolis, Curitiba, São Paulo and

Rio. But you'll need the hotel room and rest between each long leg anyway. On most-traveled routes, service is frequent and inexpensive. Between São Paulo and Rio (6½ to 7 hours), for example, there is a bus every half hour all day long costing about $4, and night "sleeper" at $8.

CAR RENTALS. Most major cities have local or international Rent-A-Car Services. Avis and Hertz have extensive operations throughout the country, and there are several good local car-rental services in various cities. Prices in Rio range from $20 a day for a small Volkswagen "Fusca," plus 5% municipal tax, mileage charges, and insurance fees.

Car Rental Agencies in Rio at the airport and on Rua Princesa Isabel, Copacabana: *Avis*, 542–4249/4349; *Hertz*, 275–4995; *InterLocadora*, 542–1043 or 275–6546; *VIP's*, 275–3095 or 295–0040; *Localiza*, 275–3340.

Leaving Brazil

CUSTOMS RETURNING HOME. U.S. residents who are out of the U.S. at least 48 hours and have claimed no exemption during the previous 30 days are entitled to bring in duty-free up to $400 worth of bona fide gifts or items for their own personal use.

The duty free allowance is based on the full fair *retail* value of the goods. You must now list the items purchased and *they must accompany you when you return.* So keep all receipts handy with the detailed list, and it is obviously wise to pack the goods together in one case. The $50 mailed gift scheme (see below) is also based on the retail value. Every member of a family is entitled to this same exemption, regardless of age, and their exemptions can be pooled. Minors do not receive exemptions on alcohol and tobacco.

One liter of alcoholic beverages and up to 100 non-Cuban cigars may be included in the exemption if you are 21 years of age or older. You may bring in up to 200 cigarettes for your personal use. Alcoholic beverages in excess of one quart are subject to customs duty and internal revenue tax.

Only one bottle of certain perfumes that are trademarked in the United States (Lanvin, Chanel, etc.) may be brought, unless you get written permission from the manufacturer to bring more. Other perfumes are limited by weight or value.

You do not have to pay duty on art objects or antiques provided that they are over 100 years old, so be sure to ask the dealer for a certificate establishing the age of whatever you buy. Remember, however, that many countries regulate the removal of cultural properties and works of art, and that in recent years the trade in pre-Colombian art everywhere in the Americas has come under very severe regulation subject to criminal penalties if violated.

Under the GSP (Generalized System of Preferences) plan some 2,800 items from *developing* countries may be brought into the U.S. duty free, quite outside the regular exemptions. The purpose of this is to help the economic development of such countries by encouraging their exports. Brazil is a GSP country. For more information, write to Department of the Treasury, U.S. Customs Service, Washington, D.C. 20229, and ask for the latest edition of the leaflet, *GSP & the Traveller.*

Do not bring foreign meats, fruits, plants, soil, or other agricultural items into the United States. It is illegal to bring in foreign agricultural items without individual permission because they can spread destructive plant or animal pests and diseases. For more information, read the pamphlet *Customs Hints,* or write

PLANNING YOUR TRIP 45

to Quarantines, Department of Agriculture, Federal Center Bldg., Hyattsville, MD 20782, and ask for Program Aid No. 1083, entitled "Traveler's Tips on Bringing Food, Plant and Animal Products into the United States."

Register (including serial numbers) with U.S. Customs your furs, jewelry, watches, rings, cameras, tape recorders, and other merchandise that might be mistaken as items purchased abroad. If not, obtain a registration at the U.S. Customs office at your departure airport. Otherwise, you many have to pay duty and then file for a refund once you can provide proof of purchase in the U.S.

British subjects, except those under the age of 17 years, may import duty-free from *any* country the following: 200 cigarettes or 100 cigarillos or 50 cigars or 250 grams of tobacco; 1 litre of spirits or 2 litres of alcoholic beverages under 22% volume and 2 litres of still table wine. Also: 50 grams of perfume, ¼ litre of toilet water, and £28 worth of other normally dutiable goods.

Canadian residents: In addition to personal effects, people 16 years and older may bring in the following articles: a maximum of 50 cigars, 200 cigarettes, 2 pounds of tobacco, and 1.1 litres of wine or liquor, provided these are declared to customs on arrival. The total exemption is $150, and unsolicited gift mailings may be up to $25 in value. Canadian customs regulations are strictuly enforced; you are recommended to check what your allowances are and to make sure you have kept receipts for whatever you have bought abroad. For complete details ask for the Canadian Customs brochure "I Declare."

EXPLORING
BRAZIL

RIO DE JANEIRO

Rio de Janeiro has been called the most beautiful city in the world by many experienced travelers. With a natural setting surpassing even Hong Kong and San Francisco, it has everything. There are long stretches of soft sandy beaches and lines of tall palm trees. There are mountains covered with deep green untouched jungle and birds, butterflies, and flowers in profusion. There are great fleecy clouds floating lazily over the ocean, which pushes in cool breezes and an occasional rain storm. There are warm days and cool nights and starlit skies and huge full moons.

What nature has given, the Brazilians have embellished with their own personalities. Along the black and white mosaic promenades walk some of the loveliest women in Latin America. The men, well built and tanned from hours on the beach, add their note of masculine grace. Colonial buildings vie for space with modern air-conditioned skyscrapers. There is music everywhere, from the honking of taxi and automobile horns to soft singing voices. There is an excitement in the air, curiously mixed with a tropical languor.

But Rio is more than just a beautiful setting. It is a city that boasts its own ballet company, magnificent opera house, and dozens of cultural centers. It is a mecca for artists and enterprising businesspeople. It also calls the international drifter, the expatriate, and the fortune hunter. And in recent years, with the construction of many luxurious hotels, it is South America's tourist capital as well.

BRAZIL

São Sebastiao do Rio de Janeiro is 15 miles long and varies from 2 to 10 miles wide. Nestling between the tall green mountains and the deep blue-green sea, the city offers a breathtaking sight, by day or night. During the day the sun plays on the sand and palm trees, and the white buildings with their red tile roofs serve more to ornament the city's natural beauty than to detract from it. At night the city wears strings of glowing lights, giving the impression that strands of diamonds have been lazily entwined around the buildings and the mountains by some benevolent giant.

The most obvious attraction for the visitor is the beach. Just the name Copacabana inspires romantic images, and rare is the tourist who doesn't arrive in Rio and immediately jump into a swimsuit. Rio has 23 different beaches, scattered from the international airport in the north to the other side of the mountains in the south. Most popular are the beaches at Copacabana, Ipanema, and Leblon. There are no bathing fees for any of the beaches. Oceanfront hotels provide cabanas, towels, chairs, umbrellas, and security guards for their guests. Waves at the beach come in hard and fast most of the time, so don't expect to do much swimming, just a lot of splashing. Also be prepared to confront lots of people on the weekends. Take nothing of value to the beach—no cameras, no jewelry, no passports, no airline tickets, and only enough cash in cruzados for a drink or a snack, which you can buy from one of the roving vendors.

Assuming you've had enough sun and that you want to see some of the city itself, a good plan is suggested in the following pages.

Botafogo and Sugar Loaf

Take a taxi or a bus to Botafogo and the Museu do Indio, or the Indian Museum open 10 A.M. to 6 P.M. Tuesday to Friday, 1 to 5 P.M. on weekends (admission is free). Located in an old home at Rua das Palmeiras 55 (286–0845/2097), it is a storehouse of Indian work (feathers, ceramics, stone, and weaving), as well as a growing archive of films and recordings of the indigenous people's way of life and music. The museum's collection gives a taste of the enormous contribution of indigenous tribes to Brazilian culture. Indian women were genetically and emotionally the mothers of Brazil, and photographs of them and their children, blown up to life-size, panel the walls, interspersed with enlarged lithographs by early artist-explorers depicting the natives as white men first encountered them. These reveal how much has changed and how much has remained the same.

Artifacts displayed in glass cases stir the imagination: Elaborate headdresses made from the brilliant plumage of jungle birds shade from purple, to blue, to green, to bright orange and yellow. Some are arc-shaped like the Indian chief's headgear familiar to North Americans, while others are feather cloches that cover the scalp like a bathing cap or cascade across the shoulders in downy waves. Smaller pieces of feather jewelry add scarabs, bones, and shells to the designs, so modern in their simple, so-called primitive way that they could fetch high prices in a chic Ipanema boutique.

RIO DE JANEIRO 51

The indigenous peoples loved to adorn themselves well before the Portuguese influenced them to cover their nakedness. Exquisite intricate body paintings and complex facial designs in shiny red and black or shimmering aqua served to designate social status, protect the wearer against evil spirits and disease, distinguish and attract the sexes—and beautify.

This small, well-laid-out exhibition analyzes the economic, symbolic, and social worlds of the best known tribes through these and other artifacts.

Close by, at Rua São Clemente 134, is the Casa Rui Barbosa (286–1297), former home of one of Brazil's leading citizens of the 19th century. Barbosa, a diplomat and politician, wrote Brazil's first constitution and supported direct elections, abolition, educational reform, federalism, the equality of nations and their right to remain neutral during war. A museum since 1930, Barbosa's house is open to the public from 10 A.M. to 4 P.M. Tuesday through Friday, and from 2 to 5 P.M. on Saturdays, Sundays, and holidays.

In this pink neoclassical mansion that sits behind a high wrought-iron fence, Barbosa and the assembled leaders of his day signed the first Constitution of the Brazilian Republic, which Barbosa also wrote. Barbosa was an erudite man; his 35,000-volume collection in seven languages testifies to his depth of knowledge and love of books. These tomes, with Barbosa's marginal notes written in the different languages of the texts, are available to the public through the museum's lending library—a continuing tribute to their owner's respect for scholarship. The rooms of the house each have a name, reflecting the preoccupations of its owner and the social structure of the time. The women's salon is separated from the men's salon, as women were expected not to mix in affairs outside the domestic sphere. The music, dressing, visitors' and family rooms, plus different dining rooms for lunch and dinner, each imply a social order and standard of propriety no longer practiced. Labels such as the "religious question room," the "constitution room," the "federation room," and rooms named for family members and places where Barbosa lived all suggest the range of his travels and concerns.

Next, head for Sugar Loaf, which is right nearby. It is advisable to get there early for there are usually many people who want to make the visit—especially during school holidays, January to March and June to August. Once you are borne upward you'll have the pleasant sensation of space all around you and a vivid panoramic display of Rio and her natural beauties below. The car makes a half-way stop on Urca mountain, where there is a pleasant restaurant and a small amphitheater that has shows and popular concerts. Starting in 1978, this peak also became the site for a spectacular pre-Carnival ball. You can either linger here or transfer to the next car to go to the top, where you have the city at your feet and can identify the other points of interest that you must see before you leave. It is best to visit Sugar Loaf *before* you visit the Corcovado Christ statute, or you will remember Sugar Loaf only as an anticlimax.

A nice family way to sightsee is on a "Bateau Mouche," which cruises Guanabara Bay. Bateau Mouche cruises leave from Avenida

52   BRAZIL

Repórter Nestor Moreira, 11 in Botafogo, daily except Mondays (295–1997/1947/1896). You can choose a morning tour that includes lunch which leaves at 9:30 A.M.; an afternoon cruise that leaves at 2:30 P.M.; or an all-day excursion combining the sights of the two shorter ones. Prices range from $20 to $40.

There are taxis waiting at the platform where you will return and ask the driver to take you—slowly—to the Gloria Church (Igreja da Gloria). On the way down Avenida Pasteur you will pass the high-walled Yacht Club (admittance strictly to members only but you can peer over the chain-barred entrance-way) and the pink-painted colonial buildings belonging to the Brazilian University. Coming out in front of the tunnel of Pasmado, you'll go along Botafogo beach and after going around a bend you'll be in the Flamengo beach district where a major face-lifting has taken place. Here they have built the largest public park in Latin America on land reclaimed from the sea. Every ounce of earth was carted in by truck. The planting was done by master landscape gardener Roberto Burle Marx. Thanks to the Flamengo *aterro,* as it is called, you can now drive to and from Copacabana in a matter of minutes. The park is a delightful place for a late afternoon stroll. You can also explore it by tractor-drawn minitrain, and if you have small children with you, there is a fine playground, and a special space for model aircraft enthusiasts. Be sure to use the overpasses and under-passes to cross the main freeways; accidents are frequent on the *aterro* and just about everywhere else in Rio.

Favorite Church of the Imperial Family

The driver will turn off and climb a steep hill that is lined on both sides with houses harking back to the days of the Portuguese colonials and will let you off in front of the big wooden doors of the Gloria Church. Built in the 18th century, it was the favorite spot of the Imperial Family and contains many fine examples of art from both the Old and the New Worlds. The site of the church was once the hut of a hermit who, in 1671, with the help of two mysterious youths (angels), sculptured a beautiful statue of Our Lady of Glory. Seventeen years later, when the image had been accredited with miraculous powers, the hermit returned to Portugal, taking the image with him. But the ship sank into the ocean, and the statue washed ashore at Lagos, Portugal. In 1924 a copy was enshrined in its place in the Gloria Church. The Brazilians still want the original image returned. On August 15, the church is lit up like a baroque birthday cake and silhouetted against the dark sky and palm trees it is one of the loveliest sights in Brazil.

Walk down the street you drove up and then along the Praça (park) Paris. Laid out by a French architect a good many years ago, it reminds many Parisians of home, with its marble statues, trimmed hedges, reflection pools, and water fountains. On the opposite side of the avenue you'll see the contrast in the ultramodern Monument to the Brazilian Dead of World War II. Brazil sent troops to fight in Italy and suffered heavy losses. Construction of Rio's controversial and long-overdue subway, which tore up much of this area, is now finished. Despite a series of financial crises and floods, the final stations have

RIO DE JANEIRO 53

been completed, linking the downtown area with the edges of the north and south zones of the city.

Museums and Historic Sites

Have lunch in the area, perhaps in the rooftop restaurant of Mesbla, Rio's largest department store, right across the street from the Passeio Público, oldest public park in the city. Filled with tall shade trees, small lagoons and rustic bridges, it is a pleasant place to get out of the sun. It also has its share of tramps and beggars and a large collection of alley cats.

Leave the park by the upper right-hand sidewalk and keep walking right over to Rio's main commercial heartline, Avenida Rio Branco. Walk up Rio Branco Avenue and you will pass the National Library (Biblioteca Nacional at #219/239 Av. Rio Branco, 240–9229; open Monday to Friday from 10 A.M. to 9 P.M. and Saturday, noon to 6 P.M.) and the Museum of Fine Arts (Museu Nacional de Belas Artes, Av. Rio Branco 199, 240–0160; open Tuesday and Thursday from 10 A.M. to 6:30 P.M., Wednesdays and Fridays from noon to 6:30 P.M.. Saturdays, Sundays, and holidays from 3 to 6 P.M.) on your right and the Municipal Theater (Teatro Municipal, Praça Floriano, 210–2463) on your left. If this theater looks familiar, it is because it is an exact one-quarter scale copy of the Opera House in Paris. If you are here at lunchtime, drop in for an unforgettable meal at the Café do Teatro, downstairs in the opera building. Good cuisine mixes here with an incredible setting, reminiscent of a Cecil B. De Mille Biblical epic. Two blocks farther down the Avenue on the left rises the 34-floor, air-conditioned, glass-paneled Edificio Avenida Central, Rio's first skyscraper.

If you walk through the arcades to the other side of this modern building and look across the street, you'll see the old Convent of Santo Antonio (Igreja do Convento de Santo Antonio, Largo da Carioca, 262–0129/0201; open weekdays except Tuesdays, 8 A.M. to 6:30 P.M., and Saturday from 7 to 11 A.M. Built between 1608 and 1619, it contains, aside from priceless colonial art objects, the tombs of Leopoldina, the first Empress of Brazil, and the Infante Dom Pedro de Bourbon. Beside the convent is the richest little church in Rio, the São Francisco da Penitência (Igreja de São Francisco da Penitência, Largo da Carioca, 5; 262–0197. Open Monday through Friday from 1–5 P.M.). Its interior is completely hand sculpted and covered in gold foil. It also has a remarkable altar and sacristy. The climb up the hill is worth it.

The former hill of Santo Antonio was removed, its earth used to form the Flamengo *aterro*. The site was transformed into a double avenue bordered by new buildings. These include the Metropolitan Cathedral —still unfinished—the aluminum-block headquarters building of Petrobrás (the government oil monopoly) and, across the avenue, the high-rise headquarters of the National Housing Bank. Behind this modern setting you will see the colonial arches built in 1723 to carry water down to the city.

Go back down Rio Branco, until you come to Rua Ouvidor. There are no automobiles permitted on this street and it buzzes like an overactive beehive.

54   **BRAZIL**

Five blocks from Ouvidor is Avenida Presidente Vargas. Be careful crossing the street here, because Brazilian drivers are notorious for disobeying traffic lights. To your right is the back entrance of the squat, attractive Church of Candelaria. (Igreja de Nossa Senhora de Candelária, Praça Pio X at the beginning of Getulio Vargas, 233–2324; open Monday to Friday from 7 A.M. to noon and 2 to 4:30 P.M.; Saturday from 7 to noon only; Sunday from 10 A.M. to noon). The front of the building once overlooked the waters of Guanabara Bay, but the view is now obstructed by buildings and elevated drives. The inside is dark and relaxing after a walk in the sun.

Continuing downward on Rio Branco you will come to Praça Mauá and the beginning of miles of docks that have made the city such an important world trading center. Praça Mauá is peopled by all sorts, with heavy emphasis on foreign sailors. Now take a bus marked Copacabana, Ipanema, or Leblon and go back to your hotel and have a tall, cool drink. You've earned it today.

The Jardim Botânico, Jockey Club, and Santa Teresa

Another full day could start with an hour at the beach, a shower, and then a visit to the Botanical Garden on Rua Jardim Botânico. Take any bus marked "Joquei" or "Jardim Botânico"—they all run along Rua Jardim Botânico. The garden is one of the best in the world, say noted horticulturalists, and is carefully kept up. Covering an area of 567,000 square meters, there are over 135,000 plants and trees. There are 900 varieties of palm tree alone. Founded in 1808 by the prince regent Dom Joao, there stood near the entrance gate the famous *palma mater* transported from the West Indies and planted by the monarch. There is also a strikingly beautiful avenue of palms that is 740 meters long and contains 134 royal palms. Also be sure and see the bronze fountain dating back to 1820 and the mammoth Victoria Regia water lilies that measure 21 feet around. There is also a peaceful jungle atmosphere, lake and waterfall, a small greenhouse filled with flesh-eating Venus flytrap plants, and some rare trees from Indonesia, whose huge roots spread atop the ground like writhing cobras.

This area of the city has a long history. After fleeing with his family to Brazil, Prince Regent Dom João VI ordered this garden prepared for the cultivation of spice seeds from the East Indies. Many foreign species were later introduced by Luiz de Abreu Vieira e Silva, who was shipwrecked in Goa, captured by the French, and sent to the Isle de France, site of the Gabrielle Garden. When Luiz escaped, he had the foresight to steal some plants, which he managed to save. Thanks to Luiz, Brazil began to grow nutmeg, clove, avocado, litchi, cinnamon, grapefruit, breadfruit, ciruela, and various kinds of nonindigenous palm trees. Later, in 1812, one of the accomplices in Luiz's escape sent along some tea seeds, whereupon Chinese workers were imported to teach their time-honored cultivation techniques. In what was perhaps the first farm subsidy in the New World, Dom João created a system of incentives to introduce new plant species to Brazil. He awarded medals to successful growers of exotic plants and made farmers exempt

RIO DE JANEIRO

from taxes levied on the imported goods needed to develop agriculture. Sugarcane from Cayenne entered the country in this way.

Dom João had to return to Portugal in 1821 when summoned by his court, but he left the Royal Botanical Garden well established. In 1842, the Avenue of the Royal Palms was planted, a majestic and towering canopy which is just as impressive now as when Mrs. Louis Agassiz, a noted chronicler among Brazil's early travelers, lamented in 1869, "I wish it were possible to give in words the faintest idea of the architectural beauty of this colonnade of palms, with their green crowns meeting to form the roof. Straight, firm and smooth as stone columns, a dim vision of . . . some ancient Egyptian temple rises to the imagination as one looks down the long vista."

A great place for salads nearby is Alfaces, at Rua Visconde da Graça 51, a few blocks east off Rua Jardim Botânico.

From there take a taxi to the Laranjeiras Palace, the residence of the governor of Rio. You probably won't be allowed past the guard, but the drive through the Guinle Park and past the luxurious private apartment houses that line it is worthwhile. Now still in your cab, take a quick look at Catete Palace on Rua Catete, Praia do Flamengo. Built of granite and rose-colored marble in 1862 by a wealthy coffee baron, it was purchased 32 years later by the federal government and used as the Foreign Office. Dictator Getulio Vargas, when he returned to power as duly elected President of the Republic, insisted on living there rather than at the other palace where he had been tossed out. It was also at Catete that he killed himself in 1954. The palace, with its magnificent gardens, was converted into the Museum of the Republic when Brasilia was inaugurated. The Museu da República, Rua do Catete, 179, has been closed temporarily for restoration and reorganization of its collection. Call 265–9747 if you're interested in seeing restoration work.

Now you can have lunch downtown and hop into another cab for a better look at the old aqueduct, over which little trolley cars cross on their way to the lovely residential area of Santa Teresa. Santa Teresa, unlike many of the communities clinging to Rio's hillsides, is not a slum. The cobbled streets, clean air, cooler temperatures, and absence of traffic make Santa Teresa a haven for artists and others seeking a good place to work. Many old mansions and lovely gardens line the winding streets, where stone stairways carved into the hillside provide shortcuts so that residents on foot can avoid the circuitous climb.

Santa Teresa's main attraction, apart from its feeling of antiquity and its superb view of the city below, is the Museu Chácara do Ceu, 224–8981, run by the Fundação Raymundo Ottoni de Castro Maya at Rua Murtinho No. 93. Raymundo was born in Paris in 1894, the son of Brazil's vice consul there. After studying law, he turned his attention to business, where he successfully enlarged his ample inheritance. Always a pillar of the community, Raymundo was a great patron of the arts, amassing an eclectic collection unified only by its owner's consistent good taste. Raymundo published many fine art books, for which he commissioned illustrations by Portinari, Santa Rosa, and numerous other noted contemporary Brazilian artists. Among his other accom-

56 BRAZIL

plishments, Raymundo founded and was president of the Museum of Modern Art in Rio, was a member of the French Legion of Honor, and edited a book of prints by Jean Baptiste Debret, whose originals he had acquired.

The museum's exhibition includes works by European greats such as Degas, Dali, Dufy, Matisse, Miró, Modigliani, Monet, Morisot, and Picasso. The Brazilian artists represented are of comparable stature: DiCavalcanti, Djanira, Isabel de Jesus, Pancetti, and Portinari. The whimsical, poignant series of 21 Don Quixote drawings in colored pencil by Portinari occupy an entire room of Raymundo's former residence and are absolutely not to be missed. The museum has a beautiful garden and outdoor patio from which can be seen the New Cathedral, which strongly resembles an upside-down beach pail.

To reach Santa Teresa, take a cab or the number 206 or 214 bus from the Menezes Cortes terminal near Praca XV and get off at Rua Dias da Barras. Signs will direct you to the museum, which is located at the cul-di-sac on top of the hill, to your left as you get off the bus. It is not advisable to take the trolley itself, since many tourists (and Cariocas) have been ripped off by street vandals on the slow-moving, open cars. The museum is open from Tuesday to Saturday 2 to 5 P.M. and on Sundays 11 A.M. to 5 P.M.

The best place to absorb the ambience of Santa Teresa is the Bar do Arnaudo, Rua Almirante Alexandrino 316-B, 252–7246, for over 15 years a hangout for artists, intellectuals, and political activists. During the repressive '70's, its reputation as a meeting place for bohemians and radicals meant that it was always under police surveillance. At that time, almost any conversation between artists was regarded with suspicion. Today, however, Brazil's political climate has eased to the point where newspaper features frankly describing this aspect of the bar's past are reproduced and posted on the walls. One such article noted that Arnaudo himself was grilled behind closed doors and that it was not unusual for two police guards to be posted outside the swinging, saloon-style entryway.

That tense epoch has passed, but Bar do Arnaudo's role as a good-time community gathering spot hasn't. The walls of this restaurant, which specializes in food typical of Brazil's northeast, still serve as a showcase for struggling artists who can't find galleries to show their work. And a handwritten notice kindly requests: "Please, don't use the tables as percussion instruments." The prices are low, and the food is tasty.

The parks and fountains of the Lapa district, inaugurated in 1975, are on a site that was once the center of Rio's bohemian nightlife and samba. Many of the surrounding buildings have escaped the march of progress; indeed, some have been protected as examples of Rio's architectural history. Look for the Automóvel Club, the Sala Cecilia Meireles music conservatory and the large white Convent of Santa Teresa, built in 1970 and now the home of a Carmelite order of nuns who have no contact with the outside world.

Now for a visit to one of the most charming corners of the city, the Largo do Boticário just off Rua Cosme Velho. Everyone will tell you it dates from colonial times, whereas in fact only one of its houses dates

RIO DE JANEIRO 57

from earlier than the 1920s. It is a pleasantly shady spot, one of its attractions being an English-owned antique store.

Now comes the treat, Corcovado. You can do one of two things. Continue in your taxi to the top of the mountain, which will give you a slow, unwinding, breathtaking view of all angles of the city, or go to Rua Cosme Velho 513 and take a tiny cogwheel train to the top. Trains leave every half hour and the ride is almost straight up through dense vegetation. When you arrive you'll have to climb a number of stairs to get to the base of the statue. The statue is impressive up close and the view from the top simply indescribable. The statue, inaugurated in 1931, has a height of 120 feet and weighs 700 tons. The head alone weighs 30 tons; each arm weighs 30 tons and each hand 8 tons. The statue was designed by Frenchman Paul Landowski and paid for by contributions of the people of Rio.

The best time to visit the statue is in the late afternoon about one hour before sunset. The effect of the reddening sun against the buildings and the sea far below is stunning. Wait patiently and one by one the lights of the town will start to come on, like fireflies awakening for the evening. Within half an hour the city will be dressed in sparkling diamonds and silhouetted against the dark shapes of Sugar Loaf and the blackening waters of the bay and ocean. **Warning:** The last trolley leaves at 7 P.M. and is always crowded. If you go up in a cab have him wait.

You may want to visit the Maracanã soccer stadium, the biggest in the world. Built in 1950 for the World Championship Games, it can hold—and has held—as many as 200,000 people at one time. While the designers looked after the comfort of the spectators, they also considered the players, and there is a wide moat around the field to protect the athletes should they lose.

Within walking distance is the Quinta da Boa Vista and the Museu Nacional, a beautiful old pink and white building that used to be the Imperial Family's Rio palace, in a gemlike setting of landscaped parks, lakes and marble statues. The museum is open from 10 A.M. to 4:45 P.M. every day except Monday and is filled with traces of Brazil's past, both historical and archeological. There are Indian funeral urns, reconstructed fossils, and a fine collection of Amazon reptiles and insects, and one of the best collections of birds in the world (264–8262).

Right beside the museum is the zoo. Open Tuesday to Sunday from 9 A.M. to 4:30 P.M., it keeps most of its more important animals in unwalled natural settings. Be sure to note the colorful Amazon parrots as you go in (their squawking for attention will force you to notice them) and the hungry leer on the face of the jungle jaguar. Also don't miss the shaded jungle pool with the colorful red cranes and little white scavenger birds. The monkeys have an island of their own, as do the Amazon boa constrictors and the alligators. Telephone for the Jardim Zoologico is 254–2024.

Now here you need another cab to visit the Church of Penha just as the sun goes down. Perched high atop a mountain, and with 365 steps, it is a favorite place for repentant pilgrims to crawl on their knees. The inside is hung with crutches and silver charms representing parts of the body that were cured, thanks to the intervention of Our Lady of Penha.

58 BRAZIL

The view from the top is superb. Igreja de Nossa Senhora da Penha is located on the Largo da Penha, 19, and is open from 7 A.M. to 5 P.M.

The Emperor's Picnic Table

On the fourth day, call another cab and make the voyage to the Tijuca Forest. On leaving Copacabana, you will pass through the neighborhoods of Ipanema and Leblon, climb higher to go around the Two Brothers mountain on Avenida Niemeyer, and go past the Gavea Golf Club and several restaurants selling coconuts and fresh oysters at São Conrado. Have your driver stop at the Emperor's Table (Mesa do Imperador). Here is a mammoth concrete picnic table where the Emperor used to bring his royal court to dine. It has an unequaled view of the south zone of the city. Nearby is the Chinese View (Vista Chinesa), which also is impressive.

The forest itself was once part of a private estate belonging to the Baron de Taunay and is studded with exotic trees, thick jungle vines, and a delightful waterfall. Also be sure and see the tiny little Mayrink Chapel with an altar painting by Brazil's famed Candido Portinari. This chapel is very popular with Brazilians and, in spite of its cramped quarters, has seen many society marriages.

Another Side to Rio

Brazil is a country of contrasts in its geography, its peoples, and its economic levels. Though it has a large and rapidly growing middle class it is still a country of the very rich and the very poor.

At first glance the favela slum sections in Rio, nestling into the mountainsides in the south zone, seem to be pastel-painted, enchanted summer cottages with magnificent views of the ocean. Then on closer inspection you can see that there is no enchantment, just bleak despair and resignation. It is not advisable to explore the favelas under any circumstances.

The favelas themselves began back in the year 1897 when soldiers of the new Republic, having put down a revolt of the Monarchists in the state of Bahia, suddenly found themselves without a cause, without money and without a place to live. They had been encamped on a hill they named Favela because of the abundance of a wildflower with the same name. So when they arrived in Rio, they called their first settlement of shacks "favela" too. The soldiers assumed they had the right to any land that wasn't being used, and once their shacks were built there were few politicians willing to incur their wrath by driving them off.

The years from 1920 to 1940 saw the favelas grow alarmingly. Brazil was entering into world trade and needed more coffee, cocoa, and fruit to export. Workers deserted the cities for the farms, cultivating the land and shipping the produce to the coast. Then prices began to fall and with the fall the workers returned to the cities, along with other peasants who had lost their jobs. They took up residence in the favelas. When Dictator Getulio Vargas set the wheels of industry into motion, he made great promises to the Brazilian people. More flocked to the

RIO DE JANEIRO 59

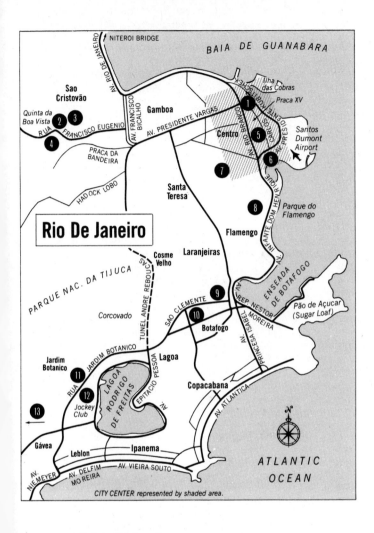

Points of Interest

Botanical Garden (Jardim Botanico) **11**
Casa Rui Barbosa **9**
Candelaria Church (Igreja da Candelaria) **1**
Chacara do Ceu **7**
City Museum (Museu da Cidade) **13**
Indian Museum (Museu do Indio) **10**
Jockey Club **12**
Maracana Stadium (Estadio do Maracano) **4**
Museum of Modern Art (Museu de Arte Moderna) **6**
Museum of the Republic (Museu da Republica) **8**
National Museum (Museu Nacional) **3**
National Museum of Fine Arts (Museu Nacional de Belas Artes) **5**
Zoological Gardens (Jardim Zoologico) **2**

BRAZIL

cities to work. From the north, truckloads of "nordestinos" converged upon Rio, anxious for employment but unlettered and untrained. They found little work and much misery.

As Rio expanded her metropolitan area, cut through roads and erected new buildings, the poor were routed and tenements demolished. Land was plentiful in the far suburbs, but the working groups (maids, bus drivers, washerwomen) could not afford to live away from the centers of activity. Transportation was sporadic and expensive. The free schools and clinics were in town, not in the outlying suburbs. People were not truly free to move to the fresh air of the distant suburbs, for necessity bound them to the favelas.

The racial mixture of the favelas has been classified by the Census Department as 28 percent white, 36 percent black, 35 percent mulatto, and 1 percent Oriental. These statistics point up the difference between Brazilian concepts of racial identity and the U.S. attitude. In the United States, all people of mixed black-white ancestry are regarded as "black," a classification which does not take into account proportions or percentages of racial ancestry. In Brazil, on the other hand, anyone lighter than "café au lait" in skin color is classified as "white," and anyone darker with a discernible trace of European ancestry is mulatto. Brazilian "blacks" are apparently of purely African descent.

Although some major favela eyesores have been entirely removed in the last few years, many still remain and nearly a fourth of Rio's population still lives in them.

The choice sites in any favela are at the bottom near the road and water supply. Many times there will be just one pump for hundreds of people, and those living at the top have to fill empty cans with water and carry them on their heads to their homes.

As would be expected under such conditions, normal sanitation practices are almost non-existent.

Welfare groups have been active in building better housing and in giving free lessons in mechanics, carpentry, and the manual arts. A number of the poor of Rio have been moved into individual concrete houses, financed originally through the Alliance For Progress but now under projects financed domestically. Unfortunately, while these moves have solved some problems, they have created others. Many ex-favelados now live up to 25 miles out of town, making transportation a heavy expense, and although they are being encouraged to buy their new homes on the installment plan, many cannot afford the low monthly payments and once again face eviction.

Like all pockets of poverty, these hillside slums have become breeding grounds for crime and in recent years Rio's crime rate has soared. Tourists can be prime targets for the legions of pickpockets and purse snatchers. While we do not wish to sound an undue alarm, it is always best to be cautious. Besides the *favela* area, other favorite hangouts for thieves in Rio are the beaches, the Santa Teresa trolley, the Maracanã soccer stadium, and popular tourist attractions such as Sugar Loaf Mountain and Corcovado (here be careful on the train to the top). When visiting any of these spots take only the essentials, no jewelry, as little cash as possible, no large bags, and hold on to your camera at all times. When on the beach watch out for overly friendly kids hanging

RIO DE JANEIRO

around your blanket. They work in groups and while one distracts you another will be off with your valuables.

Carnival

Though Carnival is celebrated everywhere in Brazil, it is in Rio that the tourist will find its most fantastic expression. Carnival is a fast-moving, mad, unbelievable, music-filled, sleepless time when the entire nation rockets off into orbit and doesn't come back to earth for four days and five nights.

The official season is actually the Saturday night before and the days leading up to Ash Wednesday, but in practice the action starts Friday at 11 P.M. when the first "bailes" (balls) begin. Usually this period falls in February but can also come in March; however preparations are going on months before.

The visitor to Rio will start hearing the strains of Carnival in late December. At first it's nothing more than the gentle throb of drums from the hillside shanty towns, mingled with the ordinary sounds of the city at work. At night the drums get louder and voices are added, chanting a fast, spirited refrain. Soon the visitor notices little dark children parading through the streets, beating on old tamborines, tin cans, or the hoods of parked automobiles. Their naked feet dance in the dust of the streets and the sands of the beach. In front of the hotels they go through the motions of a fast samba looking not only for tips and praise but also for a good time. Then, as the actual season draws closer, their parents and older brothers and sisters will parade through Copacabana in a cacophony of drums, whistles, triangles, and a weird, yelping instrument called the *cuica*. They will actually block the entire avenue, causing traffic to come to a halt while people hang out of their apartment windows and encourage them. The police do nothing to set the flow of cars in motion again, for usually they have left their posts and are dancing right in the midst of the revelers.

Stores that normally sell pens, books, and ink blotters suddenly deck their windows with coils of serpentine streamers and bags of confetti. Fabric shops, their wares spilling out onto the sidewalks, are crowded with men and women buying bright-colored silks and cottons. Other shops sell laces, stiff crinolines, masks, gold and silver chains, and decorated hats. Seamstresses double their prices and sew into the dawn, and all through the city runs an electrifying current of excitement. It affects not only the young but the oldsters as well, not only the Brazilians but the visitors.

Samba Schools Get Ready

The two months before Carnival are a good time for the tourist to arrange for a visit to a Samba school, for they are at the peak of their practice sessions and admit anyone who is willing to pay a small admission and sit on a hard bench. The school usually belongs to a certain favela slum, and most of the dancers, nearly all blacks and

62   **BRAZIL**

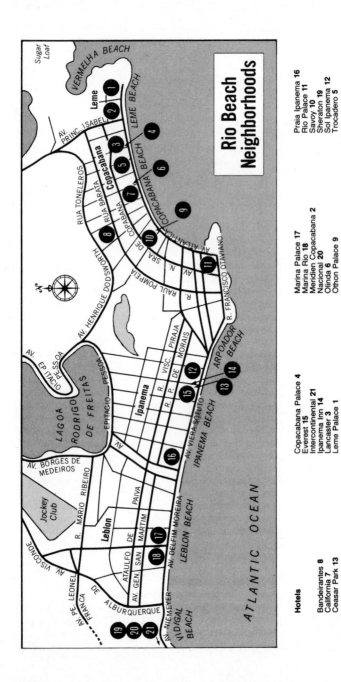

Rio Beach Neighborhoods

Hotels

Bandeirantes 8
California 7
Ceasar Park 13
Copacabana Palace 4
Everest 15
Intercontinental 21
Ipanema Inn 14
Lancaster 3
Leme Palace 1
Marina Palace 17
Marina Rio 18
Meridien Copacabana 2
Nacional 20
Olinda 6
Othon Palace 9
Praia Ipanema 16
Rio Palace 11
Savoy 10
Sheraton 19
Sol Ipanema 12
Trocadero 5

RIO DE JANEIRO 63

mulattoes, live right there. They rehearse after work far into the night or on Saturdays and Sundays. For a complete listing of where each samba school is located and/or performing, consult Riotur's monthly *Guide*. Most Samba schools are located in the Zona Norte (north side) of Rio. Talk to your hotel concierge about which to attend and transportation arrangements. Alternatively, the Beija Flor Samba school rehearses on weekends for the public in Botafogo near the Estrela do Sul Churrascaria and, off-season, performs at the Concha Verde on Sugarloaf mountain on Monday nights. The Clube do Samba, Estrada da Barra (Barrada Tijuca), 399–0892, features well-known names in samba, dancing, performances, and a dining room. It's closed Tuesday, Thursday, and Sunday and offers a different format nightly, each emphasizing a uniquely Brazilian style of entertainment.

Because they live in poverty throughout the year, they want to "act rich" during the throbbing night of glory. A specially written Samba and a complete dance routine are also centered around the theme or "enredo." A Samba school can have as many as 3,000 people in it, each with his own job to do in the over-all pageant. Each school has a "batería" or marching band of percussion instruments and drums, some of which number up to 300 men.

Such an organization costs money and the members show great ingenuity in scraping up the needed funds. Costumes alone can cost as much as $500 apiece, a lot of money especially to someone who earns but $80 a month. Much of the financing for the samba schools comes from a technically illegal but highly popular form of gambling, the "jogo do bicho," governed by Mafia-style dons who distribute part of the proceeds. In 1984, the Rio state government built a modern, concrete stadium to serve as permanent home to the samba school parade with top-quality facilities including a special section for foreign tourists to enjoy at ease what is truly an incomparable event. Tickets for this section are sold only to foreign tourists through tour operators and travel agents, and can cost as much as $100. Tickets can be purchased from scalpers for an average of $190 and up. These *cambistas,* as they are called, station themselves around the principal tourist hotels and approach foreign-looking folks.

The parades start around 8 P.M. and end the following morning. Bleacher tickets are sold, at cheaper prices, to the general public. If you don't get tickets, the *Daily Post, O Globo,* or *Jornal do Brasil* will tell you where the "secondary" Samba schools fighting to win a place in next year's top 12 will parade. You can watch these for nothing, and they are just as authentic.

The schools have their one night of glory as they vie with one another for the top prize offered by the Carnival commission. To win that top prize is just as important for them—and they practice just as hard—as the pennant is for any U.S. baseball team.

Days of Delirium

The city of Rio goes all out to stage Carnival events, in the same way that New York City pulled out all the stops for the celebration of the Statue of Liberty's birthday. All everyday activities come to a halt as

BRAZIL

Cariocas prepare for Brazil's most famous national holiday. Understandably, a shindig of this magnitude can be overwhelming for residents year after year, so while half the city has been eagerly awaiting the party they've spent all year preparing, the other half streams out of town in search of more peaceful holidays elsewhere. For the tourist, this means that many of the best shops and restaurants will be closed for much of your stay, and the streets will alternate between being totally deserted and being crammed with cars and revelers. Those who opt to visit Rio during Carnival neither want nor expect to find business as usual and are prepared for crowded restaurants, altered traffic patterns, and minor lapses in service, which all appear a small price to pay for so much high-spirited fun.

The city goes insane the weekend before Ash Wednesday. Samba is everywhere. Down from the hills stream the poor of Rio, gaudily bedecked in satins and tinsel, their faces powdered or smeared in paint. Out of swank apartment houses come the rich in their costumes costing many hundreds of dollars, laughing and embracing everyone they meet. Entire streets are blocked off from traffic, and Samba bands play 24 hours a day for anyone who wants to dance. And everybody does.

The Carnival Samba has no rigid routine of steps that one must follow. The feet move fast, the body shakes from the hips and the arms are thrown overhead in complete abandon. The music penetrates to the very bones and the Brazilians give themselves to it much as a canoe gives itself to a river's rapids. Tourists seeing this for the first time are aghast; but as their feet start beating out the music, they discover themselves trying some of the steps, and then they, too, are carried by the crowd into the very midst of the laughing, sweating bodies. By this time all reserve is gone, and only hours later, when they have collapsed onto the moonlit beach, do they realize how far away from home they really are. The next day, now bitten by the bug, they go completely native.

Although Cariocas of all social classes celebrate Carnival, creating a kind of democracy of revelry, money still determines who participates in which events. The Passarela do Samba, or parade of samba schools, is for everyone, but people with money can enjoy the show from box seats ("camarotes") and get catered meals at the Sambadromo. Despite a trend toward middle-class participation in the samba schools, they are still predominantly made up of working-class poor, favela dwellers who scrimp all year to pay for their Carnival costumes.

Carnival is for everyone. The largely black poor have their street dancing and their parties in wooden-walled, tin-roofed shacks. The middle class give blow-outs in their apartments or visit a friend who has a home in the suburbs with a backyard to expand in. The rich have their parties at their sumptuous homes in the surrounding hills or go to one or all of the fancy dress balls.

These nearly all-white balls give the visitor a true and intimate picture of upper-class, movie-star-struck Brazilians at play. Crowded, hot, reeking with perfume and whisky, they are one never-ending confusion of noise, music, and bare flesh. Tickets should be purchased in advance from hotels or tourist agencies rather than taking a chance of buying them at the door. Most tickets are sold out weeks in advance

RIO DE JANEIRO 65

for the most prestigious balls, but may also be procured from cambistas. Business suits and ordinary dresses are not permitted at the better balls. Men wear shorts and other cool, comfortable clothing. Women wear elaborate, skimpy, sequined costumes which can be purchased in Rio or concocted of bikinis, garter belts, stockings, corsets, and other erotic apparel. Guests of honor are usually Brazilian movie stars, top models, or television personalities. Many costumes competing for prizes and notoriety are extravagant versions of legendary or imaginary "royalty" and represent investments of tens of thousands of dollars.

The Samba Parade—Passarela do Samba

Without doubt, the parade of the Escolas de Samba (samba schools) is the single most spectacular event of Carnival week. Samba is the soul music of Brazil, and it is in this outpouring of joy and energy that the visitor can best sense the profound influence of Africa on Brazilian culture.

While you can enjoy the show for its musical and visual impact alone, the parade of the samba schools is more than just show biz. The excitement of the Samba Parade, beyond the sheer joy of movement and frank eroticism, is in the contest, for this is a competition as emotional and hard-fought as any soccer playoff. The dozens of samba schools, each based in a particular city neighborhood, compete and are ranked into classes or groups. Groups IA and IB perform in the Sambadromo, Groups IIA and IIB parade along Avenida Rio Branco, and groups in lesser-ranked categories do their stuff at various other locations. A samba school can upgrade its grouping from one year to the next, and making it into the first group is cause for great rejoicing in the neighborhood. In this intense competition, one of the samba schools will emerge the winner of the "Primeiro Grupo" (first group, determined by the previous year's performance) to cop the "World's Cup" of Carnival. After all the samba schools in Group I have had their chance to parade before the public (this usually occurs on the Sunday and Monday before Ash Wednesday), the judges reveal and tally their scores before an impassioned, packed crowd in Maracanã Zinha Stadium, a smaller field adjacent to Maracanã in the same athletic complex. Supporters of each samba school, clad in the school's official colors, wait as the fate of their favorite is decided during a daylong process of balloting that is televised for those who can't be at the bowl. Once the best have been chosen, the public gets a chance to see the victors parade again the next Saturday.

Watching the parade of the samba schools without knowing the rules is a little like watching a soccer match without understanding the object of the game. A group of ten judges, each marking the samba schools in a single area of expertise (music, choreography, or floats and costuming, for example), pool their votes at the end of several days of performance, and the school with the highest total ends up as the year's champion.

Every samba school's presentation must conform to guidelines established for the competition. Like the Miss America contest, there are separate categories, each of which is evaluated on its own merits. First

BRAZIL

is the "enredo," or plot, around which all the costumes and floats (called "alegorias" and "adereços") are designed and constructed, using the school's official colors. By definition, the plot must have a Brazilian theme, but this is interpreted broadly to include anything in past or present history. The floats are large, elevating the spectacularly dressed and undressed featured figures (called "destaques," or "stand-outs") to the eye level of people in the uppermost box seats, a height of several stories. The floats, as ornate as the costumes, are pushed and pulled by members of the samba schools and sometimes feature special effects such as waterfalls, showers of perfumed water, and smoke-spewing monsters. The samba school is judged on the overall cohesiveness of its movement down the avenue and on whether it completes the parade within the allotted time, usually 45 minutes.

Although most plots focus on tributes to historical characters or famous entertainers, political commentary is implanted in many. The International Monetary Fund and Uncle Sam's modern-day cultural imperialism get their noses humorously tweaked with regularity. Patriotic sentiments are prominent, as the parade provides an outlet for ordinary people to express their fondest hopes and feelings. The music and words to the samba songs, written anew each year, are also judged in the competition and reveal much about the Brazilian dream. Sung loudly and repeated like an incantation or choral refrain, the songs are opera and political protest in one. "I want our people well-nourished, a country that is developing, my child well-educated," proclaimed the Imperio Serrano samba in 1986. "Enough of earning so little, enough suffocation and cowardice."

Caprichosos, another samba school, has called for Brazil to be spelled with an "s," the way it is in Portuguese, rather than with the Americanized "z." "Brazil with a 'z' never more," demand the singers and dancers. But the title of Salgueiro's samba best summarizes the spirit of Carnival: "You must draw from your imagination what you don't have in your wallet," a tribute to the tenacious of Rio who make do with the little they have and manage to live joyfully in spite of material poverty.

The overall harmony of the various parts—words, music, the concept being acted out, choreography, costumes, floats, drum corps, or "bateria"—is an important factor in the judging, as are the Porta-Bandeira (standard bearer) and her partner, the Mestre-Sala, a couple in rich colonial dress who represent the entire samba school. Little girls in favelas aspire to carry the flag of the neighborhood samba school in the Carnival parade the way American teens yearn to be cheerleaders, and it is as much an honor for a boy to be chosen as "Dance Master."

The samba schools you want to see are in Grupo I (A or B). Each samba school is a permanent social club with 2,000 to 4,000 members, sometimes more. In quick succession, they will fill the broad boulevard of the Passarela (which, during off-season, serves as a school for needy children) with the collective excitement of 50,000 total participants. Nothing rains on this parade, the show goes on no matter what the weather, and nothing dampens the enthusiasm of the dancers. Bring an umbrella, just in case. Downpours can be heavy, but they usually don't last long.

RIO DE JANEIRO

Unless you have come with a tour group that includes tickets to the samba parade in the package (be sure to ask about this and the other tickets you want *specifically*), you will wind up getting a ticket from a scalper at a greatly inflated price. Tickets are only a few dollars if purchased well in advance from Banerj, the usual official outlet, but few tourists have the opportunity to buy them this way. What happens is that tickets are snatched up weeks before the first Carnival tourist arrives and are hoarded. The going price can range from $10 to $150, depending on the location of the seat, the number of tickets generally still available, the number of tickets remaining in any particular cambista's cache, and your skill as a bargainer. The original price of the ticket in cruzados is always printed on the ticket; make sure to take a look at it and haggle accordingly. If you prefer, the concierge at your hotel can help you procure tickets, but not necessarily for the most advantageous price.

Food is sold from stalls near the Sambadromo and by vendors within the amphitheater-like facility, but if you're fussy, you may wish to pack your own snack or get a box supper, which is provided by some hotels.

The easiest way to get to the Sambadromo in the Zona Norte, where the Samba Parade takes place, is by Mêtro. During Carnival, the Mêtro runs continuously, 24 hours a day. Even if you never use public transportation any other time, go by Mêtro during Carnival. Added police patrols guarantee safety, and altered traffic patterns make it extremely difficult to reach the Passarela by car. Don't even think about parking nearby. From the Zona Sul, take a taxi or bus to Botafogo, where you will pick up the subway. Buy a round-trip ticket ("ida e volta" or "duplo") to avoid standing in line on the way back. This will cost about 35 cents. If you have tickets for even-numbered gates, get off at Praça Onze; if odd-numbered, Estação Central do Brasil is the closest stop.

In addition to ease and safety, the Mêtro is the best bet from the standpoint of economy. Cabbies are likely to charge you an arm and a leg for the trip to the Zona Norte. Your hotel may run a bus to and from the Sambadromo, but this is expensive (about $15 per person round trip) and you will be obliged to stay until the very end to catch the bus back—assuming the bus driver hasn't been smitten with samba fever and danced off into the night. The parade lasts until about 7 A.M. If you wish to leave before dawn, you'll forfeit your return trip and wind up paying for another mode of transportation.

The Street Scene

Historians of Carnival point out that it was originally a popular street celebration, not the organized competition it has become under Riotur's aegis. Although purists lament the passing of the spontaneous, homespun quality that used to characterize Carnival on the grounds that luxury, bureaucracy, and superficialities have supplanted and undermined the true spirit of samba, it is difficult to quibble when, as a tourist, you are treated to the greatest show on earth. Nevertheless, it is also undeniable that the samba parade turns almost everybody into spectators.

BRAZIL

For those who wish to get into the swing of Carnival as participants rather than observers, there are the neighborhood "bandas," block parties without prizes, just for the fun of it. Carnival festivities in the street not only are free, they are frequently the most fun of all. A liberating sense of common energy dominates the neighborhood "bandas," as these miniparades are called. Each is organized by local people, who begin partying at an appointed spot and collect revelers like a snowball as the group proceeds along its circuit. People in apartments along the banda's route, unable to resist the call of samba, spill from buildings to swell the singing throng. Everyone is welcome to join the troupe, costumed or not, and it is a rare opportunity to find out what dancing in the street is all about. Many of the men take advantage of the "anything goes" atmosphere of Carnival to dress in women's clothing; ingenious and witty homemade costumes release the creativity of others, to the delight of neighbors and strangers alike, a tropical Halloween where costumes are the personal expression of the wearer and not designed to fit into the concept dictated by a formal samba school.

Traffic crawls along, accommodating the partyers, but motorists don't mind. It's Carnival, after all, and everyone is prepared to fall into the folly. To catch one of these bands, hang around Posto 6 in Copacabana or the Garota de Ipanema bar on the corner of Vinicius de Morais and Prudente de Morais in Ipanema.

Much more structured, the "Blocos" are organized by Riotur but are not as well financed or fancy as the groups in the samba school competition. Blocos are those neighborhood clubs ranked below Grupo I or Grupo II, vying for promotion. Carnival officially opens the weekend preceding Ash Wednesday with a parade of decorated cars and carnival clubs on Avenida Rio Branco downtown, followed by the Baile Popular ("Popular Ball") at Cinelandia. Throughout the first three or four days of Carnival, Avenida Rio Branco is the scene of "Blocos" parades, which unlike those held in the Passarela, are free. Clubs featuring the dance and music styles of "frevo" and "rancho," dances from Brazil's northeast, are also held there. Another event that takes place both in Centro and in the neighborhoods harnesses the spontaneity of the community bandas to the theme of competition; the "Concorso Folião Original" is where Cariocas display the humor and imagination for which Brazilians are famous. Hard-core "carnavalescos," or Carnival celebrants, gravitate to this event, where many believe the original, animated, for-the-love-of-it spirit of the festival lives on in a compromise between the competition of the other events and the fluidity of the bandas.

There are also countless events for children during Carnival, and if you have little ones traveling with you, you can find out about these either in the local newspapers or by asking your hotel concierge.

It is not humanly possible to see and do everything during Carnival. But don't worry—the wonder of modern communications ensures continuous coverage of Carnival by major television networks both in Rio and in key cities around Brazil. You may buy video cassettes of the Samba Parade as well as tapes and records of the samba music from Group I schools. Chances are, the incredulous folks at home won't put much stock in your stories without some visual evidence, so this might

RIO DE JANEIRO 69

be the best souvenir investment of all. If you plan to take pictures, take special care with your camera in crowds and make sure to bring at least twice as much film as you think you'll need. Whatever you bring won't be enough, and film is expensive in Brazil.

Carnival's Lavish Balls

Only timidity is castigated at the Carnival balls, declared one Carioca commentator, and it's definitely true that this aspect of Carnival is not for the prudish or old at heart. As spectators at the samba school parades visitors can marvel from afar at the Brazilian beauties' ease with nudity, but at the balls you become a participant as well as an observer. Thousands of seminude people boogeying until dawn make these among the hottest spots on the planet. Whether the heat generated at these parties results from overstimulated hormones or the close proximity of packed, dancing bodies is moot—the devil-may-care attitude is assiduously cultivated. Unless you're prepared to participate in an event that's a cross between a Fellini movie and an orgy waiting to happen, you'd best stick to the milder manifestations of Carnival. No puritanical soul will feel comfortable here, for the scent of sex is in the air and many who attend are looking for action. Ephemeral friendships are an implicit outcome of these extravaganzas, where the freedom and anonymity of a masked ball prevail despite the fact that very few are concealing anything at all.

Sex sells, and the promoters of these lavish parties lure the largest number of beautiful women through a price structure guaranteed to skew the male-female ratio, which is usually no less than three women for every man and is sometimes as lopsided as ten to one. Admissions are even sold in units of three, made up of one man and two women, and in most cases single women are admitted at a nominal price. The resulting harem effect is heaven for men interested in women, and although probably not a conscious intention on the part the men who plan these bashes, the preponderance of females frees the women from the justifiable fear of excessive violence that can be expected from a large group of drinking men.

Women fully relish their majority at the balls, where they not only outnumber but outshine the men. Costumes for men are relatively unimportant—what you wear should, above all, be cool. But for the ladies, it's no holds barred. Exhibitionism is the order of the day. Now's the time to outvamp your favorite movie or rock star. Be more outrageous than Marilyn or Madonna or Bette Midler. Vent your feminine powers, using as much makeup, tinsel, and feathers—and as little covering—as possible. Like a high school reunion, the women who show up at these parties are the ones who are proud to present themselves, and you should be, too.

You will not find the same racial rainbow at the Carnival balls that is so striking a feature of the Samba Parade. These affairs are strictly for the affluent, those who can afford both an adequate costume and the price of admission, and despite Brazil's cherished myth of racial equality, the wealthy here are predominantly white.

BRAZIL

One of the most exclusive Carnival balls is the "Hawaiian Night" at the Rio Yacht Club. It is held one week earlier beside the swimming pool under the tall palms—and the pool is where most of the sweating bodies end the night's festivities around dawn.

Each year there is an infusion of new balls as Rio's top showmen compete with each other to turn out the biggest and most lavish carnival ball.

The best balls are held at Rio's showhouse/club, the Scala, Avenida Afrãnio de Melo Franco 296, Leblon, 239–4448 (Baile de Gala da Cidade; Grande Gala Gay) and Monte Libano, Avenida Borges de Medeiros, 701, Leblon, 239–0032 (Baile do Champagne; Vermelho e Preto). But every night there are dozens of less expensive balls at other clubs—all open to the public and equally crowded and frenzied. Also popular is the ball held at Pão do Açucar (Sugarloaf), which offers a breezy, spectacular view of the bay along with the elaborate costumes. You will pay from $25 to $55 per person at the more expensive balls; tables for four cost between $200 and $275.

When the dawn of Ash Wednesday finally comes to put an end to the revelry for another year, Rio looks as if it has been attacked by Roman hordes. Sleeping bodies lie everywhere. Drunks sit on curbstones holding their heads. Arabs wander dazedly down the center of the avenue accompanied by exhausted clowns, dishevelled Pierrots, and stumbling African slaves. And while an army of street cleaners starts sweeping up the tons of debris, somewhere a never-say-die Samba band can still be heard playing.

Some advice to the inexperienced attending Carnival balls and processions: Leave your inhibitions at home or at the hotel. Dress lightly. Be sure your shoes or slippers are comfortable. Leave papers and your "14 karat hardware" in the safe! Take along only as much money as you intend to spend and your credit card.

PRACTICAL INFORMATION FOR RIO DE JANEIRO

WHEN TO GO. Almost any time is a good time to visit Rio, for the climate is not that variable and there is something interesting going on almost all the time. The hottest months of the year are Jan. to Mar. when the temperature can rise to a sweltering 104 degrees in the shade. But these months are also the months with the most rain, and even though the rain's cooling effects lessen as the water evaporates, the sudden showers do give pleasant respites. The beaches are heavily populated during these months, and the sun can be unbearably hot for fair-skinned tourists after 10 A.M. The coolest months of the year are July and Aug. when there is occasionally a gray cast to everything and the ocean comes crashing up over the sidewalks and fills the main avenue with sand. At this time Brazilians stay away from the beaches, wear heavy Italian sweaters, and complain of the cold. Visitors from more northern climates find the air comfortable and many even prefer it to the blistering heat of Jan.

Of course the big event in the Rio calendar is Carnival, that impossible spectacle of madness that takes place from Friday night to the morning of Ash Wednesday. Carnival can be as early as the first week in Feb. or as late as Mar. These are the hot months, remember, so come prepared to sweat while you Samba. Make reservations well in advance, at least a year ahead for top hotels, if you are not traveling as part of a package tour.

The cultural year begins in Apr., with stars of international magnitude drawing capacity audiences during concert seasons for performance after performance. This is also the beginning for the artists and the galleries and hardly a week goes by without an important new showing of Brazilian painting or sculpture. Movie houses show many European and American films, but remember that the movies are in their original language with Portuguese subtitles.

GETTING AROUND RIO. From the airport. Vouchers are issued at set prices for taxis at the airport, depending on your final destination. Inside Rio, **taxis** are the best way to travel. Your hotel can arrange with Avis, National, or Hertz to rent a Brazilian-made Volkswagen beetle for about $20 a day. Most require a valid driver's license and credit cards. Rio taxis have meters that start at around 25 cents as we go to press. Between 11 P.M. and 7 A.M. the number 2 on or above the meter indicates the higher night fare. This fare is also charged for driving you up steep hills, such as to the Corcovado, although some Rio taxi drivers refuse to climb hills. The price registered on the meter is keyed to a table which must be affixed to the left rear window. You pay the amount that corresponds to what appears on the meter.

By bus. In general, tourists in Rio should avoid city buses when alternatives such as taxis or comfortable air-conditioned buses are available. In particular, the 553 bus should be avoided like the plague. The Santa Teresa Trolley should not be used.

You get onto a bus at the rear and leave at the front, paying the conductor as you go through the turnstile. Buses only stop if you pull the cord by the side windows. Most bus fares start around Cz$4.80 (15 cents US) and it is wise to have change ready. They won't change anything over Cz$10 and often they have no change at all. So keep plenty of small change handy for bus fares. Air-conditioned buses, called "frescões" (big fresh ones), go to most sections of the city, for a fare of about 40 cents US. You must hail buses from regularly marked stops—they will not stop automatically just because people are standing there. The **Mêtro** from Botafogo to the Zona Norte passes through Centro and is the quickest way to get around downtown.

For a glimpse of the real Brazil in comfort, take an **intercity bus trip.** Deluxe coaches are now available on a few main routes, and bus travel in general within Brazil is fast, reliable and cheap. Book well in advance, however, and check your reservation. The main bus station, known as the *Rodoviaria* (Novo Rio), is five minutes from Praça Mauá by taxi.

A **hydrofoil** goes across the bay to Niteroi, or drive across the impressive bridge, paying a toll each way. There are ferries to Paqueta and other islands. You can also take a boat tour of Guanabara Bay, with lunch included.

HOTELS. Hotels in Rio range from sumptuous to simple, with the most luxurious concentrated in Copacabana, Ipanema, Leblon, and São Conrado. The cost of hotel rooms in Rio is directly proportional to the grandeur of the ocean view and the height from which the sea can be seen. Rooms are classified standard, superior, or deluxe as a function of their location within the hotel as well as their size and furnishings. Beachfront hotels are generally more expensive than those with no view of the ocean. The categories used below indicate price range: *Super deluxe* hotels begin at $95 per night; *Deluxe* hotels charge from $70 to $95; *Expensive* hotels range from $45 to $70; *Moderate* hotels range from $15 to $45; and *Inexpensive* hotels are $15 or less. Continental breakfast is generally included in the room rate. Most hotels add a 10% service charge to their room rates.

Vidigal- São Conrado (Gávea)

Super Deluxe

Inter-Continental Rio, Prefeito Mendes de Morais, 222, on Gávea Beach (322–2200). Opened its 500 air-conditioned rooms overlooking the beach and golf course in October 1974. Among its many attractions are a brasserie, snack bar, one of Rio's smartest cocktail lounges, lighted tennis courts, discotheque, French and Italian restaurants, swimming pool with underwater bar stools, convention rooms. Convenient parking. Satellite dish.

Rio-Sheraton, Av. Neimeyer 121 between Leblon and São Conrado (274–1122). The only hotel that can claim a near-private beach, with no street to cross to bathe in the Atlantic surf; in addition, it has its own fresh-water pools and two lighted tennis courts. Rio's first luxury-class hotel, 617 rooms, three restaurants, featuring Brazilian and international cuisine, highlighted by the newly opened Valentino's, outdoor amphitheater, health club, satellite dish, shops.

Deluxe

Nacional-Rio, Av. Niemeyer 769, also on Gávea beach (322–1000). First to be built in the area, this tower has 520 wedge-shaped rooms, as well as 25 luxury suites and one floor of presidential suites. Three restaurants serve Brazilian and international specialties, and the nightclub usually features a Brazilian Samba floor-show. Across the lobby is Rio's biggest hotel convention center, theater, shops, heliport.

RIO DE JANEIRO 73

Copacabana

Super Deluxe

Copacabana Palace, Av. Atlântica 1702 (255–7070). A Rio landmark, with 400 rooms, 2 restaurants, 24-hour service, a sidewalk cafe with view to the beach on the one side and pool on the other, theater. (Price—not necessarily comfort— puts this hotel in the Super Deluxe category.)

Meridien-Rio, Av. Atlântica 1020 (275–9922). A late 1975 inauguration, this one near the beginning of Copacabana; its 36 floors make it the tallest building on the beach. It counts 552 rooms, including two presidential suites, 130 more in the luxury class and 29 cabanas. Panoramic rooftop restaurant and rotisserie serving international and French cuisine, pool, bars, nightclub, sauna, shops, beauty parlor, satellite dish.

Rio Othon Palace, Ave. Atlântica 3264 (255–8812). Opened in 1976, this hotel soars 30 stories above the center of famed Copacabana Beach and combines traditional Brazilian charm with the latest advances in hostelry. Largest in the beach area, it has 606 air-conditioned rooms, two presidential suites and a variety of other luxury suites. Rooftop bar and pool with panoramic view, international restaurants, bars, nightclub, banquet facilities for up to 700, shopping gallery, beauty parlor.

Rio Palace, Av. Atlântica 4240 (521–3232). Most luxurious of all Brazilian-owned hotels. The 416-room facility is at the end of Copacabana Beach in a multi-story shopping complex. Numerous bars, restaurants, nightclubs, meeting rooms, and auditoriums. Two pools, satellite dish.

Deluxe

Luxor, Av. Atlântica 2554 (257–1940). Terrace restaurant.
Luxor Continental, Rua Gustavo Sampaio 320, Leme (275–5252).
Luxor Regente, Av. Atlântica 3716 (287–4212). Recently renovated.

Expensive

California, Av. Atlântica 2616 (257–1900). Modern rooms, bar, restaurant.
Leme Palace, a posh establishment at Av. Atlântica 656 (275–8080) in the Copacabana Beach area known as Leme. 194 rooms, good restaurant and sidewalk bar, cozy rooftop bar. Entirely air-conditioned. *H. Stern* store.
Miramar, Av. Atlântica 3668 (247–6070). Restaurant, rooftop bar, marvelous view.
Ouro Verde, Av. Atlântica 1456 (542–1887). One of 8 hotels in the world that retain the "discreet charm of the small hotels," according to *Fortune* magazine, this 66-room Swiss-owned and -managed jewel enjoys international prestige. Exquisite decor, all-round comfort, and courteous service.
Trocadero, Av. Atlântica 2064. (257–1834). Fine Brazilian restaurant, Moenda.

Moderate

Acapulco, Rua Gustavo Sampaio 854 (275–0022). 120 modern rooms, with a view of the back side of the Merídien across the street.
Apa, Rua República de Peru 305 (255–8112). Near Copacabana beach.
Biarritz, Rua Aires Saldanha 54 (255–6552). Near Copacabana beach.
Canada, Av. Copacabana 687 (257–1864). Near Copacabana beach.
Castro Alves, Av. Copacabana 552 (257–1800). Near Copacabana beach.
Debret, R. Almte. Gonçalves 5 (521–3332). Air-conditioned, ocean view.
Excelsior, Av. Atlântica 1800 (257–1950). 220 rooms, fine restaurant and bar with ocean view. Rates include one meal in addition to Continental breakfast.

BRAZIL

Lancaster, Av. Atlântica 1470 (541–1887). Family atmosphere.
Martinique, Rua Sá Ferreira 30 (521–4552). Near Copacabana beach.
Olinda, Av. Atlântica 2230 (257–1890).
Plaza Copacabana, Av. Princesa Isabel 263 (275–7722). Near Copacabana Beach.
Rio Copa, Av. Princesa Isabel 370 (275–6644). 110 air-conditioned rooms in new hotel on busy street leading to the beach.
Savoy Othon, Av. N.S. de Copacabana 995 (257–8052). 160 rooms. Fine restaurant and bars.
Toledo, Rua Domingos Ferreira 71 (257–1990). Near Copacabana beach.

Ipanema

Super Deluxe

Caesar Park, Av. Vieira Souto 460 (287–3122). 242 all air-conditioned rooms with TV and refrigerator. Two excellent restaurants, bar, beauty salon, barber shop, sauna, pool. Private security guards patrol beach on foot and with binoculars from hotel roof to protect guests and other bathers from "beach rats" out to relieve them of their valuables.
Everest-Rio, Rua Prudente de Morais 1117 (287–8282). 22-story hotel has 176 rooms and everything to make guests comfortable. Near beaches. (Although comfortable, only price range puts this hotel in the super deluxe category.)

Deluxe

Praia Ipanema, Av. Vieira Souto 706 (239–9932). Beachfront.
Sol Ipanema, Av. Vieira Souto 320 (227–0060). Restaurant, bar, beauty parlor, sun deck, and children's pool on roof. Beachfront.

Moderate

Arpoador Inn, Rua Francisco Otaviano 177 (247–6090). At the beginning of the beach. Casually elegant, with 50 air-conditioned rooms and restaurant.

Leblon

Deluxe

Marina Rio, Av. Delfim Moreira 696 (239–8844). On the beach beyond Ipanema. Modern new hotel with 100 air-conditioned rooms, bar, restaurant.
Marina Palace, Av. Delfim Moreira 630 (259–5212). Brand new beach hotel, Rio's newest with 165 rooms.

Moderate

Carlton, Rua Joao Lira 68 (259–1932). Quiet surroundings.

Downtown

Expensive

Gloria, Rua do Russel 632 (205–7272). In Flamengo not far from the city's center. 730 deluxe and first-class rooms. Fine colonial-style restaurant, bars, pool, terrace with view. Convention center. Overlooking Flamengo Beach.

Moderate

Aeroporto, Av. Beira Mar 290 (262–8922). Near city airport.
Ambassador, Rua Senador Dantas 25 (297–7181).
Ambassador Santos Dumont, Rua Santa Luzia 651 (240–1222). In the Clube de Aeronáutica building downtown.

RIO DE JANEIRO

Center, Av. Rio Branco 33 (296–6677). Opened late 1975. Air-conditioned, with refrigerator-bar in each room.
Flamengo Palace, Praia do Flamengo 6 (205–1552). 60 rooms, opened in 1975.
Grande Hotel OK, Rua Senador Dantas 24 (292–4114).
Novo Mundo, Praia do Flamengo 20 (225–7366). Restaurant, bar. *H. Stern* store.
Regina, Rua Ferreira Viana 29 (225–7280).
Sao Francisco, Rua Visconde de Inhauma 95 (233–8122). Air-conditioned, restaurant.

Apartment hotels are also available with maid service. The top residential hotels are: **Apart Hotel,** Rua Barata Ribeiro 370; 256–2633. **Rio Flat Service,** Rua Alm. Guilhem 332 (Leblon); 274–7222. **Apart Hotel Barramares,** Av. Sernambetiba 3300 (on the beach in Barra da Tijuca); 399–5656.

Inexpensive

Argentina, Rua Cruz Lima 30 (225–7233).
Florida, Rua Ferreira Viana 81 (245–8160).
Paissandu, Rua Paissandu 23 (225–7270).

RESTAURANTS. Typical Brazilian food is varied, unusual and delicious, but one of the biggest troubles for the tourist is trying to get some of it. Almost all the good restaurants in Rio serve international-type food only and shy away from the home product. The Brazilian wants to eat something different from everyday fare when going out to dine. Try at least one *feijoada, vatapá,* or the mouthwatering *muqueca de peixe.* Our restaurant grading system has four categories: *Deluxe,* $15 and up; *Expensive,* $10 to $15; *Moderate,* $5 to $10; *Inexpensive,* under $5. These prices are for a full meal for one person excluding wine, beer, or other drinks.

Brazilian

Sal e Pimenta. *Deluxe.* Rua Barão da Torre, 368, Ipanema (247–7178 and 521–1460). Above the "Alô-Alô" Piano Bar, next to the Club Hippopotamus, and owned by the same entertainment tycoon, this restaurant also features Italian specialties. Reservations needed, all credit cards accepted, open for lunch and dinner.

Chale Brasileiro. *Expensive.* Rua da Matriz, 54, Botafogo (286–0897). Traditional colonial setting, Bahian cuisine, waitresses in costume, less spicy food also available. Open for lunch and dinner, accepts major credit cards, reservations advisable on weekends.

Maria Tereza Weiss. *Expensive.* Rua Visconde de Silva, 152, Botafogo (286–3098). Maria Tereza Weiss is Brazil's Betty Crocker and Julia Child rolled into one. Many traditional dishes, plus international selections. Open daily except Monday from noon to 1 A.M. Major credit cards accepted.

Moenda. *Expensive.* In the Trocadero Hotel, Avenida Atlantica 2046, Copacabana (257–1834). Bahian specialties and traditional cuisine. Open noon to midnight, accepts major credit cards.

Arataca. *Moderate.* Rua Dias Ferreira, 135, Leblon (259–5846). Specializes in the cuisine of the Amazon state of Pará, including fish from the Amazon River. Open 11 A.M. to 2 A.M., major credit cards accepted, no reservatioins.

Bar do Arnaudo. *Moderate.* Rua Almirante Alexandrino 316-A, Santa Teresa (252–7246). Typical dishes from Pernambuco, including dried, salted beef with fried manioc, lamb stew, roast pork. Diners are requested not to use the tables

BRAZIL

as percussion instruments. No reservations, cash only. Open Tues. through Sat. from noon to 10 P.M.; Sun. until 9 P.M.

Seafood

Barracuda. *Deluxe.* Marina da Gloria, Parque do Flamengo (265–3997). An elegant luncheon spot for businesspeople, specializing in shrimp and *frutos do mar.* A small bar and piano music at night. Reservations at lunch, all major credit cards accepted.

Candido's. *Deluxe.* Rua Barros de Alarcão, 352, Pedra de Guaratiba (395–1630). An hour's drive south of Rio, go for an afternoon-long lunch after the beach. Open Tues-Fri. from 11:30 A.M. to 7 P.M., Sat. and Sun. from 11:30 A.M. to 11 P.M. You *must* make reservations. Diner's Club accepted.

Grottammare. *Deluxe.* Rua Gomes Carneiro, 132, Ipanema (287–1596). Noted for grilled fish and salads. Closed Mon., open from 6 P.M. to 2 A.M. Weekdays, from noon on Sunday. Reservations recommended, credit cards accepted.

Quatro Sete Meia. *Deluxe.* Rua Barros de Alaracão, 476, Pedra de Guaratiba (395–2716). Reservations are obligatory at this small, simple seafood restaurant that takes its name from the numbers of its address. Open noon to 5 P.M. Tues. through Thurs., noon to 11 P.M. Fri. through Sun. Cash only.

Sol e Mar. *Expensive.* Avenida Reporter Nestor Moreira, 11, Botafogo (295–1997). Dine on a pier overlooking Guanabara Bay and Sugarloaf. Many Spanish specialties. Reservations and credit cards accepted. The Bateau Mouche leaves from here.

Albamar. *Moderate.* Praça Marechal Ancora, 184, Centro (240–8378). In the former Mercado Municipal, a green octagonal building near Praça XV de Novembro. Deviled crab, fish chowder, fish filet in black butter are all recommended. Crowded at lunch but not at dinner. It closes by 9:30 P.M. Nice view of Guanabara Bay. No reservations needed, accepts American Express.

Cabaça Grande. *Moderate.* Rua do Ouvidor, 12, Centro (231–2338). Unpretentious Portuguese-style restaurant with steaming fish and seafood stews called *caldeiradas,* generous portions, and good service Ice cold beer. No reservations, no credit cards.

A Marisqueira. *Moderate & Expensive.* Rua Barata Ribeiro, 232, Copacabana (237–3920) and Rua Gomes Carneiro, 90, Ipanema (227–8476). Broiled and fried fish, fish and seafood stews, many beef and chicken dishes as well. Open 11 A.M. to 1:30 A.M. No reservations.

Shirley. *Moderate.* Rua Gustavo Sampaio, 610, Leme (275–9013). Be prepared to wait at this small, hidden restaurant featuring seafood and fish prepared Spanish style. No reservations. Open noon to 1 A.M.

Tia Palmira. *Moderate.* Rua Alvaro Ribeiro de Souza, 18, Pedra de Guaratiba (310–1169). Open for lunch only and closed Mon. Prix fixe menu.

Salads and Vegetarian

Natural. *Moderate.* Rua Barão da Torre, 171, Ipanema (267–7799). Inexpensive daily vegetarian plate includes rice or grain, beans, vegetables, and soup. Also serves chicken and fish, which are more expensive but still extremely reasonable.

Super Salads. *Moderate.* Av. Armando Lombardi, 601, Barra da Tijuca (399–1026). Prix fixe all-you-can-eat buffet of salads, including meat, fish, chicken, fruits, vegetables, and several hot entrees.

RIO DE JANEIRO 77

Alfaces. *Inexpensive.* Rua Visconde de Graça, 51, Jardim Botânico (no phone). Fresh, tangy fruit and vegetable salads sold in quantities of 100 grams, cheeses, cold meats, hot baked potatoes with stuffings, desserts.

Delírio Tropical. *Inexpensive.* Rua da Assembléia 36, Centro (no phone). Sandwiches, cold cuts, and salad plates for under $5, are well seasoned, fresh, and tasty.

Japanese

Mariko. *Deluxe.* Av. Vieira Souto, 460, in the Caesar Park Hotel, Ipanema (287–3122). Rio's choicest sushi bar, also serves sashimi and tempura. Open from 6 P.M. to 1 A.M., closed Sun.

Akasaka. *Moderate.* Av. Copacabana, 1391, Copacabana (287–3211).

Portuguese

Negresco. *Expensive.* Rua Barão da Torre, 348, Ipanema (287–4842). Elegant atmosphere and cozy bar, authentic Portuguese entrees and desserts. Open every day for lunch and dinner, Fri. for dinner only, Sat until 4 A.M. Reservations accepted.

Churrascurias

Buffalo Grill. *Expensive.* Rua Rita Ludolf, 47, Leblon (274–4848). Dinner only except on Sun., when lunch is also served. Open until 3 A.M., live music, bar. A la carte.

Mariu's. *Expensive.* Av. Atlântica, 290, Leme (542–2393). If you only go to one churrascuria during your stay in Rio, make it Mariu's. Great meats and accompaniments; Rodizlio. Reservations advisable on weekends and during high season. Open every day, 11:30 A.M. to 1:30 P.M.; credit cards accepted.

Porcão de Ipanema. *Expensive.* Rua Barão da Torre, 218, Ipanema (521–0999). Rodizio-style service, open every day, 11 A.M. to 2 A.M.

Rodeio. *Expensive.* Av. Alvorada, 2150, Bloco G, Cassa Shopping, Barra da Tijuca (325–6163). A branch of the well-known São Paulo charrascuria, with the same high-quality meats. Open for lunch and dinner, most major credit cards accepted.

French

Rio's best restaurants are French, both classical and nouvelle cuisine. All tend to be on the high end of the price scale.

Le Bec Fin. *Deluxe.* Av. Copacabana, 178, Copacabana (542–4097). Over 30 years of classical French cooking. Reservations suggested, all major credit cards accepted, dinner only.

Claude Troisgros. *Deluxe.* Rua Custodio Serrão, 62, Jardim Botânico (226–4542 or 246–7509). Nouvelle cuisine on a "menu confiance"—you don't know what you'll be eating until it arrives, but everything is delicious. Reservations are a must. Open noon to 3 P.M., Mon. through Fri., 7:30 P.M. to midnight, Mon. through Sat.

Clube Gourmet. *Deluxe.* Rua General Polidoro, 186, Botafogo (295–3494). Nouvelle cuisine, prix fixe menu, and the best wine cellar in town. Comfortable, converted townhouse with/outdoor dining area. Reservations essential. Open for lunch (except Sat.) and dinner.

Monseigneur. *Deluxe.* Av. Prefeito Mendes de Morais 222 (322–2200). In the Inter-Continental Hotel, nouvelle cuisine in the hands of a master chef, Domi-

78 BRAZIL

nique, coupled with a luxurious setting and the romance of strolling violins. Dinner only, 7 P.M. to 2 A.M. All major credit cards accepted.

Ouro Verde. *Deluxe.* Av. Atlântica, 1456, Copacabana, in the Ouro Verde Hotel (542–1887). Traditional French cuisine, open noon to 1 A.M., make reservations.

Le Pré Catalan. *Deluxe.* Av. Atlântica, 4240, Copacabana (521–3232). Located in the Rio Palace Hotel, this restaurant is a branch of the Paris original from which it takes its name. Nouvelle cuisine. Dinner only, open 8 P.M. to 1 A.M. Major credit cards.

Saint Honoré. *Deluxe.* Av. Atlântica, 1020, Copacabana (275–9922). The Hotel Meridien's pride and joy, this restaurant is overseen by French chef Paul Bocuse and in addition to great food you get a spectacular view of the beach and bay. Prix fixe menu at lunch, à la carte at dinner. Make reservations. Closed Sun.

Italian

Alfredo's. *Deluxe.* Av. Prefeito Mendes de Morais, 222 (322–2200). In the Inter-Continental Hotel. A branch of the world-famous Alfredo's of Rome, and absolute tops in Rio for pasta, especially fettuccine. Make reservations.

Enotria. *Deluxe.* Rua Constante Ramos, 115, Copacabana (237–6705). Classical Italian cuisine made fresh on the premises daily, from pasta to bread. Fine wine selection. Choose from the prix fixe menu of the day. Reservations suggested, closed Sun., dinner only, most credit cards honored.

Le Streghe. *Deluxe.* Prudente de Morais, 129 (Praça General Osório), Ipanema (287–1369). Fine, carefully prepared food, relaxed, sophisticated atmosphere, bar/disco named Caligula for after dinner. Open 7:30 P.M. to 2 A.M., reservations advisable, all major credit cards accepted.

Valentino's. *Deluxe.* Rio Sheraton Hotel, Avenida Niemeyer, Vidigal (274–1122). Beautifully served nova cucina entrees in an elegant atmosphere with excellent service. Open 7 P.M. to midnight, all major credit cards, reservations accepted.

La Mole. *Moderate.* Av. Copacabana 552, Copacabana (257–5593) and Rua Dias Ferreira, 147, Leblon (294–0699). A chain of restaurants serving excellent pasta, pizza, and many other choices at reasonable prices. No reservations. If there is a line, you are given a number. All major credit cards.

Pizza Palace. *Moderate.* Rua Barão da Torre, 340, Ipanema (267–8346). Good homemade pasta, pizza, meat, and chicken dishes available in an open, sidewalk cafe setting. No reservations.

International

Café do Teatro. *Deluxe.* Av. Rio Branco in the Teatro Municipal (262–4164). Marvelous Assyrian decor makes dining here a special experience. Open for lunch only, 11 A.M. to 3:30 P.M., closed Sat., Sun., and holidays.

Rio's. *Deluxe.* Parque do Flamengo (551–1131). American bar with live music, good view of Sugarloaf and the bay. Open daily, noon to 2 A.M.

Un, Deux, Trois. *Deluxe.* Rua Bartolomeu Mitre, 123, Leblon (293–0198). Open daily for dinner, lunch on Sat. and Sun. only. Live music and bar make dinner here a full evening.

Antonio's. *Expensive.* Av. Bartolomeu Mitre, 297, Leblon (294–2699). Has a faithful following of regulars. Open daily from noon to 2 A.M.

Lord Jim's Pub. *Expensive.* Rua Paul Redfern, 63, Ipanema (259–3047). A meeting place for English speakers and the foreign community featuring British food, drinking, darts, and afternoon tea, for which you should make reservations. Open Tues. through Sat., 4 P.M. to 1 A.M. and Sun. from 11 A.M. to 1 A.M.; closed Monday. Cash only.

Neal's. *Expensive.* Rua Sorocaba, 695, Botafogo (266–6577). A Manhattan-style bar-restaurant in a renovated townhouse serving American favorites like hamburgers, ribs, and T-bone steaks. Videos of American stars, posters from *New Yorker* covers and museum exhibitions. Open until the wee hours, usually around 4 A.M. Lunch weekdays; Sat. and Sun., dinner only, from 7 P.M. on; closed Mon.

Café Colombo. *Moderate.* Rua Gonçalves Dias 32–36, Centro (232–2300). Lunch only in a historic belle époque setting with an aura of the past. Large portions, reasonable prices, good food. No reservations. Closed Sat. and Sun.

TOURIST INFORMATION. Riotur, the official tourism agency of the city of Rio, operates information posts in the following locations: Main Office, Rua da Assembléia, 10, 8th and 9th floors, Centro (297–7117). Open Mon.-Fri., 9 A.M. to 6 P.M. Branches: *Estaçao Rodoviária Novo Rio,* Av. Francisco Bicalho, 1, São Cristovão (291–5151, Riotur), open 24 hours a day. Pão de Açucar, Av. Pasteur, 520, Urca, Estação do Teleférico, open from 8 A.M. to 7 P.M. *Marina da Gloria,* Aterro do Flamengo (205–6447), open 8 A.M. to 5 P.M. English, French, Spanish, German, Italian, and Japanese are spoken. **Flumitur,** the state of Rio's official tourism bureau, also has main offices at Rua da Assembléia, 10, on the 7th and 8th floors (252–4512), open from 9 A.M. to 10 P.M. Branches: International Airport, Disembarkation, Sections A, B, and C (398–4073/7). Open from 6 A.M. to midnight. Same languages spoken as above.

TOURS. You can easily book a tour around Rio and its environs through your hotel. There are many tour operators licensed by Embratur who cater to tourists in English, Spanish, and other languages. Most tours are by air-conditioned bus, which will pick you up and drop you off at your hotel. Tours are run to Corcovado/Floresta de Tijuca ($17), Pão de Açucar and the Botanical Garden ($18), Petropolis ($20), Petropolis and Teresopolis ($30), downtown and Niteroi Bridge ($13), and various other combinations of these sights. Night and special tours include Rio by Night ($50), Samba Show ($40), football game ($17), Paradise Island Tour around Sepetiba Bay ($36), Macumba, or African Spiritist cult ceremonies ($38), and Buzios/Cabo Frio ($50).

Tour operators offering these itineraries include: **Brasil Italia Turismo,** Rua Alcindo Guanabara 24, suite 208–209, Botafogo (240–5886 or 240–6436). **BrazilRio Viagens e Turismo, Ltda.,** Avenida Copacabana 300A, Copacabana (541–5099). **Ékoda,** Avenida Rio Branco 277, 1306, Centro (240–7067). Specializing in service to Búzios. **Gray Line,** Avenida Niemeyer 121, suite 412, São Conrado (central reservations: 274–7146, 294–0393, 294–1196). **Kontik-Franstur,** Av. Atlântica, 2316A, Copacabana (237–7797). **SulAmerica Turismo,** Av. Copacabana 441, suite 201, Copacabana (257–4732, 257–4735, 236–6947). **Vikings,** Rua Barata Ribeiro, 383, sobreloja, Copacabana (255–9242). **Walpax,** Rua Visconde de Pirajá, 547, suite 725, Ipanema (511–1242).

For a more culturally-oriented approach, the **Projecto Roteiros Culturais,** supported by the Associação Brasileira de Educação (Brazilian Education Association), sponsors guided tours by Prof. Carlos Roquette in English and French, for $20. In-depth explanations are available in tours of Colonial Rio, Imperial Rio, the Botanical Garden, Chácara do Ceu Museum, the Teatro Municipal, and other points of interest. Information is available 24 hours a day at 322–4872, and offices are located at Rua Santa Clara 110, suite 904, Copacabana.

BRAZIL

SIGHTS AND MUSEUMS. Rio is divided into the Zona Norte (North Zone), Zona Sul (South Zone), and Centro (Center), and it makes sense to see the points of interest in each zone at the same time. Many of these have already been described in the Rio narrative. The Zona Norte is the poorer section, with the lower economic classes and small individual homes. Away from the breezes of the ocean it can also be sticky hot. But it does have interesting and important spots to visit like the **Church of Penha**, the **Museu Nacional**, in the former Imperial Palace, **Quinta da Boa Vista**, the **Zoo**, **Maracanã** (the world's biggest soccer stadium); and the **Feira Nordestino at São Cristovao**, held Sun. from 6 A.M. to 1 P.M., a fair which features food and articles from Brazil's Northeast.

The central part of the city is the commercial area, with bustling Avenida Rio Branco and Avenida Presidente Vargas. Here are all of the banks, important department stores, and office buildings. Here also is the **Museum of Modern Art**, (Museu de Arte Moderno–MAM), Parque do Flamengo, Av. Infante Dom Henrique; 210–2188; open Tues.–Sun., hours depending on event, with a fine restaurant and cafeteria, daily film showings, and a lovely garden; the **Museum of Fine Arts** (Belas Artes), Av. Rio Branco 199; the **National History Museum** (Museu Historico Nacional), Praça Marechal Ancora, near Praça XV; 240–7978; 240–7928; open Tues–Fri., 10 A.M. to 5:30 P.M. Sat., Sun., and holidays from 2:30 to 5:30 P.M. Under partial restoration and reorganization; the classic **Municipal Theater;** all the old **Congress and Supreme Court buildings** from when Rio was the nation's capital; and an area with movie houses called **Cinelandia**.

Other museums and sights in this area include: **Paço Imperial** (Royal Palace), Praça XV de Novembro, Centro (no phone listing). Currently used as an exhibition and concert hall, the Paço Imperial was the site of many historic events, including the signing of the "Lei Auréa," Brazil's Emancipation Proclamation, by Princesa Isabel in 1888. Open Tues. through Sun. from 11 A.M. to 5 P.M., and other days according to ongoing events (check newspaper listings), it also features an exhibit on the archeological research carried out during the building's recent restoration. **Aqueduto da Carioca** (Aquaduct), located in Lapa, near Centro, was completed in 1750 and is part of the National Historic Register. The Santa Teresa trolley tracks run on it. **Museu do Palácio do Itamarati** (Itamarati Museum), Av. Marechal Floriano 196, Centro (291–4411, ext. 6) is open Tues. through Fri., 11 A.M. to 5 P.M. The palace itself is considered one of the best examples of classical architecture in Rio and was built in 1853. After the proclamation of the republic, it was purchased by the Federal Government and served as the President's residence until 1897. Remodeled in 1930, the building now houses a museum with a varied collection of art and artifacts. **Museu da Cidade** (City Museum), Estrada de Santa Marinha (Parque da Cidade, Gávea), 322–1328 is open Tues. through Sun. and holidays from noon to 4:30 P.M. Objects illustrating the history of the city are displayed by century, with a special room on the pharmaceutical industry. **Museu Chácara do Ceu**, Rua Murtinho Nobre, 345, Santa Teresa (224–8981) is open Tues. through Sat. from 2 to 5:30 P.M., Sun. from 1 to 5:30 P.M. In addition to a beautiful view of Rio from a peaceful garden, this museum offers a select sample of the art collection of Raymundo Castro Mayer, which includes works by prominent European painters and the Don Quixote series by Portinari, considered one of Brazil's great artists. **Museu do Folclore Edson Carneiro,** (Edson Carneiro Folklore Museum), Rua do Catete, 181, Catete (285–0891) is open from Tues. to Fri., 11 A.M. to 6 P.M.; Sat., Sun., and holidays from 3 to 5 P.M. Collection includes artesanatos, household and religious objects, musical instruments, and

RIO DE JANEIRO

popular literature (broadsides) from all over Brazil. **Museu da Imagem e do Som** (Museum of Image and Sound) Praça Rui Barbosa, 1 (near Praça XV de Novembro), Centro (262–0309), is open Mon. through Fri. from 1 to 6 P.M. Varied collection of recordings, photographs, and archives reflecting the life of the city of Rio and Brazilian Popular Music.

The south of Rio is the chic and expensive place to live. Here are the best hotels, restaurants, and beaches. Here is Copacabana, Ipanema, and Leblon. A little farther are Avenida Niemeyer and São Conrado beach, where the newest hotels are located. Here also is the beautiful **Lagoa (lagoon) Rodrigo de Freitas,** the traditional **Jockey Club,** the calm and well-kept **Botanical Gardens, Presidents' and governors' palaces,** and, rising from the bay's blue water, **Sugar Loaf.** The **Villa Riso,** open every Tues. to the public, at Estrada da Gávea 728, São Conrado, operates as a museum, performance space, and concert hall and features employees in colonial dress, (à la Williamsburg, VA) who give a tour of this former fazenda.

Out of town via private car or taxi you have the junglelike **Tijuca Forest** with its Emperor's Table, Chinese View, and impressive waterfall.

BEACHES. Visitors to Brazil are always surprised to see how important the beach is to the Brazilians. Not just for those who live in the coastal cities, but even for those who live deep in the interior. Copacabana Beach or fashionable Ipanema Beach are focal points of life in Rio. The beach permeates the lives of Cariocas the way winter conditions the lives of Canadians. Everyone falls under the influence of the beach, which is cocktail party, college mixer, soccer field, and backyard all in one.

Rio's beaches—all 23 of them—are all public. There are rest rooms but no private cabanas or changing rooms. You either arrive in your suit at the beach or else you peel off your clothes right there with your bathing suit on underneath. There is no color line drawn, the rich lie on the none-too-clean sand with the poor, as fruit and soft drink sellers walk over them equally. As one uppercrust American tourist once put it: "It is probably the most democratic beach in the world."

The undertow is strong, making swimming difficult, but the waves are prized by surfers. And lifeguards are stationed along Copacabana, Ipanema, and Leblon in numbered *postos,* or posts, which also serve as landmarks by which you can orient yourself.

Brazilians begin their beach life early. It is not at all unusual to see tiny babies in wicker baskets soaking up the sun alongside their bikini-clad mothers. When they get old enough to walk they are usually accompanied by a maid who hovers over them. Once they are able to leave their maids they go to the beach with their friends. The boys learn to play soccer, boys and girls learn volleyball, windsurfing, and surf boarding. Later on, these same children will do their homework on the beach, listen to rock music on the beach, meet a "steady" on the beach, and when the cycle is completed bring their newly born babies to the beach.

Almost anything goes on there. Early in the morning you can see old men still trying to keep young by a sunrise dip or jogging. Muscle boys cavort there. Crooks steal there and politicians even campaign there. Many business deals are closed there too. Often a weary executive will arrange to meet a client at the beach. The client also shows up in a swimsuit and with his briefcase. In spite of the sand, the fleas, and the noise of the shouting people, they manage to get their business done.

BRAZIL

There are also many things to buy on the beach. A short list would include Coca-Cola, beer, ripe coconuts, skewered bits of shrimp, peanuts, ice cream, natural sandwiches (ricotta cheese and carrot, tuna or chicken salad on whole wheat), corn on the cob, bright-colored kites, sunglasses, beach umbrellas, and hats and visors to protect you from the sun. The vendors wander among the bathers and call attention to their wares by blowing on whistles, shouting, singing, beating a small drum or whirling a metal rachet that clatters loudly. Keep your eye on your belongings. There may be fast-working kids around, ready to snatch the unguarded purse or camera.

Another annoyance that Brazilians take for granted is the volleyball games that seem to spring up just as you have gotten comfortable and drowsy on the sand. From out of nowhere will appear eight to a dozen young people, their arms loaded down with poles, nets, rope and a leather ball. They plant the stakes, string up the net and mark off their boundaries in a matter of minutes. Brazilians, with a disinclination for trouble, just pick up their towels and move elsewhere; it is the foreigners who get furious and threaten to take on both sides of the team at once. There have been laws passed that say a volleyball game cannot be played in certain sections of Copacabana Beach or started before 2 P.M., but they are frequently ignored.

Apart from Copacabana, Ipanema, and Leblon, which are all close to hotels in the Zona Sul, the best beaches are further south: Barra da Tijica, Recreio dos Bandeirantes, Prainha, and Grumari. For a change, try the beaches on the Ilha de Paqueta, an island in Guanabara Bay which permits no automobiles, only horsedrawn carriages and bicycles. Take a ferry boat or hydrofoil from Barcas Estação da Praça XV (224–0001). Boats leave and return Mon.-Sat., 5:30 A.M. to 11 P.M. and Sun. from 7:10 A.M. to 11 P.M.

SPORTS. Tennis is popular. See the manager of the Rio Country Club or the Caiçaras in Ipanema or the Paissandu Club in Leblon for special permission to play. Only hotels with courts are the Inter-Continental, Sheraton, and Nacional.

Surfing is popular at Copacabana Beach, Ipanema's Arpoador Beach, and at Praia dos Bandeirantes. The sea is rough and dangerous.

Golf hasn't really caught on in Brazil as yet, but the two clubs that exist for it are stunning, beautifully trimmed places in the hills of Gávea. The Gávea Golf Club (322–4141) has many American and English members and a number of foreign firms keep memberships for their executives. The tourist can visit the club and admire the majestic scenery without being accompanied by a club member, but to play you must be invited or have your hotel make reservations for you. The Itanhanga Golf Club (399–0507) is nearby.

Ocean fishing goes on year-round, and if you don't know someone who has a boat you can always rent one at the Marina da Gloria (205–6447). There are marlin as well as other ocean gamefish awaiting either your hook and sinker or your spear. No license is needed and the fish are so big you won't have to throw any of them back.

Horse racing events are held Thursday nights and weekend afternoons at the Jockey Club (274–0055). An impressive place with excellent grass and dirt tracks, it runs the best horses in the nation for your pleasure. Betting is not only permitted, but encouraged. The first Sunday in August is reserved for the Grande Premio Brazil, which draws the finest bluebloods from all over Latin America. It is also an occasion for ladies to wear elaborate hats and gowns, and for the top brass, from the President on down, to show up glittering in medals.

RIO DE JANEIRO

Soccer rules supreme in Brazil, and will remain so for years to come. The best players in the world (this is no exaggeration) are on hand to delight the visiting soccer fan. Rio's clubs have top players and any game that has teams like Vasco, Flamengo, Botafogo, or Fluminense can be counted on for plenty of excitement.

Yachting is a major sport in Rio and there are two yacht clubs in the Botafogo area that lies halfway between Copacabana and the center of town. Most exclusive and interesting is the Rio Yacht Club. Clubs are open to members only and gate crashing is not easy.

MUSIC AND DANCE. Rio has a solid program of classical music and dance, and offers concerts by visiting performers as well as resident artists. The **Teatro Municipal** Praça Floriano, Centro (210-2463) houses the city's Opera and Ballet companies and is the favored performance space for touring orchestras and dance troupes as well—at Christmas time, the house troupe features the Nutcracker, snowflakes and all, and the Bolshoi performed there in May, 1986. The **Sala Cecilia Meireles,** Largo da Lapa, 47, near Cinelandia (232-9714), frequently features classical music concerts with guest artists and Brazilian music festivals; and the **Sala Sidney Miller** at Rua Aruajo Porto Alegre, 80, near the Teatro Municipal (297-6116, ext. 255), runs various jazz and Brazilian Popular Music series featuring new performers and regional music.

Events sponsored by Funarte, Funarj, Fundação Roberto Marinho, and Fundação Calouste Gulbenkian are consistently high caliber and worth seeking out. Listings of current performances appear daily in *O Globo* and *Jornal do Brasil* in the entertainment section. Programs are scheduled year-round, but the cultural "season" begins during Rio's autumn in April and extends until the end of December.

ART GALLERIES. Rio has a lively art scene, with many openings (listed in the newspaper entertainment section under "Artes Plasticas" and in Riotur's monthly *Rio Guide*), especially during the cultural season, which begins in April and extends through the Brazilian autumn and winter. Galleries and antique stores are concentrated in the Shopping Center da Gávea, Rua Marquês de São Vicente, 52, Gávea; the Shopping Cassino Atlantico, Avenida Atlantica 4240, Copacabana; and the Rio Design Center, Avenida Ataulfo de Paiva, 270, Leblon. Opening and closing hours are idiosyncratic, varying from gallery to gallery and opening to opening. But in the shopping centers, schedules tend to conform with normal business hours. It is best to check the newspaper or call.

In the Shopping Center da Gávea: **Ana Maria Niemeyer,** store 205 (239-9144); **Art Poster Gallery,** store 214 (259-8147); **Beco da Arte,** store 368 (259-1449), also in Rio Design Center, store 314 (511-1746); **Borguese,** stores 138-139 (274-3245), also in Rio Design Center, store 201 (259-6793); **Bronze,** store 220 (259-7599); **Contorno,** store 261 (274-3832); **Paulo Klabin,** loja 204 (274-2644); **Saramenha,** store 165 (274-9445); **Toulouse,** store 350 (274-4044).

In the Cassino Atlântico: **Aktuel,** store 223 (287-4693); **Basilio,** store 224 (267-9791); **Gauguin,** store 233 (227-4738); **Gravura Brasileira,** store 129 (267-3747); **Investiarte,** stores 101-104 (521-1442); **Juan Luis Zaffaroni,** stores 331-332 (287-6899); **Maria Augusta,** store 131 (227-8461); **Ralph Camargo,** stores 112-113 (521-1727); **Rejane,** store 130 (521-1896); **Scopus,** store 207 (247–6999); **Versailles,** store 109 (247–2185); **Villa Bernini,** store 214 (247–5198).

In the Rio Design Center: **Montesanti,** store 114 (239–9391) and **Museum,** store 305 (239–1032). **Francisco Brennand** is at Rua Marquês de São Vicente, 75, Loja N. (274–5943).

In Ipanema, on Visconde de Pirajá: **Andréa Sigaud,** no. 207, store 307 (247–2921); **Arte Maior,** no. 547, store 203 (274–5624); **César Aché,** no. 282, store H (287–1663); **Maria Eugenia,** no. 207, store 209 (287–5748); **Olivia Kann,** no. 351 store 105 (521–3695).

Elsewhere in the Zona Sul: **Acervo,** Rua das Palmeiras, 19, Botafogo (266–5837); **Artespaço,** Rua Conde Bernardotte, 26, store 116 (266–5837); **Atelier Hélio Rodriques,** Rua General Dionisio, 47, Botafogo (246–2591); **Bahiart,** Rua Carlos Góes 234, store G, Leblon (239–4599); **Banerj,** Av. Atlântica 4066, Copacabana (267–3046); **Bonino,** Rua Barata Ribeiro, 578, Copacabana (235–7831); **Centro Cultural Candido Mendes,** Rua Joana Angélica, 63, Ipanema (267–7098); **Claudio Gil,** Rua Teixeira de Melo, 30A, Ipanema (227–8975); **Domus,** Rua Joana Angélica 184, Ipanema (227–3446); **Ibeu,** Av. Copacabana, 690, 2nd floor, Copacabana (255–8332 or 255–4283); **Irlandini,** Rua Teixeira de Melo, 31D-E, Ipanema, (267–7891); **Petite Galerie,** Rua Barão da Torre, 220, Ipanema (287–0231). Also; **Funarte** has several galleries at Rua Araújo Porto Alegre, 80, Centro (297–6116); **Centro Cultural Itaipava,** Av. Epitácio Pessoa, no number, in front of Parque Catacumba (267–3839); **Centro Municipal Calouste Gulbenkian,** Rua Benedito Hipólito, 125, Cidade Nova (221–7760 or 232–1087); **Galeria de Arte Jean-Jacques,** Rua Ramon Franco, 49, Urca (542–1443).

SHOPPING. Brazil is considered a "developing country" under the GSP customs exemption plan so many of the things you buy here may be able to enter the U.S. wholly duty free. Get the latest list from the U.S. Customs Service before you go. Precious stones, clothing, and leather goods are all good buys. Most shops will accept traveler's checks and dollars in cash at close to the black market rate.

Gems and Jewelry

Top gem seller is **H. Stern,** who in the last 30 years has built an international organization with branches all around the world, including New York and St. Thomas (V.I.). Their headquarters are on Rua Visconde de Pirajá 490, tel. 259–7442, with branches at Galeão International Airport, downtown Santos Dumont domestic airport, the Touring Club (landing pier), Sheraton, Inter-Continental, Meridien, Othon Palace, Gloria, Nacional, Leme Palace, Copacabana, Marina, and all other principal hotels. They and other leading jewelers offer a one-year guarantee and worldwide service. Stern's has the largest selection in town at reasonable prices, from the low-priced to the extremely expensive. They also let you see their artists at work in the lapidary and jewelry workshops of their headquarters.

Stern's also has stores in these other principal Brazilian cities: São Paulo—Praça da República 242, Hotel Brasilton, Hotel São Paulo Hilton, Shopping Center Iguatemi, Shopping Center Ibirapuera; Brasilia—Hotel Nacional; Salvador—Hotel Othon Palace, Hotel Meridien, International Airport; Manaus—Hotel Tropical, International Airport; Foz do Iguaçu—Hotel das Cataratas, International Airport.

RIO DE JANEIRO   85

For over thirty years the **Amsterdam-Sauer** Company has been a pioneer in lapidary art and the leading Brazilian specialist in emeralds. The owner, Jules Roger Sauer, is a well-known gemologist who has reactivated some old mines and opened a series of new ones. His company today has its own mining, cutting, designing, and jewelry divisions, as well as shops. Their headquarters are at Rua Mexico 41, downtown. Showcases at the hotels: Leme Palace, Savoy, Ouro Verde, California, Trocadero, Olinda, Lancaster.

Roditi, whose slogan is "The fastest growing jeweler in town," has branches in New York and Geneva. His main showroom is downtown at Av. Rio Branco 39, fifteenth floor. Shops are at Av. Rio Branco 133, Av. Atlântica 1702 (Copacabana Palace), Av. Atlântica 994 (next to Hotel Meridien), Av. Atlântica 2364, Rua Xavier da Silveira 22-A (Rio Othon Palace), and Av. Niemeyer 769 (Hotel Nacional Rio).

Maximino, a traditional jeweler and gemologist, has his head office with a magnificent gem museum downtown at Av. Rio Branco 25, and two branches at Copacabana: Rua Santa Clara 27 and Rua Figueiredo Magalhães 131. A couple of small but outstanding traditional jewelers, all with many years' experience, are **Joalharia Schupp** on Rua Gonçalves Dias 49, which has no branches but owns mines, and **Franz Flohr** on Rua Miguel Couto 23. The late Franz founded the shop back in 1936; his two sons, Gunther, a stonecutter, and Werner, a designer, are the present owners.

Ernani and Walter's ad says "No luxury store," meaning that his prices are highly competitive. His shop is at Praça Olavo Bilac 28, second floor, near the Flower Market. A number of small jewelers are to be found in this neighborhood, such as **Gregory and Sheehan.**

Burle Marx, whose head office is downtown at Praça Mahatma Gandhi 2, sells only at Rua Rodolfo Dantas 6 (next to Copacabana Palace). His specialties are unusually shaped semiprecious stones in one-of-a-kind settings. His necklace and bracelet designs have won prizes. The government often purchases jewelry from him as gifts for visiting dignitaries—the French premier's wife and the Empress of Japan, for example.

A relatively new addition to Rio's gem scene is **Mayer** at Av. Copacabana 291-E, just next to the theater of the Copacabana Palace Hotel. For collector specimens try *Edwin* at Rua Xavier da Silva 19-A behind the Othon Palace Hotel in Copacabana.

Souvenirs

The best way to acquire souvenirs is to windowshop around your hotel on Copacabana, where there are numerous shops, such as **Casa de Folclore, Macumba Souvenir,** and **Liane,** that carry Indian artifacts, butterfly trays, wooden statuettes, stuffed snakes, silverware, etc. Souvenir shops in Copacabana are concentrated along Avenida Copacabana itself, especially between Rua Paula Freitas and Avenida Princesa Isabel, and in Shopping Cassino Atlântica.

For articles made of alligator skin, look for the specialty shop, Souvenir do Brasil, on Av. Rio Branco 25. For beautiful leather handbags visit Rozwadowski, Av. Rainha Elizabeth 152, suite 101. *Copacabana Presentes,* Av. Copacabana 331-A, specializes in leather and alligator items, stones, skins, rugs, handbags, and belts. Copacabana Couros e Artesanatos, nearby at Rua Fernando Mendes 45, also features alligator goods and has exclusive designs for handmade bags and belts. Although you will see alligator goods for sale, it is against the law in Brazil to hunt the animal. Check to see whether you will be able to bring these goods home with you or into the next country on your itinerary. Brazilian artistic wood carvings and native paintings by *Batista and Mady* are

BRAZIL

excellent souvenirs; visit their studio on Rua Pacheco Leão 1270 in Ipanema where an appointment may be made to see their works.

Malls

Copacabana and Ipanema are loaded with chic boutiques and shops. To capture the flavor of the city, wandering up and down Avenida Copacabana or Visconde de Pirajá and their cross streets, which constitute the main shopping drag, can't be beat. But there are a number of malls, too, for those short of time or for days when you simply wish to get out of the rain or sun. **Rio Sul,** Avenida Lauro Muller 116, Botafogo, has over 400 shops, including the best stores of the Zona Sul. The biggest and newest mall is **Barra Shopping,** Avenida das Americas, 4666 in Barra da Tijuca. Ask at your hotel about free bus service to these malls. Other malls include:

Casa Shopping, Av. Alvorada, 2150, Barra da Tijuca, specializing in household items.

Rio Design Center, Av. Ataulfo de Paiva, 270, Leblon. Interior design and home decoration.

São Conrado Shopping Mall, Estrada da Gávea, 899, São Conrado. Built to serve the hotels Nacional and InterContinental.

Shopping Center Cassino Atlântico, Av. Atlântica 4240, Copacabana. Attached to the Rio Palace Hotel, this mall features art galleries, antique stores, and souvenir shops.

Shopping Center da Gávea, Rua Marquês de São Vicente, 52, Gávea. Notable for leather shops featuring women's clothing and shoes, and galleries.

Malls are generally open from 10 A.M. to 10 P.M. on weekdays, smaller malls until 6 P.M. on Sat. Stores are not open on Sun.

Clothing

Most of the leading shops in Rio are concentrated in Ipanema, but they also have multiple branches in Copacabana and major malls. High fashion, good quality clothing for women can be found at the following Ipanema stores: **Aspargus,** Rua Maria Quiteria, 59 (cotton jersey ensembles and knits); **Krishna,** Rua Garcia D'Avila, 101 (linen and silk suits and dresses); **Maria Bonita,** Rua Vinicius de Morais 149 (linen, cotton, and silk outfits); **Georges Henri,** Rua Visconde de Pirajá 525; **Chocolate,** Rua Visconde de Pirajá 550, entrance on Anibal de Mendonça; **Spy & Great,** Rua Garcia D'Avila 58; **Alice Tapajós** and **Marcia Pinheiros,** both in the Forum de Ipanema, Rua Visconde de Pirajá, 351.

Casual wear for women and teens is available at **Evelyn's,** Avenida Copacabana 706, Copacabana and nine other branches; **Cantao, Smash, Smuggler, Yes Brazil,** and **Toot,** all with branches in Rio Sul. Many boutiques also carry bikinis, but **Bum Bum,** Rua Vinicius de Morais 130 and **Agua na Boca,** Rua Visconde de Pirajá, loja 117 in Ipanema both specialize in swimwear.

Stores carrying clothing for both women and men: **Dijon,** Garcia D'Avila, 110 (and many branches in Rio); **Company,** Garcia D'Avila 56; **Van Gogh,** Visconde de Pirajá 444, loja 101; **Philippe Martin,** Rua Visconde de Pirajá, 338; **Elle et Lui,** Rua Garcia D'Avila, 393; and **Bee,** Rua Visconde de Pirajá 483 (T-shirts for the whole family).

Elegant men's wear at: **Richard's,** Rua Maria Quiteria 95; **Georges Henri,** Rua Maria Quiteria 77; **Eduardo Guinle,** Rua Visconde de Pirajá 514a.

Leather

The Shopping Center da Gávea is the place to go for women's leather clothing. Try **Frankie Amaury** and **Sang.** Also in Gávea Shopping are **Marco Aurelio** and **Bottega Veneta** for fine leather shoes and bags. In Ipanema, **Rotstein** and **Pucci,** both at Visconde de Pirajá 371, carry excellent women's shoes, as do the following stores, all on Visconde de Pirajá: **Mariazinha,** no. 365B, **Lele de Cuca,** no. 430, and **Beneduci,** no. 423B. In Rio Sul, **Altemia Spinelli, Birello, Germon's,** and **Sagaro** all have good women's shoes. Two shops in Rio Sul specialize in bags for women: **Victor Hugo** and **Santa Marinella,** both with branches in Ipanema.

Fairs

Popular fairs, selling food, clothing, and household items are held throughout the city every day of the week. In Ipanema, the fair is held on Fri. on Praça Nossa Senhora da Paz; in Copacabana, on Thurs. on Rua Ronald de Carvalho between Avenida Copacabana and Rua Barata Ribeiro. The **Feira Nordestino** is held every Sun. from 6 A.M. to 1 P.M. at São Cristovão in the Zona Norte. You will hear the distinctive twang of Brazil's northeast in the conversation and "frevo" music played there, sometimes by a live band. Food of the region is also available. The **Feira de Antiquidades,** or Antique Fair takes place every Sat. at Praça XV de Novembro, Centro, from 8 A.M. to 5 P.M. **Feirarte,** formerly known as the "hippy fair," continues on Sun. at the Praça General Osório, Ipanema, from 8 A.M. to 6 P.M.

NIGHTLIFE. The typical memorable Rio evening is simple; it begins at dinner with a group of friends shooting the breeze and laughing together, having a grand time entertaining themselves and each other. Soon the restaurant with live music or the nightclub with food—it's hard to tell the difference—has filled up with a critical mass of cliques, which seem to melt into one another as friends and acquaintances spot each other across the room. Suddenly you've got a party on your hands. Add a musical performance, impromptu or professional, to the merry hum of conversation and people enjoying themselves, and it's only a matter of time before the dancing begins.

Music, food, and friends are the key ingredients in Rio's varied nightlife. There's always music going on, whether it's a bunch of guys at the corner bar singing samba a cappella and using anything available as percussion instruments or a star-studded show staged with the latest audio technology and visual effects. Brazil has its own panoply of pop music stars, few of whom are well known outside Portuguese- and Spanish-speaking countries, despite their contributions to the world of music. Although you may miss the meaning of the frequently very beautiful lyrics, you can make up for it by concentrating on the musicianship of these talented performers. Any show by an established artist will include a reprise of past hits. It's a treat to be among warm, emotional Brazilian fans as they respond to their own golden oldies, each person reliving private moments en masse as the tunes evoke their individual and collective pasts. It is often said that the senses of smell and taste stir our most profound memories, but any former adolescent who can recite by heart words from the hit songs of youth well into middle age will attest that the power of music is at least as strong—and equally unaffected by language barriers. If you miss the chance to hear real Brazilian music, you will miss the essence of Brazil. Rio's varied nightlife gets started late, around 10 or 11 P.M. and goes until 4 or 5 in the morning, or until

BRAZIL

the last customer leaves. Shows, concerts, and club performances begin around 9 or 9:30 P.M., sometimes later. Many nightclubs also serve food, and quite a number of restaurants also have live music and dance floors—there is sometimes a fine line between one definition and another.

Samba Shows

If you can't make it to Rio at Carnival time, samba shows designed for tourists will give you an idea of the extravagant costumes and booming samba beat that make Carnival what it is. Mostly, the shows consist of attractive mulatas prancing around in "fantasias," as the costumes are appropriately called, acting out various scenes from Brazilian folklore. Tableaux and dance numbers based on capoeira, Bumba-meu-Boi, and homage to Iemanjá are typically included in the program. If you wish to dine before the 11 P.M. show, restaurants are part of the premises, and you may stay after the performances to dance until 4 A.M. The three samba showhouses are Las Vegas-slick and unabashedly commercial, tailoring their shows to foreigners. The masters of ceremonies address audiences in English, Spanish, Italian, and other languages, to the delight of those assembled. This is definitely not the real thing, but some think it is the next best thing to being there. The shows don't even come close to approximating the radiance and excitement of the samba parades, however.

Samba Shows begin at $20 per person and go up. **Scala,** Av. Afranio de Mello Franco, 292, Leblon (239–4448); **Plataforma I,** Rua Adalberto Ferreira, 32, Leblon (274–4022); **Oba Oba,** Rua Humaita 110, Botafogo (246–2146 or 286–9848); **Concha Verde,** Pão de Açucar, Morro de Urca, Praça General Tibúrcio, Botafogo (541–3737 or 295–2397). The guided tours of Rio by Night generally include one of these Las Vegas style shows, but you can make reservations yourself and go without paying the additional cost of the tour. Also for samba, the **Clube do Samba,** Estrada da Barra da Tijuca 65, Barra da Tijuca (399–0892); Thurs. through Sun.

Concerts

Tickets range from $10 to $20, more for foreign performers. **Canecao,** Av. Venceslau Braz, 215, Botafogo (295–3044), near Rio Sul, features the best in national and international performers. Seats are at tables or in a gallery, with drinks and snacks available to all. **Scala** (details above) also stages shows of noted performers; **Circo Voador,** Arcos da Lapa Lapa (265–2555), presents top Brazilian popular and jazz artists, and after the concerts you can stay and dance. Limited seating—you may wind up sitting on the dance floor. Musical concerts are also presented in various stadiums, museums and parks around town. Consult newspaper listings and posters for information.

Nightclubs and Bars

Arco Da Velha, Praça Cardeal Câmara 132, Lapa (252–0844), is an important spot for Brazilian Popular Music. The best places to hear jazz are **Jazzmania,** Av. Rainha Elizabeth 769, Ipanema, (227–2447 or 287–0085) and **People Jazz Bar,** Av. Bartolomeu Mitre, 370A, Leblon (294–0547). Cover charges average $3 to $5. Make reservations on weekends, other days access depends on the popularity of the performer. **Mistura Fina Studio,** Rua Garcia D'Avila 15, Ipanema (259–9394) also has jazz and popular music. For Rock n' Roll as well as jazz, **Let It Be,** Rua Siqueira Campos, 206, Copacabana, draws a young crowd. Many other piano and jazz bars cater to professional people with more disposable income. These include **Biblo's Bar,** Av. Epitácio Pessoa, 1484,

RIO DE JANEIRO 89

Lagoa (521-2645); popular with singles; **Alô-Alo,** Rua Barão da Torre, 368, Ipanema, (521-1460); **Caligula,** Rua Prudente de Morais, 129, Ipanema (287-1369); **Un, Deux, Trois,** Av. Bartolomeu Mitre, 112, Leblon (239-0198).

The following are private clubs, but if you're staying at one of the 5-star hotels, you can arrange to be admitted (ask the concierge): **Hippopotamus,** Rua Barão da Torre, 354, Ipanema (227-8658), has dancing, dinner, and music; **Regine's,** Hotel Meridien, Copacabana (275-9922); **Le Streghe,** Rua Prudente de Morais, 129, Ipanema (287-1369).

Discotheques

Discos are called "danceterias" in Brazil, and generally draw a young crowd, playing a good many American and British tunes in addition to Brazilian rock. The biggest in Rio is **Help,** Av. Atlantica 3432, Copacabana (521-1296). Also, **Mistura Fina,** Estrada da Barra da Tijuca, 1636, Barra (399-3460), open every night. **Papillon,** in the Inter-Continental Hotel (322-2200), is also open every night of the week.

Dancing to live band music tends to draw a more mature group. **Sobre As Ondas,** Av. Atlantica 3432, Copacabana (521-1296); **Vogue,** Rua Cupertino Durão, 173, Ipanema (274-8196); **Vinicius,** Av. Copacabana, 1144, Copacabana (267-1497); **Carinhoso,** Rua Visconde de Piraja, 22, Ipanema, (287-3579). **Asa Branca,** Av. Mem de Sá, 17, Lapa (252-0966), also has dinner and shows, closed Mon. and Tues.

Gafieiras

Asa Branca, described above, is sometimes categorized as a "gafieira," despite its luxuriousness. Most gafieiras are funky dance halls with live Brazilian band music and a heterogeneous clientele not necessarily from the Zona Sul. **Elite,** Rua Frei Caneca, 4, 1st floor, Centro (232-3217), open Fri.–Sun. nights from 10 P.M.; **Estudantina,** Praça Tiradentes, 79, 1st fl., Centro (232-1149), open Thurs.–Sat.; and **Forró Forrado,** Rua do Catete, 235, 2nd fl., Catete (245-0524), closed Mon. and Wed. All are unpretentious, genuine, and cheap, and cost about a dollar at the door.

Karaoke

Karaoke is a Japanese word meaning "empty stage or orchestra" and has been adopted by Brazilians as a popular form of entertainment. In a karaoke club, the customers are the performers, and a menu of songs is delivered with the food menu. You sing to a back-up tape, with words provided. Good clubs for English speakers: **Canja,** Av. Ataulfo da Paiva, 375, Leblon (511-0484); **Limelight,** Rua Ministro Viveiros de Castro, 93B, Copacabana (542-3596); and **Manga Rosa,** Rua 19 de Fevereiro, 94, Botafogo (266-4996).

BRAZIL

EXCURSIONS FROM RIO

Like San Francisco or Boston, Rio is close to mountains as well as beautiful beaches on the north and south shores. No one would go all the way to San Francisco and miss the chance to see Point Reyes, Sausalito, or Big Sur and Carmel, just as no one would travel to Boston and miss Tanglewood, Cape Cod, or scenic, quintessentially New England towns such as Ipswich and Rockport on the north shore. Yet countless tourists get to Rio without taking in the city's fabulous environs. Like any old port city, Rio is surrounded by quaint fishing villages, mountain getaways, seaside second-home communities, and places as rich in history as Rio itself. Three areas outside city limits are of major interest and are only an hour or two away by car.

THE MOUNTAINS—SERRA DOS ORGÃOS

Petrópolis, Teresópolis and Nova Friburgo are popular mountain resorts offering Cariocas a break from the summer heat. Located in the Serra dos Orgãos mountain range north of Rio, these towns were settled by German and Swiss colonists, giving them a decidedly Alpine appearance.

Petrópolis

Petrópolis is a city of considerable historic significance. Emperor Dom Pedro II liked the climate and fresh air of the area so much that he ordered a residence built in 1845 and sent for German emigrants to found a city around it. Today, his former summer palace is the Museu Imperial, Avenida 7 de Setembro, 220 (42–7012), open Tuesday through Sunday from noon until 5 P.M. The museum is full of royal memorabilia, including the Imperial Crown, weighing in at 1,720 grams, 639 diamonds and 77 pearls. It's hard to imagine anyone wearing tights in the tropics, even in the mountains, but Dom Pedro did it, along with heavy silver and velvet robes trimmed with toucan feathers, all on display now in carefully lit cases. Upstairs, you'll see the royal cradle, an ornate, gilded basket in the shape of a shell, carved of madeira wood, draped with lace, held up by a female figurehead that could have graced the prow of a boat. You will be given felt slippers as you enter to wear over your shoes so that you won't damage the wooden floors. Women should not wear high heels. The House of Santos Dumont, Brazil's father of aviation, Rua do Encanto 124, is open from 9 to 5 Tuesday to Friday, 11 to 5 Saturday and Sunday. Brazilians believe that Dumont, after whom the Rio airport is named, was the first to fly—not the Wright Brothers. This leprechaun of a man never married, and he built this tiny vacation cabin for one on his own scale so that it looks like a dollhouse. He used to sleep on the top of a table that doubled as his desk during the day, and all the furniture is noticeably low to the ground. An original and inventive Frenchman,

RIO DE JANEIRO 91

Dumont constructed what the museum claims is the first hot shower in Brazil, a funnel-like contraption terminating in a sieve. The stairs between the first and second floors are so narrow that you must climb up and down sideways. Dumont carved out semicircles in the steps so he wouldn't hit his knees or ruin the high heels he always wore. The Crystal Palace, a great greenhouse at Praça da Confluencia at Rua Alfredo Pacha, was the scene of a gala ball attended by former slaves and Princesa Isabel, after she signed Brazil's emancipation proclamation in 1888. The Crystal Place was made in France of genuine crystal, then transported and assembled in Petrópolis, where it opened in February 1884 to serve as an exposition hall for Petrópolis's agricultural products. When the royal era ended, the building was abandoned and vandalized, so that today only the structure and the crystal chandelier inside are original. In 1970, it was rehabilitated and opened to the public. The Catédral, Rua São Pedro de Alcântara 60, holds the earthly remains of Dom Pedro II, the Empress Dona Teresa Cristina and Princesa Isabel. Petrotur, the city's tourist bureau, is located at Rua Barão do Amazonas, 98, telephone 42–1466 (located around the corner from the House of Santos Dumont). Petrópolis is also a center for cotton jersey ("malha") fashions at bargain prices, concentrated on Rua Teresa. Chartered buses bring shoppers here from all over Brazil on Saturdays, so go midweek to avoid crowds.

Teresópolis

Teresópolis, an hour's drive from Petrópolis past wooded hillsides and lovely homes and farms, belonged at one time to an Englishman named George March. In 1855 he sold his ranch to the government who cut it into lots and encouraged immigration. The town gets its name from the Empress Teresa, the same way Petrópolis took its name from Dom Pedro. The most memorable thing about Teresópolis is the string of mountains it's on, the Serra dos Orgãos, which became a national park in 1939. Here is the 1,650-meter Finger of God pointing straight to Heaven, as well as the Finger of Our Lady, the Fish Mouth, and the Priest's Nose. Tallest of them all is The Rock of the Bell, which towers 2,263 meters above sea level. Alpinists climb these mountains every weekend, and if you're interested, ask your travel agent to put you in contact with a group.

Nova Friburgo

Nova Friburgo, farther east in the same mountain range, came into being by command of the Imperial Family, but years before either Petrópolis or Teresópolis (in 1818 to be exact). The man responsible for laying out the city, with its parks and beautiful homes, was the Count of Nova Friburgo. The three main squares are symphonies in marble, eucalyptus, and bamboo. Be sure and visit the park of São Clemente with its pools and wide shaded paths, currently being used as a country club. The Paço Catete, former residence of the Count of Nova Friburgo within the park, is being renovated and will eventually function as a museum. The gardens were designed by Glasioux, who also did the Quinta da Boa Vista in Rio. Of special interest in Nova Friburgo is the Cão Sentado (Sitting Dog), which perches atop a promontory reached after a hike of over an hour. The trail is clearly marked, although in disrepair, but the climb is worth it both to see this natural rock formation that looks like sculpture, and to get a good view of the countryside. The city itself sponsors many fairs featuring the immigrant groups that have settled there.

PRACTICAL INFORMATION FOR SERRA DOS ORGÃOS

PETRÓPOLIS

HOW TO GET THERE. Guided bus trips are offered by various tour agencies and the city's sights can be covered in a day, minus shopping. From Rio, public buses leave from Castelo (Praça XV de Novembro) from the Terminal Menezes Cortes, Platform A, leaving 5:30 A.M. to midnight, every half hour. Telephone 242–5414 for information.

HOTELS. Casa do Sol, Estrada Rio/Petrópolis, Km. 115, Quitandinha, (0246–43–5062)—a huge resort complex, turned condominium, with a lake in front, this is considered a landmark. A travel agent may be able to get you a reservation; **Riverside Parque Hotel,** Rua Hermogêneo Silva, 522, Retiro, (0246–43–2312 or 42–3704).

TERESÓPOLIS

HOW TO GET THERE. Public buses to Teresópolis leave from Castelo. Telephone 221–6328 for information. Also, Viação Teresópolis runs buses from 6 A.M. to 10 P.M. every half hour, 233–4625.

HOTELS. Alpina, Rua Candido Portinari, 837 (742–5252); **Rosa dos Ventos,** Estrada Teresópolis/Friburgo, Km. 22.6 (742–8833); **São Moritz,** Estrada Teresópolis/Friburgo, Km. 36 (742–4360).

NOVA FRIBURGO

HOTELS. Sans Souci, Jardim Sans Souci (0245–22–7752); **Park Hotel,** Parque São Clemente (0245–22–0825); **Mury Garden,** Estrada Rio/Nova Friburgo, Km. 70 (0245–42–1120); **Bucsky,** Estrada Rio/Friburgo, Km. 76 (0245–22–5052); **Fazenda Garlipp,** Estrada Rio/Friburgo, Km. 70.5 (0245–42–1173). These resort hotels include full meal plans and offer recreational facilities.

THE NORTH SHORE—CABO FRIO AND BÚZIOS

On the coast north of Rio, Cabo Frio has wide white sandy beaches, long enough and hard enough to drive on. It is studded with architectural relics from the colonial days, including forts, a 17th-century Franciscan convent, and an ancient cemetery. All places are open to the public and tourists can wander around undisturbed to their hearts' content. If you like water-skiing or fishing, make friends with someone

RIO DE JANEIRO 93

from Rio who has a boat, or else convince a salty old fisherman that he should rent you his. You might also visit the little fishing village of Barra de São João and watch the men working with their long woven nets. The thatched roof cottages are mixed with modern summer homes of Cariocas who have discovered it as a weekend spot. Seven miles south on the beach is the fishing village of Arraial do Cabo. Here scores of Japanese fishermen live and bring in giant whales during the cold months from June to September. One of the best beaches is Praia do Peró in Ogiva, a long, empty stretch of white sand perfect for a long walk or run.

Armação dos Búzios, once just a small village on the peninsula of Cabo Frio, is the cape's chic retreat. Beware of Búzios; it's the kind of place people intend to go for a weekend visit. But there are so many tales of folks who returned to where they came from, packed their bags, quit their nine-to-five's, and came back to Búzios to stay that you begin to believe those who tell you Búzios is enchanted. Does the sun shine bewitchingly in Búzios, or is it just your imagination making it seem brighter? No matter.

Whether the magic is real or the result of cosmic special effects, the self-selected Argentineans and Europeans who have settled here and transformed this spot from a sleepy fishing village to an enclave of polylingual professionals have devoted their considerable talents and energies to their new home. Búzios has grown through the collective enthusiasm of each person for whom it was a personal discovery.

Twenty years ago, the fine restaurants, homey but plush pousadas, and unique architectural style that place Búzios in the same league as St. Tropez or Mykonos didn't exist. First Cabo Frio (Cape Cold), from which the hamlet of Búzios protrudes into the sea, served as a hideout for French pirates. Later it became a holding station where Africans were fattened up before their sale into slavery in Rio. For generations thereafter it was off the circuit, completely forgotten. Only fishing families lived in Búzios until Brigitte Bardot appeared with her Brazilian boyfriend of the moment back in 1964.

It was a fateful visit for Búzios, which was never the same again. What with the international papparazzi crawling about snapping pictures of Bardot in the buff, someone was bound to notice the raw, sensual beauty of the cape's 23 beaches, each one offering a vista of cove and sky lovelier than the last.

Búzios' destiny was sealed when *Paris Match* published the photos and made the town instantly and internationally famous. A French colony formed, and a British colony grew. The peso was strong back then, and many Argentineans bought land. Those who came early were searching for relaxation and peace. Many, as was common in the '60's, had examined themselves and had chosen to make a radical change in their lives, to find a new, gentler way. People bought modest fisherman's cabins and remodeled them. Luxurious private homes and pousadas were built. Growth was consistent, gradual, and inexorable. Until 1980, there were only three public telephones in town, with numbers 1, 2, and 3. Those days are gone.

Size has transformed Búzios as completely as Brigitte once did. A permanent population of 12,000 swells to 50,000 during high season.

BRAZIL

Fancy boutiques line the small grid of the Centro district, replacing the bohemian feel of old. New restaurants open every season, and huge vacation complexes are being constructed. The boom has begun in earnest, and Búzios has leapt from savage, unspoiled beaches and solitude to sophisticated international watering hole in a brace of fleeting years. Today, José Hugo Celidonio, Brazil's noted food critic, believes that there are three great restaurant towns in Brazil: São Paulo, Rio, and Búzios, in that order.

PRACTICAL INFORMATION FOR THE NORTH SHORE

HOW TO GET THERE. Rent a car to get to Búzios; you'll need it to get to the various beaches, and bus service from Rio extends only as far as Cabo Frio. Or you can arrange through a travel agent for a round-trip transportation and excursions around the cape. *Ekoda*, on Rua José Bento Ribeiro Dantas, 22, in Búzios, 0246–23–1493, or Av. Rio Branco 277, Loja E, in Rio, 240–7067, will provide transportation to and from Cabo Frio as well as jeep tours of Búzios, rides to the beaches, boat tours, and water sports equipment, including snorkeling gear, surfboards, wind surfers, and water skis. Many of the prices are negotiable, but the beach tour price is fixed and depends on the number in your group.

CABO FRIO

HOTELS. Accommodations in this area are available at pousadas, small, owner-operated inns; **Porto Peró**, Av. dos Pescadores 2002 (0246–43–1395); **Ponta de Areia**, Av. Espadarte 184 (0246–43–2053); **Portoveleiro**, Av. dos Espadartes, 129 (0246–43–3081). Prices depend on high or low season, but range between $25 and $40, not including meals. This area is still simple, casual and quiet.

BÚZIOS

HOTELS. Búzios, sometimes considered Rio's "Côte D'Azur," is a watering hole for affluent Cariocas and international jetsetters. **Pousada nas Rocas,** Ilha Rasa, Marina Porto Búzios, occupies its own island and offers a 5-star restaurant, swimming pool, running track, nautical sports, breakfast, dinner and all activities included in the daily rate, beginning at $150. Make reservations in Rio, (021) 253–0001.

In Armação dos Búzios or Centro, comfortable, elegant lodging is available at **Pousada Casas Brancas,** on a hill overlooking Praia da Armação. Casas Brancas is noted for its special breakfasts and warm hospitality, starting at about $70 a night (0246–23–1458). Also, **Pousada La Chimère** on Praça dos Ossos, (0246–231043) in Búzios or book in Rio (220–2129), prices begin at about $35 per night. There are many more pousadas in existence and under construction.

RESTAURANTS. Búzios is noted for great dining. French: **Au Cheval Blanc,** Rua Bento Dantas, Centro. Italian: **Le Streghe,** Rua Bento Dantas 201, a few doors down from Au Cheval Blanc, and **Satiricon,** on the road from Centro to Praça dos Ossos. All of these are *expensive*. For simpler, *moder-*

RIO DE JANEIRO 95

ate fare: **Gostinho Natural,** Rua Manoel Toribes de Farias, 233 and **Restaurante do Davide,** right across the street. No telephone reservations—Centro is so small, you can drop in and make them in person.

THE SOUTH SHORE—SEPETIBA BAY, ANGRA DOS REIS, AND PARATÍ

Rio's south shore, like Cabo Frio to the north, is walking the fine line between rational development and ruination. It is the Midas touch of tourism that the very bohemian spirit or natural wonders that attract people to a place are irrevocably altered or destroyed by those who would appreciate them. Ecologists warn that fishing will be extinct in the waters between Rio and Angra dos Reis in six years—that Sepetiba Bay will soon be as polluted by traffic and sewage as any city beach. Brazilian scientists and officials are aware of the problem, and it is hoped that with careful management this recreational treasure can be preserved.

Fortunately for visitors in the near future, paradise is not yet lost. Thirty-six islands dot Sepetiba Bay, and scores more extend down the coast in the Baia da Ilha Grande between Angra dos Reis and Paratí, two colonial towns that have preserved the treasures of the past.

A convenient way to explore Sepetiba Bay is to take the Tropical Island Tour, a one-day excursion from Rio. These day trips cost between $15 and $30 for the day, depending on the tour operator, and are an excellent value in addition to being a relaxed way to meet visitors from all over the world. You'll cruise the bay, stop for a sumptuous luncheon buffet at one of the islands, and while away the afternoon swimming and sunning on the beach with newfound companions.

Make Angra dos Reis your headquarters for visiting some of the 300 islands in the Ilha Grande Bay. Although today Angra dos Reis is known principally for the wild, beautiful beaches of the hundreds of islands off its coast, during the seventeenth-century it was a haven for pirates and one of the most important ports of Brazil. By 1749, there were 15 sugar mills and 91 related factories, evidence of a substantial agricultural, commercial, and industrial base. Angra began to stagnate after a railroad connecting Rio and São Paulo shriveled the shipping trade. With the emancipation of the slaves in the late 1800s, Angra's manpower-intensive economy foundered. The town turned to fishing and faded into obscurity.

The tables turned around 1970 when the Rio–Santos highway opened, linking Angra easily to Brazil's two population centers and making the area accessible for tourism. Today Angra is alive with boating, fishing, and water-related recreational activities, especially around Carnival, when it becomes a floating celebration.

Ilha Grande, one of Angra's major attractions, was once a place to which people were banished. According to legend, Jorge Grego, one of the most successful pirates to ply these waters, was sailing toward the straits of Magellan, when he was attacked by the British Armada. He escaped his ruined ship with his two young daughters and a former slave, came to live on Ilha Grande, gave up the life of a pirate, and became a prosperous merchant-farmer. His little girls were growing up, and one day Jorge became crazed with jealousy when he realized that

BRAZIL

his old companion was in love with one of his daughters. Jorge killed his friend and himself became the lover of both girls, causing a great curse to fall upon Ilha Grande.

Suddenly, a wind storm more ferocious than any within memory swept through the island, destroying all the farms and houses on it. Everyone living on the island disappeared, except Jorge Grego, old and alone, who wandered around the island until he died, burying, in the meantime, all the treasures he had accumulated.

Today the treasure of Ilha Grande is nature, unburied and free. Wander along paths away from sandy white beaches and discover parrots, hummingbirds, monkeys, butterflies, and other wildlife living among the thick, wanton vegetation.

There are many hotels concentrated in the Angra area, and the best are those of the Frade Hotel chain, whose hotels are really complete vacation complexes. The most famous is the Hotel Portogalo, which offers a vista so beautiful that it is featured prominently in the $50 picture books on sale in the region's souvenir shops. The luncheon buffet is delicious, imaginative, and generous, with enough variety for a vegetable-hungry foreigner to eat green things instead of just the beans, rice, and French fries that are the inevitable accompaniments at every Brazilian meal. The dinner buffet is completely different from what has been served at lunch, and just as good.

You can leave on a day cruise of the islands early every morning directly from the hotel or sign on to Frade's floating hotel, the schooner Frade-Mar, on a Monday or Friday and not set foot on earth again for several days. The schooner has 12 cabins, a large deck for meals and sunbathing, and equipment for wind surfing, fishing, and diving. If you prefer, you can rent a small sailboat and be your own skipper. Scuba diving lessons are also available, and tennis courts are open for play day and night.

The Portogalo is geared toward adults who want to relax. If you are traveling with children or want other leisure options, the Hotel do Frade, on the road to Paratí, offers horseback riding, a nine-hole golf course, biking, and soccer in addition to a full range of water activities and cruises.

The coastal village of Paratí was founded way back in the early 16th century. Its calm, natural little harbor was the perfect jumping off point for adventurers looking for the gold and precious stones in Minas Gerais. For decades the town flourished while it catered to the needs of the miners and helped them spend their money. But the boom calmed down, Santos rose in importance because of its superb harbor, and over the years Paratí was forgotten. The same forces that caused the decline of Paratí in the 1700s also preserved it: economic winds changed and left it stranded. Considered by UNESCO to be one of the world's richest preserves of eighteenth-century architecture, it is also protected by the Brazilian government as a national monument. Nothing can be built, and nothing can be changed. Paratí remains as it looked when time passed it by.

In its heyday, around 1670, Paratí was a city of 16,000 inhabitants, a wealthy, busy port through which passed slaves, tobacco, pork, coffee, corn, beans, sugar cane, manioc, and the renowned pinga manu-

RIO DE JANEIRO 97

factured locally. One million kilos of gold and 100 kilos of precious stones were shipped via Paratí, explaining why the town is surrounded by forts. A serious blow to Paratí's economy is what saved her: In 1723, a new road between Rio and Minas Gerais cut 15 days off the trip, circumventing Paratí, previously the principal axis for jewel traffic. Business at the port dropped precipitately, and the old Indian trails over which so much lucre had been carried were abandoned.

When the law freeing the slaves was signed in 1888, causing the collapse of Paratí's sugar cane and coffee plantations, Paratí was consigned to a state of arrested decay. Then, in 1954, another new road was opened, bursting rather than sealing Paratí's isolation. Artists and tourists discovered its peace, beauty, and historical atmosphere, and the city revived. Today it is famed for its artistic and folkloric events and is still considered the cachaça capital of Brazil.

As you walk through these quiet, carless, cobbled streets, you can hear birds singing and, if you listen, the clip-clop of horses and the clang of the old iron city gate that used to close at nightfall at the signal of a cannon still echo. The single small pier gives no hint of Paratí's former shipping glory. Stroll to the end of it, then turn around for a priceless view of the past. You'll be charmed by the colorful painted fishing boats which make more for their sea-loving owners these days as charter boats for tourists. If you're a fan of Brazilian cinema, you may recognize Paratí as the town in Bruno Barreto's film *Gabriela,* based on Jorge Amado's famous novel and starring Sonia Braga.

The boutiques scattered among the dozens of pousadas feature artwork depicting Paratí, the distinctive papier mâché masks used during the Festa do Divino, and models of the saveiro boats in all sizes, painted just like the real ones in tricolor combinations of blue, red, yellow, and earthy tones in between. The Fazenda Murycana, a pinga factory, was built in colonial times and is still producing the potent sugar cane liquor (variously called aguardente, pinga, and cachaça throughout Brazil) for which Paratí is known. The Fazenda today also has a zoo, a museum of artifacts from colonial times, a playground, and a riding stable. Dispensers of insect repellent are placed around the grounds so that visitors can ward off numerous, aggressive mosquitoes. Today it is important as a tourist center. With the Rio-Santos Highway passing close by, traffic jams became so great that cars are now banned from most city streets. Those who have taken the time to visit it come back with glowing tales of baroque churches, charming squares, and an unspoiled old-world charm. Many houses have been restored by private parties and the mandate is to preserve as much of the original flavor as possible.

Many artistic and cultural festivals, including the Festa do Divino and the Festas Juninas are held in Angra and Paratí in May and June. The main attraction of Angra is as a point of departure to explore the islands of Sepetiba Bay. Paratí itself is small and can be seen in a day's walking tour. Don't miss the view of the town from the pier, where you can rent a small boat called a saveiro. Lots of mosquitoes here, bring an effective repellent.

PRACTICAL INFORMATION FOR ANGRA DOS REIS AND PARATÍ

HOTELS. Angra and Paratí are served by the Frade Hotel chain, which operates the **Hotel do Frade,** the **Portogalo** (Angra) and the **Pousada Dom João** (Paratí). Book in Rio at Rua Joaquim Nabuco, 161, Copacabana (267–7375). The chain sends a bus down from Rio regularly for about $10 to serve its hotels, which offer a full range of recreational activities. Rooms start at $30, without meals; leisure options are extra, full meal plans available. In Paratí, these inns are also recommended: Pousada Pardieiro, rua Ten. Francisco Antonio, 74, tel. 71–1370; Pousada do Ouro, rua Dr. Pereira, 145, tel. 71–1311; Pescador, Ave. Beira-Rio, no number, tel. 71–1466; Coxixo, rua Ten. Francisco Antonio, 362, tel. 71–1568. All range from $40 to $50 a night.

OTHER DESTINATIONS

Itacuruçá and Aguas Lindas

Itacuruçá is the take-off point for the saveiro boats that form the second leg of the Island Paradise Tours, offered by a number of tour operators from Rio. A bus picks you up at your hotel, drops you at the boat, and takes you back to Rio at the end of the day. Three hotels are located on tropical paradise islands in this area about 55 miles southwest of Rio. Two of these have individual bungalows. The Jaguanum occupies its own beach on Jaguanum Island, about 30 minutes by launch from Itacuruçá pier. European management. Book in advance in Rio (237–5119); meals included in rooms rates.

Aguas Lindas, also with bungalows, is in a cove where many of the wealthy have weekend cottages, on the island of Itacuruçá. Reservations in Rio (220–0007), boat transportation to island and meals included in room rates. On the other side of the island is the larger Hotel de Pierre (788–1016) with 50 air-conditioned rooms.

The hotels can help you arrange boat outings, sailing, fishing, windsurfing.

Resende

143 kms. from Rio, Resende is an excellent vacation spot near Itatiaia National Park. Among its attractions: Agulhas Negras Peak; Funil Dam, a Finnish settlement; Blue Lake waterfalls; Agulhas Negras military academy. Best hotels are the Simon, (52–1122), expensive, and the more moderate Cabanas de Itatiaia (52–1328) and Hotel do Ypê (52–1453 or reservations in Rio at 221–2022), all inside the Parque Nacional. In Resende itself, the small Avenida (54–1184) and the Espigao Palace (54–1855) are the only choices, both inexpensive.

SÃO PAULO

No matter how well you've studied Latin America and boned up on Brazil, the city of São Paulo will come as a startling surprise. There is nothing like it in any other South American nation, no other place that can come close or that even hints of coming close. It's the richest area in South America, the fastest growing, and the pride of all the Brazilians.

Nothing of importance happens in Brazil that doesn't begin in São Paulo. Brasilia may be the country's capital, but politically, economically, and culturally, São Paulo is the number one city in the country, and the largest, wealthiest metropolis in all of South America. Where Rio is beautiful, São Paulo is brilliant. Where Rio is devil-may-care, São Paulo is committed and dynamic. Where Rio is laid-back and lackadaisical, São Paulo is efficient, productive, and propelled by the work ethic.

Paulistanos, as natives of the city are called, work hard, play hard, and demand the very best in shopping, restaurants, and entertainment. Paulistanos are the shrewd, industrious Yankees of Brazil. This mighty headquarters of multinational companies and manufacturing is a craggy concrete center of skyscrapers and astute entrepreneurs. This is where Brazilians come to make it big, for everyone knows that the right place and the right time are here, and the secret ingredients to success are hard work and persistence. This giant city is a magnet for money

100   **BRAZIL**

and talent, drawing the ambitious from all parts of Brazil and all over the world.

São Paulo is a cross between New York and Los Angeles. Like Los Angeles, it sprawls over 589 square miles, is covered by a semi-permanent blanket of smog, and is connected by a giant freeway system. Like New York, skyscrapers dominate the horizon in jagged concrete clusters, the constant din of traffic and construction provides a permanent white noise in the background, and life is lived indoors, at night, in the best, most sophisticated restaurants, nightclubs, and company in all Brazil.

Like their counterparts in New York, Paulistanos have a love-hate relationship with their city. They complain that it is ugly, dirty, and threatening. On weekends, they escape to Guarujá by the sea or Campos do Jordão in the mountains the way New Yorkers flee Manhattan for Long Island or the Catskills. Some say they find it impossible to live here, yet they can't imagine living anywhere else. No other Brazilian city has the tempo, the creative drive, the excitement that comes from the pursuit of excellence.

Most tourists never get to São Paulo, as it is rarely included on a vacationer's itinerary. Yet a visit to Brazil that did not include São Paulo would be like going to the United States without seeing New York—unthinkable. Nevertheless, many settle for the seductions of Rio instead of the superlatives of São Paulo, a mistake São Paulo's 14 million residents have avoided. Seventy percent of São Paulo's inhabitants are descendents of immigrants, most of whom arrived between 1885 and 1914 as part of the great global migration from Europe and Asia to the New World. Another wave of Europeans arrived after the Second World War, while transplants from Brazil's interior and impoverished northeast arrive daily to start new lives. This is Brazil's big apple. Great expectations are what São Paulo is made of. People with dreams to realize come here, work hard, and make it happen. The city is constantly growing—demographers estimate that by the year 2000, São Paulo will have a population of 26 million.

Historically, immense wealth generated by the coffee plantation period positioned São Paulo fortuitously: when the late-blooming Brazilian industrial revolution finally burgeoned during the late 1950s and early 1960s, São Paulo boomed, growing outward from the Centro district in concentric circles of development, forming an accretion of 500 neighborhoods. Little is left from the colonial period except for the determined spirit of the Bandeirantes, hunters for Indian slaves and gold whose hardy expeditions into the interior claimed much of Brazil's territory and countless native lives. The legacy of such ruthlessness and rapid growth is relentless concrete, helter-skelter urban sprawl, a mania for achievement, and an area so rich that it is virtually a country within a country. The costs of industrialization have been as high as the profits—São Paulo also holds the dubious distinction of including within its immediate vicinity Cubatão, generally conceded to be the world's most polluted community.

São Paulo today is a cosmopolitan hybrid, manifesting layers of cultural amalgamation that distinguishes it from the rest of Brazil, where the ethnic stew is made of a different mix. To the original African

SÃO PAULO 101

and Portuguese influences—epitomized by the earthy sensuality of samba and the piety of Catholic tradition—were added the cultural traits of later immigrants, primarily Japanese and Italian. The largest Japanese community outside Japan added its industriousness and pragmatism; the Italians contributed their flair for seizing and enjoying the moment. Simmered together with the universal yearnings of the immigrant, these cultural ingredients produced the Paulistano: responsible, competent, ambitious, free from Anglo-Saxon angst at pleasure, warm and flexible in dealing with people.

The state of São Paulo, whose residents are called "Paulistas," is a fit setting for its active, pulsating, capital city. With some of the richest farmland in Brazil, it supplies almost half the nation's coffee, cotton, fruits, and vegetables. The fertile land is criscrossed by an excellent system of railways and modern highways, which the industries scattered in the small towns use to their advantage.

São Paulo is a cosmopolitan city that owes its progress to people from all nations, the richness of the soil and the temperate climate. It is a never ending source of investigation and amazement on the part of sociologists and a richly rewarding experience to those Brazilians who feel their country is capable of becoming an important world power.

From a sleepy little Jesuit colony founded in 1554 it has grown into a metropolis almost three times the size of Paris, with an industrial district that swallows up mile after mile of surrounding land annually. There is a violent energy in the air and none of the sentimentality that binds the rest of the nation to the past. For São Paulo there is only the future. The Paulistas like to say that "São Paulo can never stop." And from the way it has weathered every political crisis and change and steered its way through inflation and depression, it looks as if it never is going to stop.

But it is not an inhuman city of robots, concrete, and machines. It is a city of people who have come looking to better themselves from every nation on the globe. They are individuals who desire better living conditions and are willing to work for them. The Paulista asks nothing from anyone. He has two hands and uses them to get what he wants. Sometimes his attitude is rather Texan, in that he thinks the world comes to an end at the state's boundaries. His capital city is self-contained and thrives on the manufacture of textiles, clothes, paper, pottery, chemicals, leather, rubber, timber, cement, iron, and steel. His state alone provides one-fourth of the two million new jobs Brazil needs annually to keep unemployment from becoming a severe problem.

The city was first with enough cheap electrical power to handle any industry that was interested in building there. It also offered a direct railway connection to the seaport town of Santos, and its early governors encouraged immigration of industrial workers rather than farmers. Those Europeans who couldn't take the climate of Rio or Bahia thrived in São Paulo, built their homes there, and encouraged their children to stay on and handle the family businesses. The result is that today the city counts a number of millionaire families who are third and fourth generation Paulista, and they are proud to tell the visitor the way their grandparents worked their way up from steerage class to

102   BRAZIL

the mansions along Avenida Paulista, which are rapidly being replaced today by ultra-modern bank and office buildings.

The Times Square of Brazil

Probably the best place to "feel" the pulse of the city is right in its heart, the bridge over the vast Avenida Anhangabaú. It leads into the Praça do Patriarca. Just stand there and observe the autos and people hurrying below you in what appears to be organized confusion. This is the Times Square of Brazil, and the bridge you're on is the Viaduto do Cha (tea), named for the product once grown in this valley. The intricately worked bridge farther down the avenue is the Santa Ifigênia, recently spruced up by the city and bathed in golden light at night by the General Electric Co. Now look at the buildings that flank each side of the bridge and note especially the squat white granite, solid looking one that is partly below the bridge and partly above it. It is the Matarazzo Building, former headquarters of one of Brazil's most successful immigrant families. The first Matarazzo came to Brazil as an immigrant and arrived dripping wet when his boat overturned going to the shore. He had lost every one of his possessions. Undaunted but penniless, he started to buy and sell pork fat door to door. Soon he had a small lard company and this he parlayed into a canning factory. Not long afterward there was nothing that he wasn't manufacturing or operating. Today the Matarazzo businesses are run by his granddaughter and grandsons.

Now walk up Rua Barão de Itapetininga across the Praça Ramos de Azevedo along the front of the majestic Teatro Municipal and four blocks to Av. Ipiranga. Here is the center of the man-in-the-streets haunts, with the huge movie theaters, the elegant and well-kept Praça de Republica and the sidestreets leading off to shops and specialty stores. Most of the tourist and souvenir shops are in this area, as well as the airline company offices and better bookstores.

Edifício Italia, the tallest building in South America, is situated at the highest point in São Paulo. Visit one of its rooftop bars or restaurants on a clear day or night. Behind it, on Ipiranga, is the graceful, serpent-shaped apartment and office building designed by famed Brasilia builder Oscar Niemeyer, across the street from the São Paulo Hilton. Turning from Ipiranga and walking down São Luiz, which leads to the Hotel Jaraguá, you'll see new office buildings with shops, theaters, and luxury stores that have sprung up in the past few years. São Paulo is like New York in this respect; wherever you look there is an old building coming down and a new one rising in its place.

Parks, Museums, and Sights

In 1888 the state government purchased an old farm house and turned it over to a scientist who had some crazy notion that snake serum could be used to save the life of someone bitten by a snake. His first patients were the horses of the Paulista cavalry, and he had 64 snakes to work with. Today the Instituto Butantãn, Avenida Vital Brasil 1500, Butantã (211–8211), the largest snake farm in Latin

SÃO PAULO 103

America, counts more than 70,000 snakes in its collection, as well as thousands of spiders, scorpions, and lizards. It extracts their venom regularly and processes it so it can be flown anywhere in the world when it's needed in a hurry. The institute is open daily, 8 A.M. to 5 P.M. Be sure to see them milking the snakes between 10 A.M. and 4 P.M. You can take a bus from Praça da Republica or, of course, a taxi, for it's quite a distance from the downtown area.

The Instituto Butantã was originally founded to develop a vaccine against bubonic plague, which hit the nearby port of Santos in 1899. Once that menace had passed, the Institute expanded its scientific interests to include the study of venomous animals, the production and distribution of antidotes specific to each type of snake venom (a discovery credited to Institute founder Vital Brasil), and the treatment and prevention of poisoning accidents and infectious diseases.

Between 1933 and 1979, Butantã produced 199,333,430 doses of antismallpox vaccine. Smallpox was not eradicated in Brazil until 1971, following a campaign that entailed the vaccination of 84 percent of the population. In addition to processing serums against rabies, tetanus, diphtheria, typhoid, and cholera, Butantã annually supplies 7 million doses of tuberculosis vaccine and also runs a hospital that specializes in treating victims of snakebite, who are airlifted to the facility by helicopter.

Before the city limits of São Paulo reached Butantã during the 1950s, the Institute was a self-contained scientific farm community, complete with a primary school for the children of employees who lived on the premises, a medical office, a dining hall, and a kitchen, plus a cooperative store and a recreational club. A small museum on the grounds displays some of original instruments used and explains the Institute's history.

Today Butantã also operates the snake museum, which is dedicated to education about poisonous snakes and insects and their habits. Large glass cases contain huge boa constrictors, coiled together like intestines motionless except for an occasional undulation and a quick serpent's tongue darting toward a white mouse, destined to be lunch, that hovers in the corner. Surprisingly, the most dangerous snakes in Brazil are not these monsters but the small coral snake, no larger than a child's fat crayon. Without serum, the bite of the coral snake is always fatal, but what confuses matters is that there are two kinds of coral snake, one poisonous and the other harmless; it's difficult to tell one from the other, since both are red with black circles.

In general, however, you can tell a venomous snake from a harmless one by the position of the fangs. Nonvenomous snakes never have fangs located to the rear of the mouth or between the nose and eyes. Most snakebite accidents, according to Butantã research, occur on the hands and are caused by people handling and playing with snakes or attempting to capture them without the proper instruments.

In addition to live displays of both snakes and spiders, there are static dioramas showing snakes in various stages of swallowing birds, mice, and other small animals. A skeleton of a sucuri snake stretches 5.1 meters, 311 vertebrae and 241 pairs of ribs long.

104   BRAZIL

The Exotiquarium, Avenida Roque Petroni Junior, 1089, Shopping Morumbi, Piso lazer, 543–2611, affords a rare opportunity to see the pink freshwater dolphins of the Amazon, shown here in captivity for the first time in South America. Long snouts, a camelish hump on their backs, grayish in color despite their name, with flippers like a seal, these animals are oddly graceful in spite of their girth—they weigh up to 200 kg at maturity. In addition to the dolphins, 60 smaller tanks of tropical fish and flora make you want to take up skin diving, so beautiful is the deep-sea scenery depicted here. Exquisitely colored, exotically shaped "ornamental" fish in all sizes are displayed along with piranha, electric eels, trout, carp, the freshwater shark from Thailand, and dozens of mollusks and other denizens of the deep. Admission for adults varies from $1 to $1.50 depending on the day. Open from Tues. through Sun. from 10 A.M. to 10 P.M., the Exotiquarium is considered the best in Brazil.

Within walking distance of the snake farm is the House of the Flagbearer (Casa do Bandeirante), Praça Monteiro Lobato (211–0920). An old ranch house that goes back to the 18th cenury, the building was completely restored in 1954 and decorated with priceless furniture and pottery of the period. Even the outside buildings like the corn crib and the mill are authentic down to the last detail. If you are interested in the antiques of this era, you'll love the place. It's open from Tues. to Sat. from 10:30 A.M. to 5 P.M., Sun. from 9 A.M. to 5 P.M. There is a guide here. Entrance is free.

Ibirapuera Park is perhaps the biggest one of its kind in the world. It covers two million square meters, is decorated with natural lakes and rolling, well-watered lawns, and contains ten modern exhibition halls where one thing or another is being shown. The entrance to the park is dominated by a statue containing 36 figures of the pioneers, Indians, and horses who braved the unmapped lands and carved out a new empire. The statue, the work of Frenchman Victor Brecheret, is 50 meters long and has been given the affectionate if irreverent name of "Don't push." Inside the park you'll be able to visit the Japanese Pavilion, which is an exact reproduction of the Katura Palace in Japan and is kept up by donations of the Japanese colony. There is also a windowless dome of cement called the History Pavilion. Here are the museums of Science, Aeronautics, and Technical Arts. In the Pavilion Pereira, the world-famed Bienal art exhibits are held in odd years—the next one is in 1989. The greatest display of contemporary art in Latin America, the show attracts painters from all over the globe who compete for top honors in the art world. Don't miss the beautiful Museu dos Presépios (recently renovated, call 544–1329), a year-round display of nativity scenes. The Planetarium is also in this park and is rated the best in South America. Complete, absorbing shows are given each Saturday, Sunday, and holiday at 4, 6 and 8 P.M., and Tuesday and Thursday at 8 P.M. Tickets at the door cost about 90 cents. There is also a radio-telescope (the only one in Brazil) that lets you "listen" to the stars, as well as an interesting corner where telescopes are assembled. (For information call 544–4606.) Take any bus marked Ibirapuera.

Along the banks of the Anhembi River, at the entrance to the São Paulo-Rio Highway, is Anhembi Park, whose exposition hall is the

SÃO PAULO 105

world's largest aluminum structure. The roof is supported by 25 light columns and the hall is illuminated by 200 aluminum globes. Right beside it is a modernistic convention hall seating 5,000 persons. A 453-room hotel is also under construction nearby.

The Zoological Park is located in Avenida Miguel Estafeno, 4241, Agua Funda (276–0811). The largest zoo in South America, it displays over 400 animals and 600 birds. There are few fences or cages and Paulistas dot the lawns on Sunday afternoons with their tablecloths and picnic baskets. It is open daily from 9 A.M. to 6 P.M., and adult admission is about $1.

Near the zoo, on the same avenue at number 3031 is the Jardim Botânico, an orchid farm where there are over 35,000 species. The force of so much beauty is overpowering at times. You may visit the orchids and the zoo by taking a number 546 bus from Praça da Liberdade or Anhangabaú. Open Tues. to Sun., 9 A.M. to 5 P.M. (275–3322).

Just behind the zoo, but requiring a closed car in which to visit it, is the Simba Safari, Avenida do Cursino 6338, Vila Morais (577–6249), where lions, camels, monkeys and cheetahs roam free in their own wilderness, and only the visitors are caged. Open from 9 A.M. to 5:45 P.M. Tues. to Sun. in summer, 9 A.M. to 5 P.M. in winter.

If you are interested in collecting stamps or coins, then a must on your itinerary is a visit to the center of downtown Praça da Republica on a Sunday morning. There collectors and dealers traditionally gather to talk, swap, and sell. But today they are outnumbered by "hippies" selling their handicraft—leather goods, furniture, paintings, and trinkets made of glass, straw, and metal.

Three museums should be on your list of musts. The first is the Museu de Arte de São Paulo, Avenida Paulista 1578, (251–5644). Open Tues. to Fri. from 1 to 5 P.M., Sat. and Sun. from 2 to 6 P.M. MASP has the only collection in South America that shows a panorama of Western art from the Gothic Age to the present. Here hangs Raphael's famed "Resurrection," painted when he was just 17 years old. There is a Rembrandt self-portrait, three Frans Hals, 13 works by Renoir, 10 by Toulouse-Lautrec, and many others. There is a section of 19th-century and contemporary Brazilian painters, a selection of Gobelin tapestries, and a collection of early Italian majolica. The basement houses special exhibits, frequently changed, of art, antiques, glass collections, and other treasures. Frequent traveling and special exhibits, such as a collection of Picasso's prints, enrich MASP's program. MASP was founded in 1947 by Assis Chateaubriand to support and develop art in Brazil. Chateaubriand chose São Paulo because he believed, rightly, that this would become the major city on the continent as a result of its concentration of wealth. He also chose Pietro Maria Bardi, a colleague of Corbusier and an art historian, to create the museum from scratch and then direct it. Bardi, now in his late 80s, continues to do so to this day, overseeing a permanent collection of 750 works, revolving exhibitions, and international exchanges. "A museum does not exist to preserve art," says Bardi of his and the museum's philosophy, "but as a center creating the impetus for the growth of art." According to Professor Bardi, when he arrived from Rome in 1946, there were no galleries and no museums dedicated to art in São

BRAZIL

Paulo. Today there are over 150 galleries and dozens of museums. Admission fees of about a dollar are charged for these.

The second important museum is the Museu de Arte Contemporánea (571–9610) located in the Pereira Pavilion in Ibirapuera Park. There are over 1,650 works by such modern masters as Kandinsky, Léger, Carrá, Portinari, and various cubists of the pre-World War I era. Open every day but Monday from 1 to 6 P.M. Admission is roughly 65 cents.

Third is the Museum of Brazilian Art at Rua Alagoas 903 (826–4233). Here are copies of all the monuments and statues in the parks and buildings of Brazil, including copies of the famed Prophets of Aleijadinho. Free admission Tues. through Fri. from 2 to 10 P.M., Sat. and Sun. from 1 to 7 P.M.

Also important are the Museum of Modern Art (Museu de Arte Moderna—MAM), Parque Ibirapuera, (549–9688), open Tues.–Fri., 1–8 P.M., Sat. and Sun., 11 A.M. to 7 P.M.; and the Sacred Art Museum (Museu de Arte Sacra), Avenida Tiradentes, 676 (227–7694), a large collection of Brazilian art from the colonial period; open Tues. through Sun., 1 to 5 P.M.

SÃO PAULO

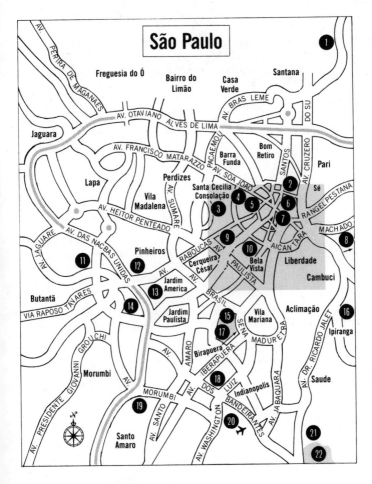

Points of Interest

Butanta Institute (Instituto Butuntã) **11**
Botanical Garden (Jardim Botânico) **21**
Congonhas Airport **20**
Forest Park (Horto Florestal) **1**
Jockey Club **14**
Marco Zero—City Center **6**
Municipal Theater (Teatrõ Municipal) **5**
Museum of Bixiga's Memories (Museu Memórias do Bixiga) **9**
Museum of Brazilian Art (Museu de Arte Brasileira) **3**
Museum of Contemporary Art (Museu de Arte Contemporanea) **17**
Museum of Religious Art (Museu de Arte Sacra) **2**
Parque do Carmo **8**
Parque do Ibirapuera **15**
Pateo de Colégio—Historic Center **7**
Paulista Museum (Museu Paulista "do Ipiranga") **16**
Praca da Republica **4**
São Paulo Art Museum (Museu de Arte de S. Paulo, MASP) **10**
Shopping Center Eldorado **13**
Shopping Center Ibirapuera **18**
Shopping Center Iguatemi **12**
Shopping Center Morumbi **19**
Zoological Garden (Jardim Zoológico) **22**

PRACTICAL INFORMATION FOR SÃO PAULO

WHEN TO GO. The weather information for Rio is also good for São Paulo, except that when it is cool in Rio, it is twice as chilly here. Since the city sits 820 meters (2,665 ft.) above sea level, it is prey to the variable winds that come northward from cold Argentina as well as those breezes coming from muggy Mato Grosso jungles. It is a stimulating climate that does not sap one's energy. There is a continuing series of interesting things like museum openings, art exhibits, industrial fairs, and sports programs. There is always something going on, and the visitor will not have to worry about killing time, in spite of the lack of sandy beaches.

HOW TO GET TO SÃO PAULO. Most people visit here after they have been in Rio. The easiest and most comfortable way to come is via the modern, efficient *Ponte Aérea* (Air Bridge), which consists of the constant arrival and departure of airplanes between Rio's Santos Dumont airport and São Paulo's Congonhas field. They leave every half-hour from 6 A.M. till 10:30 P.M. Reservations aren't needed, unless you want a certain plane. You just show up and take the next plane. It is a good idea to book in advance for a weekend flight, especially Friday evening. Tickets: about $30 one way.

In 1985, São Paulo finally inaugurated its long-awaited international airport of Cumbica, in the industrial suburb of Guarulhos, about a 45-minute drive from downtown. Most international flights now land there, although some still use Viracopos in Campinas, two hours away. Buses linking Guarulhos airport and Praça da República run about every 20 minutes and cost about $1.50.

São Paulo can also be reached by first-class buses which leave Novo Rio bus terminal every half hour and make the 253-mile trip in five-and-one-half hours on an excellent highway with one rest stop. Either *Expresso Brasileiro* or *Viaçao Cometa* will give you more than satisfactory service. The late-night sleeper buses, called "leitos," run about $10 and are extremely comfortable and modern. Regular shuttle buses are half the price of leitos. All buses arrive in São Paulo's Tietè terminal, linked by the Metrô to downtown.

Low-cost trains leave Rio's Central do Brasil railroad station. The sleeper leaves at 11:10 P.M., arriving in São Paulo about 8:00 A.M. Not fancy, but clean and comfortable, with a dining car. Sleeper seats and Pullman compartments range from $5 to $20.

GETTING AROUND SÃO PAULO. From the airport. At Congonhas city airport, there are no regular taxis. The red and white airport taxis outside the domestic wing will cost about $4 to your downtown hotel. Air-conditioned "luxury" taxis outside the international wing cost about $9. To take a regular metered cab (many are VW beetles), walk down the few steps to the street and flag one down. Cost: about $2.50 to city center. As in Rio, the system of a price table correlated with what registers on the meter is used. Avis, Hertz, L'Auto, and National rental cars are available, but São Paulo is a difficult city for the nonresident to get around in, due to its size, traffic congestion, and constant road repairs. City buses are cheap, about 10 cents for most fares, but lines are long at rush hours, and, for non-Portuguese speakers, the routes can

SÃO PAULO

be confusing. A subway crosses the city from north to south for 20 cents. It is safe, rapid, comfortable, and convenient, but only serves a small sector of the city. Tours can be arranged by a local travel agent.

HOTELS. Booming São Paulo is a city of international businesspeople and their customers; so it is only natural that the city is prepared to take care of them. There are hundreds of good hotels in town, and rates are about what they are for similar accommodations in Rio. *Super deluxe* hotels begin at $95 per night; *Deluxe* hotels charge from $70 to $95; *Expensive* hotels range from $45 to $70, *Moderate* hotels range from $15 to $45, and *Inexpensive* hotels are $15 or less. Continental breakfast is generally included in the room rate.

Super Deluxe

Brasilton São Paulo, Rua Martins Fontes 330 (258-5811). Part of the Hilton group, in the center of shopping and downtown, convenient to most everything. A popular hotel for business lunches, international stars; where the action is. Two restaurants, bars, banquet and convention facilities. Satellite dish.

Caesar Park, Rua Augusta 1508 (285-6622). On the fashionable shopping street and a few blocks from the U.S. Trade Center and Avenida Paulista business center, offers European personal service—the staff knows you by name. Restaurants, a coffee shop, bars, banquet and small convention facilities, outdoor swimming pool on the roof, and beauty shop. Conservative, for discriminating people. Satellite dish.

Grand Hotel Ca D'Oro, Rua Augusta 129 (256-8011). "Home away from home." Many American families stay in suites here until their household goods arrive. The owner Fabrizio Guzzoni and his two sons, Eugenio and Aurelio, are always available. This 400-room hotel offers the most to a family with children: tennis court, outdoor swimming pool and children's pool and play equipment. Banquet and convention facilities and one of the best formal Italian dining rooms. The only luxury hotel with kennel. Satellite dish.

Maksoud Plaza, Al. Campinas 150 (251-2233). One of São Paulo's newest hotels, located one block from the Paulista business district. Acknowledged as one of Brazil's finest hotels. Popular with business travelers, it is deluxe in every sense. Electronic temperature controls in all 420 rooms, room service, TV, and other amenities. Panoramic indoor elevators permit an excellent view of the atrium lobby as they glide to the two squash courts on the top (22nd) floor. American billiards, indoor swimming pool, sauna, VIP Club, convention facilities, as well as shops. Restaurants are *La Cuisine du Soleil* with superb French food, the *Vikings' Scandinavian* smorgasbord, and *Belavista,* the latter open 24 hours a day. Satellite dish.

Mofarrej Sheraton, Al. Santos, 1437 (284-5544). São Paulo's newest deluxe hotel overlooks a beautiful park and caters to business clients with special butler services and facilities for executives; two pools, one indoors; beautiful lobby piano bar and São Paulo's newest and best rooftop restaurant and bar. The hotel has quickly jumped into the number-two spot in São Paulo and is challenging the Maksoud for number one. Satellite dish.

São Paulo Hilton, Av. Ipiranga 165 (256-0033). Popular hotel for conventions and business people. Its 34 stories command a sweeping view of the world's fastest-growing city; four restaurants, five bars, including the *London Tavern* pub-disco restaurant, large convention center and theater.

Transamerica, Av. Nações Unidos 18591 (523-4511). Opened in 1985, close to downtown with two restaurants, swimming pool, and a convention center. Satellite dish.

BRAZIL

Deluxe

Augusta Boulevard, Rua Augusta 843 (257–7844). Another modern hotel on this famous shopping street.

Bourbon Hotel, Av. Vieira de Carvalho, 99 (223–2244). Small, elegant, comfortable hotel near the Praça da Republica. Good restaurant and service.

Bristol, Rua Martins Fontes 277 (258–0011).

Eldorado Boulevard, Av. São Luiz 234 (256–8833). Small, but elegant 157 rooms. In the popular downtown three-block hotel district. Terrace coffee shop with view of the busy avenue, fashionable. Pool, nightclub, meeting rooms, international cuisine. Loew's reservation service.

Eldorado Higienopolis, Rua Marquês de Itú 836 (222–3422). Restaurant, bar and coffee shop. Residential neighborhood. Outdoor swimming pool. Ten-minute walk to downtown commercial area. Sister to the Eldorado Boulevard.

Novotel, Rua Ministro Nelson Hungria 450 in the suburb of Morumbi (542–1244). Good for executives visiting factories on the Marginal. Outdoor swimming pool and a view of the city. Not convenient to downtown or the shopping area.

Expensive

Comodoro, on Av. Duque de Caxias (220–1211). Close to the bus station. Though in a not-too-desirable location, is popular with theater and sports groups.

Samambaia, 7 de Abril at Praça da República (231–1333). Right in the downtown area. Small but excellent service and cuisine.

São Paulo Center, Largo Santa Ifigenia 40 (228–6033). Recently redecorated in modern style, adjacent to the heart of the old city. Ifigenia Bridge immediately to the left and within walking distance of the Colegio Patio, founding site of São Paulo. 111 air-conditioned rooms. Very popular executive lunch.

Moderate

Osaka Plaza, Praça da Liberdade, 149 (270–1311). Has a good Japanese restaurant.

Othon Palace Hotel, Rua Libero Badaró 196, Praça Patriarca (239–3277). Strategically located in the center of the financial district. Part of Brazilian chain of Othon hotels, contains the *VIP Bar, The Four Seasons Restaurant,* and the *Swiss Chalet.* Three large rooms for meetings, cocktail parties, and other social occasions. All air-conditioned.

Most Paulista hotels serve continental breakfast free of charge.

As in Rio, Apartment Hotels are also available, the top ones being: **Triannon Residence,** Av. Casa Branca 363 (283–0066); **Augusta Park Residence,** Rua Augusta 922 (255–5722); and **Flat Service Morumby,** Rua Minister Nelson Hungria 600 (531–2121).

RESTAURANTS. Prepare yourselves for some of the finest international eating delights on the continent. It is difficult to choose the best when every one is so good. Your dining should not be confined to the following list, as it is merely the *crème de la crème* of the Paulista restaurants. Look around and experiment. The finest restaurant in São Paulo is generally conceded to be the *Ca D'Oro.* Our restaurant grading system has four categories; *Deluxe,* $15 and up; *Expensive,* $10 to $15; *Moderate,* $5 to $10; *Inexpensive,* under $5.

SÃO PAULO

These prices are for a complete meal for one person and do not include wine, beer, or other drinks.

There are literally thousands of restaurants in São Paulo, the gourmet capital of Brazil. Since São Paulo is a city of large immigrant communities which have retained their national cuisines, it's possible to eat any kind of food you have a yen for. In the Oriental Liberdade section, you can find Japanese restaurants in the moderate price range, and less expensive. In Bixiga, the popular name for Bela Vista, dozens of cantinas and bistros featuring pasta, pizza, and other Italian specialties at moderate prices compete for customers. Stroll around these districts, read menus, and feast. By far the largest number of fine restaurants are located in the Jardins district, where you can find anything from a sandwich to a first-class nouvelle cuisine meal.

International

A Biaúca-Jardins. *Moderate to Expensive.* Av. Faria Lima, 609, Jardim Paulista (212–6341). Open every day, Sat. for dinner only, Sun. lunch only. One of the most popular bars in the city with live music from 7 P.M. on, modest cuisine but an "in" place.

Clark's. *Moderate to Expensive.* Av. Cidade Jardim, 389, Jardim Europa (853–0609). Open daily, Sat. for dinner only. Looks like a London townhouse, specializes in filets stuffed with a variety of fillings.

Manhattan. *Moderate to Expensive.* Rua Bela Cintra, 2238, Cerqueira César (852–0947). Open for lunch and dinner. A place to see and be seen.

Massimo. *Moderate to Expensive.* Al. Santos, 1826, Cerqueira César (284–0311). Closed Mon., open for lunch and dinner the rest of the week. One of the most durable, popular restaurants in the city.

La Tambouille. *Moderate to Expensive.* Av. 9 de Julho, 5925, Jardim Europa (881–5356). Open 11:30 to 1 A.M. Reservations advised. Leans toward Italian nova cucina, but a variety of classical dishes is also available.

Terraço Italia. *Moderate to Expensive.* Av. Ipiranga, 344, 41st floor, Centro (257–6566). A spectacular view of the city from all angles is the biggest attraction here, although the food is well prepared, too. Afternoon tea, live music at night. Open daily from 11:30 A.M. to 3 P.M.

Uptown. *Moderate to Expensive.* Av. Paulista, 1499, loja 12 (Edifício Conde Andrea Matarazzo), Cerqueira César (284–3142). Sophisticated luncheon spot for businesspeople, with heavy French influence, open for lunch on workdays only, from noon until 4 P.M.

French

La Cuisine du Soleil. *Deluxe.* Al. Campinas, 150, in the Hotel Maksoud, Bela Vista (251–2233). Open Sat. for dinner only, lunch and dinner on weekdays, closed Sun. Superb service and atmosphere in São Paulo's ritziest French restaurant.

Vivaldi. *Deluxe.* Al. Santos 1301 (284–5544). São Paulo's newest top-quality French restaurant in the Mofarrej Sheraton. Rooftop with spectacular view of the city. Open for lunch and dinner.

L'Arnaque. *Moderate to Expensive.* Rua Oscar Freire, 518, Cerqueira César (280–9936). Excellent nouvelle cuisine with a Brazilian twist in friendly, comfortable, relaxed surroundings with a sidewalk bar. Closed Mon., open for lunch and dinner.

La Cocagne. *Moderate to Expensive.* Rua Campos Bicudo, 129, Itaim Bibi (881–5177). Closed Sun., Sat. only dinner is served.

112 BRAZIL

David's. *Moderate to Expensive.* Rua Oscar Freire, 913, Cerqueira César (282–2507). Open every day, noon to 4 P.M. and 6 P.M. to 2 A.M. Noted for its popular bar with live music.

Le Panache. *Moderate to Expensive.* Rua Jorge Coehlho, 129, Itaim Bibi (883–0163). Closed Mon., open for lunch and dinner. Owned by Regine's, the nightclub, but you needn't be a member to dine here. Sumptuous decor, good food.

Italian

Ca D'Oro. *Deluxe.* Rua Augusta, 129, in the Hotel Ca D'Oro (256–8011). Many consider this the best restaurant in São Paulo in all categories. Make reservations, open daily for lunch and dinner.

Boccaccio. *Moderate to Expensive.* Rua Martins Fontes, 99, Jardins (255–7573). Closed Sun., Sat. dinner only.

Gigetto. *Moderate to Expensive.* Rua Avanhandava, 63, Centro (256–9804). Open daily for lunch and dinner until 3:30 A.M. During its 50 years in business, it has become a meeting place for journalists, intellectuals, and artists.

Otello. *Moderate to Expensive.* Rua Haddock Lobo, 1550, Cerqueira César (64–0829). Closed Mon., open Fri. and Sat. until 3 A.M. Popular place for pizza.

Via Veneto. *Moderate to Expensive.* Al. Barros 909, Santa Cecilia (66–7905). Open every day, homemade pasta.

Brazilian

Many restaurants and hotels serve the traditional *feijoada* on Saturdays. In addition, try these restaurants specializing in Brazilian dishes.

Bolinha. *Moderate to Expensive.* Av. Cidade Jardim, 53, Jardim Europa (852–9526). Famous for feijoada, which has been served here daily for almost 40 years.

Made in Brazil. *Moderate to Expensive.* Al. Santos, 1518 (corner of Alameda Casa Branca) (287–5815 and 285–0231). Lunch only.

Tia Carly. *Moderate to Expensive.* Al. Riberão Preto, 492, Bela Vista (284–4372). Open for lunch and dinner. Feijoada Wed. and Sat.

Portuguese

Abril em Portugal. *Moderate to Expensive.* Rua Caio Prado, 47, Centro (256–5160). Dinner only, 8 P.M. to 2 A.M., closed Sun. Live guitar and fado music, dancing after midnight.

Alfama dos Marinheiros. *Moderate to Expensive.* Rua Pamplona 1285, 1st fl., Jardim Paulista (285–0523). Dinner only, Mon. to Sat.

Marquês de Marialva. *Moderate to Expensive.* Rua Haddock Lobo, 1583, Cerqueira Cesar (852–1805). Closed Mon., open for lunch and dinner.

Japanese

Mariko. *Deluxe.* Rua Augusta 1508, in the Caesar Park Hotel (285–6622). Closed Sun.

Suntory. *Moderate to Expensive.* Al. Campinas, 600, Jardim Paulista (283–2455). Closed Sun., overlooks a garden and fish pond.

Komazushi. *Moderate to Expensive.* Av. Brigadeiro Luis Antonio, 2050, loja 7, Centro Commercial Paulista (288–5582). Lunch only. Sushi and sashimi specialties.

SÃO PAULO 113

There are also dozens of *inexpensive* Oriental restaurants in the Liberdade section, including **Hinodê,** Rua Tomas Gonzaga, 62 (278–6633); **Yamaga,** Rua Tomas Gonzaga, 66 (278–3667), closed Tues; and **Korea House,** Rua Galvão Bueno, 43, upstairs (278–3052), open daily for lunch and dinner.

Churrascarias

Baby Beef Rubaiyat. *Moderate to Expensive.* Av. Faria Lima, 533, Jardim Paulistano (813–2703). Open daily.

Bassi. *Moderate to Expensive.* Rua 13 de Maio, 334, Bela Vista (34–2375). Large portions, excellent meat.

Buffalo Grill. *Moderate to Expensive.* Rua Bela Cintra 2231, Cequeira Cesar (853–5014).

Dinho's Place. *Moderate to Expensive.* Al. Santos, 45, Paraiso (284–5333) and Av. Morumbi, 7976, Brooklin Paulista (542–5299).

Other restaurants: For fish and seafood, **St. Peter's Pier,** Al. Lorena, 1160, Cerqueira César (881–2413), open daily, dinner only on Sat.; **La Truite Cocagne,** Rua Campos Bicudo, 141, Jardim Paulista (883–2770); **La Trainera,** Av. Faria Lima, 511, Jardim Europa (852–6333). For Arab food, **Cedro's,** Rua Oscar Freire 800, Cerqueira César (64–2123).

TOURIST INFORMATION. Until recently, Paulistur was the city's official tourism authority, but it was closed by Mayor Jânio Quadros when he took office in 1986. For information, contact the **Secretaria de Esportes e Turismo do Estado de São Paulo** (Office of Sports and Tourism of the State of São Paulo), Praça Antonio Prado, 9, Centro (229–3011) and Avenida São Luis 115, Centro (257–7248). Both are open from Mon. through Fri., 9 A.M. to 6 P.M. Also, the **São Paulo Convention Bureau,** at Rua Columbia 582, Jardins (280–2979/4523), has assumed Paulistur's functions, and is open Mon. through Fri., 9 A.M. to 6 P.M.

TOURS. There are many tour operators in São Paulo sponsoring tours within the state and beyond—inquire at your hotel. For tours of the city of São Paulo, try the "Circuito Cultural," which leaves from and returns to the Shopping Center Iguatemi (Jardim America) on Sundays. Eight distinct itineraries around the city are offered. Call one of the agencies above for more information.

SPORTS. The fitness fad has arrived with a rush in São Paulo in recent years with tennis, squash, and jogging today among the favorite leisure-time activities of the city's residents. Visitors to the city can partake of all three. **Tennis** is mainly confined to tennis clubs that are scattered throughout the city but that rent court time to all comers. Ask at your hotel. Since most of São Paulo's leading hotels are located downtown, there is little room for tennis courts. The Transamerica, however, has several excellent courts. The only other major hotel with a court is the Grand Hotel Ca'd' Oro. **Squash** is also for the most part limited to clubs where visitors can play for a fee. The Maksoud Plaza and Transamerica offer squash courts for their guests. **Jogging** has taken a strong hold in the city and the favorite spot is the giant Ibiripuera Park, Brazil's version of New York's Central Park. There are jogging paths, as well as roadways for bicycle riders. **Golf** in São Paulo is a sport for the wealthy.

All clubs are private and greens fees are stiff, although the clubs are accessible to visitors—again, check at your hotel. The city has seven golf clubs, all of them in surrounding suburbs or nearby cities. Among **spectator sports,** the most popular by far is **soccer.** In recent years, São Paulo has supplanted Rio as the most soccer-mad city in this soccer-mad country. The top teams are São Paulo, Santos, Palmeiras, Cointhians, and Guarani. **Horse racing** is held in the evenings and during the afternoon on weekends at the Jockey Club.

ART GALLERIES. The concentration of affluence in the São Paulo area has created a strong market for art collectors, lovers, and investors. Most of the better galleries are concentrated in Jardins. Check the newspaper for openings, and call for store hours, which vary. **Arte Aplicada,** Rua Haddock Lobo, 1406, Jardim Paulista (852–5128) and Avenida Cidade Jardim, 108, Jardim Europa (64–2988). Applied Art, as the name implies, specializes in well designed objects for practical use and decorations. **Arte Nativa Aplicada.** Rua Dr. Mário Ferraz, 339, Jardim Europa (813–8839) has authentic Indian designs rendered faithfully in textiles, wallpaper, pillows, clothing, sheets, and household items. **Arte & Risco,** Rua Jaoquim Tavora, 670, Vila Mariana (549–6826), contemporary Japanese art. **Gabinete de Arte Raquel Arnaud Babenco,** Av. 9 de Julho, 5719, Itaim Bibi (881–9853), contemporary conceptual and geometric sculpture and paintings. **Luiza Strina,** Rua Padre João Manoel, 974A, Cerqueira César (280–2471), modern Brazilian artists. **André Blau,** Rua Estados Unidos, 2280, Jardim America (881–6664), contemporary art. **Chelsea Art Gallery,** Rua Estados Unidos, 1591, Jardim America (852–4218). **Jacques Ardies,** Rua do Livramento, 221, Vila Mariana (884–2916), best collection of Brazilian primitives. **Skultura,** Alameda Lorena, 1593, Cerqueira César (280–5624). Modern sculpture in all sizes and materials. **São Paulo,** Rua Estados Unidos, 1456, Cerqueira César (852–8855), contemporary Brazilian artists. **Dan,** Rua Estados Unidos, 1638, Cerqueira César (883–2294). **A Galeria,** Rua Bela Cintra 1533, Jardim Paulista (853–2122). **Paço das Artes,** Avenida Europa 158, Jardim Europa (64–1728), alternative art. **Subdistrito,** Rua Arthur de Azevedo, 401 (881–8910). **O Bode: Arte Popular Brasileira,** Rua Bela Cintra, 2009, Cerqueira César (853–3184), artesanatos (folk art) from the north and northwest.

SHOPPING. As the largest industrial and commercial center of South America, São Paulo offers just about anything you want to buy. There are four major shopping malls in the Zona Sul, open from 9 A.M. to 10 P.M.; **Iguatemi,** Av. Brig. Faria Lima, 1191, Jardim Paulistano (210–1333); **Ibirapuera,** Av. Ibirapuera, 3103, Moema (543–0011); **Morumbi,** Av. Roque Petroni, Jr. 1089, Morumbi (533–2444); **Eldorado,** Av. Reboucas, 3970, Pinheiros (815–7066).

However, the city itself could easily be considered a shopping center, with a number of special streets lined with great shops. Rua João Cachoeira, Itaim, is the city's wholesale clothing center, with many small "confeccões" (factories), some with outlets that sell to the general public. Many, however, are "pronta entrega," and sell only in quantity to buyers. It is best to ask when you have doubts.

The area known as the Quadrilátero dos Jardins, consisting of 28 streets within the perimeter defined by Av. Paulista, Rua Estados Unidos, Brig. Luis Antônio, and Av. Rebouças, has the best of the best: whether you're looking for a great sandwich, French baguettes, or party clothes, you'll find it in this area.

SÃO PAULO

Worth special mention are Rua Dr. Mário Ferraz and Avenida Cidade Jardim, both of which feature expensive, fashionable boutiques.

 NIGHTLIFE. Surprisingly enough, there are better clubs and bars in São Paulo than you'll find in Rio. The Paulista enjoys going out after a day in the office and seems to have more money to spend on nighttime playing. Like New York, São Paulo has a sophisticated nightlife revolving around food and music. The functions of restaurants, nightclubs, and bars frequently overlap, and the following are general categories. The "in" places change frequently, as one group of friends moves on to a new place and another discovers the former's haunt, but the following have endured.

Bars

Lua de Tomate, Al. Santos, 805, Cerqueira César, (257–2566). Mon.–Fri., 11 P.M. to 3 A.M., Sat. 6 P.M. to 3 A.M. Live jazz, musica popular brasileira, and tango; artistic cover charge.
Piu Piu, Rua 13 de Maio, 134, Bela Vista (258–8066). Minimum consumption charge, live music, especially jazz.
Spazio Pirandello, Rua Augusta, 311, Consolação (256–5245). Open 7 P.M to 6 A.M.; Closed Mon. Restaurant and meeting place for artists, journalists.
Supremo, Rua da Consolação, 3437, Consolação (282–6142). Open Tues. through Sun., noon to 3 P.M. and 6 P.M. to 1:30 A.M. Popular bar and restaurant with Brazil's yuppies, always crowded.

Nightclubs

Calash, Rua Amauri, 328 (282–7652). Open daily from 6 P.M. to 2 A.M. Dance floor and soft music.
Cheek to Cheek, Rua Jerônimo de Veiga, 61 (282–6001). Open Tues. through Sun. from 9 P.M.
Club 150, Al. Campinas, 150, in the Maksoud Hotel, Bela Vista (251–2233). Dance floor, first rate shows with an emphasis on jazz.
Gallery, Rua Haddock Lobo, 1626, Jardim Paulista (881–3291). Open Mon. through Sat., from 8 P.M. until the last customer leaves. Dance floor, shows, restaurant. This is a private club—ask your deluxe hotel to arrange a reservation or go with a Brazilian member.
O Ponto, Al. Jaú, 1445 (280–1577). Closed Sun. and Mon. Artistic cover and minimum consumption charge on weekends.
Regine's, Rua Jorge Coelho, 129, Jardim Paulista (883–0163). Another branch of the famous nightclub, also private, but go with a member or arrange entry through your hotel. Open Tues. through Sun. from 10 P.M.
Saint Paul, Al. Lorena 1717, Cerqueira César (282–7697). Closed Sun. Mon. and Thurs. are singles' nights, couples only are admitted on weekends, from 9 P.M. on.
Shadow, Rua Pamplona, 1109 (288–7765). Open daily from 7 P.M.
Soul Train, Rua Amauri, 334, Jardim Paulista (852–6566). Open daily from 9 P.M. to 4 A.M. Fri. and Sat. couples only are allowed and there is a cover charge.
Ta Matete, Av. 9 de Julho, 5725, Jardim Paulista (881–3622). Open from 8 P.M. to 4 A.M. Closed Sun.
Talento, Av. Faria Lima 743 (210–8089). Caraoke and bar.

BRAZIL

Show Houses

Beco, Av. Paulista, 424 (287–1234). Open Mon. through Sat. from 8:30 P.M. on. Variety show with mulatas. Artistic cover charge.

Palace, Av. dos Jamaris, 213, Moema (531–4900). Open Wed. through Sun. from 8 P.M.

Palladium Eldorado, Av. Rebouças, 3970, 3rd fl. (815–7066). Bar, restaurant, dance floor, and sophisticated non-touristic floor show. Artistic cover charge. Open Tues. through Sun. from 8 P.M. to 3 A.M.

Projeto SP, Rua Caio Prado, 232 (255–2484). Entrance charge, open Thurs. through Sun.

Danceterias/Discotheques

Area, Rua Pinheiros 1275, Pinheiros (221–8698). Open Tues. through Sun. from 7 P.M. Restaurant, bar, pizzeria, game room, dance floor. Crowded on weekends.

Dancing, Av. Morumbi, 6849 (542–7889). Open every day from 10 P.M. to 4 A.M., minimum consumption charge.

Latitude, Av. 23 de Maio, 3001 (571–2250). Open Thurs.-Sun. from 9 P.M. to 5 A.M. Minimum consumption charge.

Radar Tantan, Rua Solon, 1069 (223–2621). Entrance fee; open 9 P.M. to 4 A.M., Fri. through Sun.

THE STATE OF SÃO PAULO

If one cannot understand the "Paulistas" contented "I want to be isolated" attitude from studying their capital city, then it will certainly become apparent when the rest of their domain is seen. The area has everything from sandy beaches to lofty mountain plateaus, from colonial splendor to ultramodern health resorts. To see all of it you need time, much more time than most tourists have to devote to an area. That is one of the problems of visiting Brazil. There is so much to see that it's absolutely impossible to crowd it all in one visit.

The State of São Paulo itself is about the size of Great Britain and Northern Ireland put together, covering 95,800 square miles. Slow to take root (the first colonies founded by the Jesuit fathers were complete failures), São Paulo didn't really start to grow until the coffee plant was introduced in the early 1800s. The product found a ready market, and when in 1847 a landowner near Limeira brought over a colony of Germans to work his fields, the area was on its way at last. The demand for coffee grew and more and more immigrants came from Europe to try their hand with the new plant. From Italy alone came a million people. Portugal sent half a million and Spaniards and Japanese many hundreds of thousands. From the sale of coffee came money enough to start factories, install electrical power, build railways, and clear rich forest land.

Santos is another pride of the Paulistas, for aside from having the biggest dock area in Latin America, it also has a tropical climate and some beautiful beaches. Apart from the basilica of Santo Andre, which faces the beach and the row after row of modern apartment buildings, the city has little to offer the tourist except her beaches. They are different from the ones in Rio, the sand being darker and harder.

The nearby island of Guarujá is lush, green, and lined with towering palm trees—and, increasingly, with high-rises along the ocean. Today, to reach more unspoiled areas you must go north by bus or car, crossing the ferry to Bertioga and beyond (but avoid Sundays and holidays because of long lines). There are some relatively untouched beaches, considering the proximity to Santos and the number of weekend visitors. They offer a pleasant visual and mental change from the hustle of the city. A trip around the island by automobile can be made in an hour, for the roads are paved and in good condition. The best beaches north of Guarujá are Ubatuba, Caraguatatuba, and the romantic island of Ilha Bela.

The coastal village of Paratí was founded way back in the early 16th century. Its calm, natural little harbor was the perfect jumping off point for adventurers looking for the gold and precious stones in Minas Gerais. For decades the town flourished while it catered to the needs of the miners and helped them spend their money. But the boom calmed down, Santos rose in importance because of its superb harbor, and over the years Paratí was forgotten. Then just a few years ago, the

Paulistas rediscovered this colonial village (actually located in Rio de Janeiro state), and the government declared it a national monument whose architectural style must be preserved. Today it is important as a tourist center. With the Rio-Santos Highway passing close by, traffic jams became so great that cars are now banned from most city streets. Those who have taken the time to visit it come back with glowing tales of baroque churches, charming squares, and an unspoiled old-world charm. Many houses have been restored by private parties and the tendency is to preserve as much of the original flavor as possible. (See *Excursions from Rio* section.)

São Paulo's mineral water resort area is located in the northeastern part of the state near the border with the state of Minas Gerais. The top resorts, Poços de Caldas, Caxambú and Aquas da Prata, are all within a short distance of one another and some 150 miles from the city of São Paulo. The various spas and hot spring resorts radiate northward into the higher country, away from the capital city. Most of them have a large German or Swiss population and will remind the traveler more of Europe than South America.

The hot springs attract an equal number of visitors, who go there to sit in the warm, swirling (at times rather smelly) water, rather than drink it. Campos do Jordão, Poços de Caldas, and Serra Negra all have dry climates and their waters are famous for treating such diverse ailments as rheumatism, skin diseases, and fatigue. Clean and nicely landscaped, these villages are as pleasant to the eye as they are to the skin.

PRACTICAL INFORMATION FOR THE STATE OF SÃO PAULO

For definitions of price categories see *Planning Your Trip*.

WHEN TO GO. This depends on where you are going. Because of the varying altitude of the state, which ranges from sea level to 9,000 feet, it can be hot in some spots and cold in others at the same time. If you want the seashore, then the months of Dec. to Apr. are the best. But exactly during these months you will be competing with Brazilian tourists for the best hotels in such popular vacation beach towns as Guarujá, Ubatuba, Caraguatatuba, Ilha Bela, and Paratí. During Carnival in Feb. or Mar. it is almost impossible to find a hotel room without a reservation well in advance. Those same months will be chilly in the evenings in the mountain resorts but you will have an easier time finding a place to stay. The situation reverses itself during the southern hemisphere winter months from July to Sept., when the bracing temperatures of the mountains attract Paulistas looking for a friendly fireplace to stretch out in front of. For this period, the mountains load up with vacationers while the beaches are often empty.

HOW TO GET THERE. Although the state of São Paulo is large, the concentration of top vacation spots in two areas—the beaches near Santos and the mountains near the border with Minas Gerais—make ground travel the best option. Good highways connect São Paulo with the resort areas and major bus lines serve all of the cities. The Rio-Santos highway runs along some of the most beautiful coastline in Brazil, unfortunately the upkeep of the high-

SÃO PAULO

way in recent years has not been what it should have been, making the trip more of an adventure than most international travelers are looking for. From the city of São Paulo a winding road leads down the coastal mountains to Santos. A highway link also exists from Santos to the island of Guarujá or you can take the ferry boat (30 cents) at the end of Avenida Almirante Saldanha da Gama, which is the final stop along the Santos beachfront. The boats leave every fifteen minutes or so on a first-come, first-served basis. They handle cars as well as people and the trip takes 15 minutes. On the other side there are buses waiting to transport passengers to the various beaches. A word of warning: the Paulistas love their beaches. On hot weekends in the summer huge lines form for the ferry boats to Guarujá and back and the highway up the mountain to São Paulo from Santos frequently has bumper to bumper traffic on Sun. evenings.

SANTOS

HOTELS. There are hotels and boarding houses on just about every corner. While the beaches of Santos do not compare with those of nearby Guarujá, you can find far cheaper hotels here and then cross over to the quality beaches of the island by ferry. The best bets are: **Fenicia Praia,** *Inexpensive,* Av. Presidente Wilson 184 (37-1955); **Praiano,** *Inexpensive,* Av. Barao de Penedo 39 (37-4033); **Indaia,** *Inexpensive,* Av. Ana Costa 431 (4-1134); **Avenida Palace,** *Inexpensive,* Av. Presidente Wilson 10 (4-1166).

RESTAURANTS. Admittedly the restaurants of Santos would probably never figure on anyone's dining out list. In particular avoid seafood, which tends to be vastly overpriced and of low quality. There are plenty of pizzerias and hamburger spots to satisfy your hunger. Any more serious dining out should be left for the city of São Paulo or a trip on the ferry to Guarujá.

WHAT TO SEE. Even though it has fallen out of favor with Paulistas in recent years, Santos still has the relaxed, friendly air of a beach city. It also has an extensive beach front that can be best appreciated by taking a city bus along the beach in the direction of the neighboring city of São Vicente. Santos is also the largest coffee port in the world, but avoid the temptation of visiting the port area—it is not safe for tourists.

GUARUJÁ

HOTELS. The love affair of São Paulo residents with this island has led to an explosion of hotel construction. The best are: **Casa Grande,** *Deluxe,* Av. Miguel Stefano 999, Ensaiado Beach (86-2223); **Jequitimar Hotel,** *Expensive,* Av. Marjory Prado 1100, on the beach (53-3111); **Delphin Hotel Guarujá,** *Expensive,* Av. Miguel Stefano 1295, Enseada Beach (86-2111); **Guarujá Inn,** *Expensive,* Av. da Saudade 170, Enseada Beach (87-2332); **Ferrareto Guarujá Hotel,** *Moderate,* Rua Mario Ribeiro 564 (86-1112); **Gávea Hotel,** *Moderate,* Alameda Floriano Peixoto 311 Pitangueiras Beach (86-2212).

BRAZIL

RESTAURANTS. There are several fine international restaurants in Guarujá although prices at times run well above the levels of the city of São Paulo. Among the better restaurants are: **Ancora Praia,** *Expensive,* Rua Des. Mario de Almeida Pires 450 (87–2585); **Rufino's,** *Expensive,* good for seafood, Estrada do Pernambuco 111; **Margherita,** *Moderate,* Av. Dom Pedro I 847 (87–3601); **Sobre as Ondas,** *Moderate,* Av. General, Rondon 30, on the central beach of Guarujá (86–7128).

WHAT TO SEE. Despite the growing presence of high rise-apartments on the island, Guarujá remains extraordinarily beautuful. To explore the island, rent a taxi and take a trip to the many beaches. Keep your eye out for the spectacular vacation homes built here by wealthy Paulistas.

UBATUBA

HOTELS. The boom in top quality hotels along the São Paulo coast is also visible in this once sleepy beach city. The main hotels are: **Mediterraneo,** *Expensive,* Praia de Enseada (42–0112); **Sol e Vida,** *Moderate,* Praia de Enseada (42–0188); **Solar das Aguas Cantantes,** *Moderate,* Praia do Lazaro (42–0178); **Wembley Inn,** *Moderate,* Estrada para Caraguatauba (42–0198).

RESTAURANTS. Cassino Sol e Vida, *Moderate,* seafood, in Sol e Vida Hotel. Enseada beach (42–0188); **Malibu,** *Moderate,* international food, Saco da Ribeira beach (42–0830).

WHAT TO SEE. This region is overflowing with small, beautiful beaches, both north and south of the city.

CARAGUATATUBA

HOTELS. One of the best resorts along the coast is the **Pousada Tabatinga,** *Deluxe,* on Tabatinga beach, tennis courts and, a rarity in Brazil, a 9-hole golf course (24–1411); **Guanabara,** *Moderate,* Rua Santo Antonio 75 (22–2533).

RESTAURANTS. Top restaurant in the area is the **Pousada Tabatinga,** *Expensive,* in the hotel of the same name, international cuisine (24–1411).

ILHA BELA

HOW TO GET THERE. Just north of Caraguatatuba, this island jewel is reached by a ferry boat from the mainland city of São Sebastiao.

HOTELS. Mercedes, *Moderate,* Mercedes Beach (72–1071); **Ilhabela,** *Moderate,* Av. Pedro Paula de Morais 151 (72–1083); **Devisse,** *Moderate,* Av. Almirante Tamandare 343 (72–1385); **Pousada de Capitao,** *Moderate,* Av. Almirante Tamandare 272 (72–1037).

SÃO PAULO

RESTAURANTS. Surprisingly, the island has several fine seafood restaurants: **Deck,** *Moderate,* Av. Princesa Isabel 805 (72–1489); **Fandango,** *Moderate,* Av. Dona Germana 68 (72–1109).

AGUAS DA PRATA

HOTELS. This mountain mineral water spa follows the custom of the region—all meals are included in the room rate. The best hotels are: the **Panorama,** *Moderate,* Rua Hernani Correa 45 (42–1511); **Ideal,** *Moderate,* Rua Gabriel Rabelo de Andrade 79 (42–1011); **Parque Paineiras,** *Inexpensive,* on the highway to São João da Boa Vista (42–1411).

AGUAS DE LINDOIA

HOTELS. Best hotel is the new **Nova Lindoia Vacance,** *Moderate,* with tennis courts, Av. das Naçoes Unidas 1374 (94–1193); others are the **Tamoio,** *Moderate,* Rua São Paulo 622 (94–1212) and **Hotel das Fontes,** *Moderate,* Rua Rio de Janeiro 267 (94–1511). Meals included at all hotels.

ARAXA

HOTELS. Famous mineral spa in Minas Gerais near the border with São Paulo. Best hotel is **Grande Hotel,** *Moderate,* Estrancia do Barreiro (661–2011).

Suggested side trips to springs at Barbeiro, Osario, and Cascatinha Gruta de Monje and Historic Museum of Dona Beja.

CAMPOS DO JORDÃO

HOW TO GET THERE. The most sophisticated and popular of the mountain resorts of São Paulo, Campos can be reached by bus or car from São Paulo or by a short train ride from São Jose dos Campos, one of the state's main cities located on the Rio-São Paulo Highway (Via Dutra).

HOTELS. This picturesque mountain village has become one of São Paulo's top tourist attractions, offering Swiss-style hotels and chalets amidst a setting of tabernacle pines, mountains, and streams. Tops among the hotels are the **Toriba,** *Deluxe,* expensive but worth it, located in a natural park, with meals, included in room rate, better than those served in many international restaurants with good ratings. Av Ernesto Diederichsen (62–1566); book well in advance, the hotel is a favorite of European residents of São Paulo; **Orotur Garden Hotel,** *Expensive,* meals included. Rua 3 (62–2833); **Vila Inglesa,** *Expensive,* meals included, Rua Senador Roberto Simonsenn 3500 (63–1955).

WHAT TO SEE. The natural setting is easily one of the most beautiful in Brazil and no matter how many walks among the pines you take, there will always be something else to see. Horses can be rented and there are many nearby mountains that can be easily climbed. In the month of June the

BRAZIL

city hosts one of South America's finest classical music festivals and throughout the year there are activities for the guests at the many hotels in the region.

CAXAMBU

HOTELS. This popular mineral resort is located just across the border in Minas Gerais. Recommended hotels are: **Gloria**, *Moderate*, Rua Camilo Soares 590 (341–1233); **Palace**, *Moderate*, Rua Dr. Viotti 567 (341–1044); **Grande**, *Inexpensive*, Rua Dr. Viotti 438 (341–1099). All with meals included.

WHAT TO SEE. Recommended side trips to Parque das Aguias, Colina de Santa Isabel. Chacara Rosalan, Chacara das Ucas, São Tome das Letras, Corcovado Morro de Caxambu.

POÇOS DE CALDAS

HOTELS. One of the best known hot springs in Latin America, Poços is also in the state of Minas Gerais. It boasts of 37 hotels but try to get into the **Palace**, *Moderate*, with meals, Praça Pedro Sanches (721–3392). Built by the state government, it has up-to-date facilities for the treatment of rheumatism, skin and intestinal diseases. Also the **Minas Gerais**, *Inexpensive*, Rua Pernambuco 615 (721–8686).

WHAT TO SEE. In the vicinity suggested side trips are to Cascata das Antas, Veu de Noiva, Fonte dos Amores, and Morro de São Domingos.

SÃO LOURENÇO

HOTELS. A third well-known Minas Gerais mineral water city. Recommended hotels are: **Primus**, *Moderate*, with meals, Rua Coronel Jose Justino 681 (331–1244); **Brasil**, *Moderate*, Praça João Laje (331–1422); **Negreiros**, *Moderate*, Rua Veneceslau Bras 242 (331–1533).

ATIBAIA

HOTELS. A mountain village 45 miles from the city of São Paulo, Atibaia is most proud of the fact that according to UNESCO it possesses the second healthiest climate in the world, losing out only to Switzerland. It also is home to one of the best mountain resorts in Brazil. The **Village Eldorado**, *Expensive*, Dom Pedro I Highway km. 70.5 (484–2533), is an idyllic escape for São Paulo's businessmen. Other good hotels are **Parque Atibaia**, *Expensive*, Fernao Dias Highway (484–3423); **Recanto de Paz**, *Moderate*, 10 chalets on a former farm (487–1369). The area surrounding Atibaia is one of Brazil's most popular camping areas.

THE SOUTH

The south of Brazil moves to the same upbeat, quickened pace of the city and state of São Paulo. Here in the states of Rio Grande do Sul, Paraná, and Santa Catarina, the results of heightened economic growth over the last 15 years are clearly apparent. Large, modern cities with efficient public transportation systems coexist with the ruins of colonial times and the natural beauty of one of Brazil's most fascinating areas. In the far south on the borders of Argentina and Uruguay, a mixture of Spanish, Portuguese, German, and Italian cultures has produced the fabled land of the gauchos: the flat pampas grasslands stretching as far as the eye can see, the spirited proud horses, the women in their skirts and multicolored petticoats, the thousands of grazing cattle, the lonely nights, and full moon, and the gaucho lament plucked softly on a guitar. These romantic flatlands have created their own spirit and folklore visible today in the dances, songs, and traditional dress of the region. There are the old mission cities, now in splendid ruin, built by the Jesuits in the 1600s. There is the rich grape-growing area where the best wines in Brazil are produced. And there are vast cattle ranches, source of the succulent beef that has made the gaucho barbecue—the *churrasco*—a synonym for mouth-watering steaks and sausages throughout Brazil.

While its tentacles stretch into Paraná and Santa Catarina, the color, the legend, the clothes, and the individualism of gaucho country are more closely associated with Rio Grande do Sul. In neighboring Santa

Catarina the accent is on beaches and sauerkraut in a state known for its German influence and the beauty of its coastline. Paraná, third state in the region, is home to perhaps Brazil's most spectacular natural wonder, the magnificent Iguaçu Falls.

RIO GRANDE DO SUL

The thriving state capital of Porto Alegre, home to 1,300,000 Brazilians, will surprise you. One of the most up-to-date and fastest growing cities south of São Paulo, it has modern buildings, amiable people, and well-stocked shops. Lying as it does at the junction of five rivers, it has become an important shipping port, and much of the state's leather, canned beef, and rice are shipped from here to destinations as far away as Africa and Japan. The Lagoa dos Patos on which the city nestles is the largest fresh-water lagoon in South America.

Porto Alegre

The old residential part of the city is on high ground with delightful views all around. It is dominated by the Governor's Palace (where soldiers crouched with machine guns both when "Jango" Goulart came back as President in 1961 and when he left in disgrace in 1964). Nearby there are an imposing stone cathedral and two high white towers of an old church called the Lady in Pain. The streets of the city wind in and around and up and down, and one of the best ways to enjoy Porto Alegre is to get out and walk; head toward the prisons and the electrical energy plant on General Salustiano. The huge, green-grassed park of Farroupilha is the site of a zoo and botanical gardens and on weekends and holidays is also a setting for folk dancers.

Caxias do Sul

Caxias do Sul is located 70 miles north of Porto Alegre along a highway that also passes through the mountain resorts of Granado, Canela, and Nova Petrópolis, all within 15 miles of Caxias do Sul.

The best Brazilian wine is produced in the area around Caxias do Sul, home of Italian immigrants who transported the art from their native land. Today, 28 different companies work at growing, selecting, and bottling the juices from thousands of tons of grapes grown in this region. In March the entire city stops work to celebrate the "Festival of the Grapes."

Farmers arrive to show off their products, visitors come from all over Brazil as well as France and Italy, and regional folk dances are held. There is also more beef eaten than can be imagined and more wine drunk than should be. The owners of *Michielon* (Avenida Michielon 136) welcome visitors to their bottling plant from 7:30 to 11:00 A.M. and from 1:30 to 5 P.M.

In the first years of the 1600s, the Portuguese domination of Brazil didn't go farther south than Laguna in the State of Santa Catarina.

THE SOUTH

Below this was Spanish territory, and it was here that the Jesuits came from Spain to build a series of missions. They managed to win the confidence of the Indians and soon had them making and laying bricks. The Indians stayed near the missions for protection. Then the Portuguese "flagbearers" from São Paulo came rushing south. Enemies of the Spanish, they killed the priests, enslaved the Indians, and destroyed the mission cities. What is left today—towering walls, delicately curved arches, carved angles and cornices—stands in mute testament to the grandeur that the Jesuits tried to implant on Brazilian soil. The Cathedral of São Miguel, roofless and overgrown with grass, is probably the most impressive ruin. There is a museum beside it with some of the wooden images and iron bells that were salvaged from the Cathedral. Other ruins, all reachable in one day, are at São João Velho, São Lourenço das Missoes, and São Nicolau. At this last ruin the legend still holds that the Jesuits buried a treasure chest before the Portuguese arrived.

All through this area and especially near São Borja, the home of both Presidents Getulio Vargas and João Goulart, you'll see the gauchos and their horses. They still wear the bright-colored shirts and neckerchiefs, the balloon pleated trousers, the creased leather boots, and the flat chin strap hat. They will stop and talk to you and may even offer a taste of their chimarrao, the traditional gourd of hot mate tea.

Nova Petrópolis, Gramado, and Canela

For a break from the flat pampas of the state there is nothing better than a visit to the cities of Nova Petrópolis, Gramado, and Canela, all located in the mountains that run down the coastline. Here the spirit of German and Swiss immigrants is apparent in cozy small hotels and chalets with fireplaces and surrounded by tall pines in an idyllic natural setting that inspires long walks and horseback riding. The region is famous for its homemade chocolate candy and knitted wear. Every weekend in January and February, Nova Petrópolis is alive with the Summer Festival and in June and July the Winter Festival repeats the weekend schedule of events.

Gramado, a sophisticated retreat for wealthy Brazilians who maintain vacation homes here, is the site of the Brazilian Film Festival in March. Calm and relaxing, the city is a sedate jewel tucked away amidst mountains and forests. Only four miles away, Canela is a smaller version of the same magical formula.

PRACTICAL INFORMATION FOR RIO GRANDE DO SUL

For definitions of price categories see *Planning Your Trip.*

PORTO ALEGRE

WHEN TO GO. Try not to come in the winter months from June to Aug.; cold winds from the south whip across the pampas and the temperature drops to the 30s-40s with occasional frosts and snowfall once every 4–5 years. Almost any other time is fine as the temperature is moderate, 70s-80s, and the spring (Oct.-Dec.) is especially enchanting, with the fresh green grass, the new wildflowers, and the young calves and lambs.

HOW TO GET THERE. Porto Alegre is connected with the rest of Brazil by daily **flights** via *Varig-Cruzeiro, Vasp,* and *Transbrasil* airlines. There are international flights from Santiago, Chile (Varig), Montevideo, Uruguay (Pluma, Cruzeiro), and Buenos Aires, Argentina (Cruzeiro). **Buses** make connections from Rio, São Paulo, Curitiba, Iguaçu, and Florianopolis. You can take buses throughout the state. Since the land is flat, the highways run smoothly and buses stick to a tight schedule that is bound to please. **Automobiles** can also be rented in Porto Alegre and Varig airlines has regular service from the capital to many small towns in the interior that can be explored on foot.

HOTELS. The best in town are: **Plaza San Rafael,** *Expensive,* on Av. Alberto Lins 514 (21–6100), with its 218 rooms, air-conditioning, bar, nightclub, and central location making it the ideal spot while in the gaucho capital. **Center Park,** *Expensive,* Rua Frederico Link 25 (21–5388). **Continental,** *Moderate,* Largo Vespasiano Julio Veppo 77 (25–3233). **Alfred Porto Alegre,** *Moderate,* Rua Senhor dos Passos 105 (26–2555). **Alfred Executivo,** *Moderate,* Praça Otavio Rocha 270 (21–8966). **Everest Palace,** *Moderate,* Rua Duque de Caxias 1357 (24–7355). **Embaixador,** *Moderate,* Rua Jeronimo Coelho 354 (26–5622). More modest and with no restaurants are **Sao Luiz,** *Inexpensive,* Av. Farropos 45 (24–9522); **Metropole,** *Inexpensive,* Rua Andrade Nevoes 59 (26–1800); and the **Açores,** *Inexpensive,* Rua dos Andradas 855 (21–7588).

RESTAURANTS. It's an ironclad rule that you can't go wrong anywhere in Gaucho country if you eat in the local churrascarias or steak houses. Here you can be sure that the meat is fresh and the rice is fluffy and delicious. Probably the best beef in all Brazil is served in Porto Alegre. In most churrascarias, you slice your own steak off the sizzling skewer, and eat it with a salad of lettuce, tomatoes, and hearts of palm—washing it all down with an inexpensive pitcher (caneca) of vinho verde. Start with a linguiça (grilled sausage), then move on to filet, picanha, or lombo de porco (pork loin).

There are just too many good spots with this mouth-watering specialty grilling over smoldering charcoal to list all, but start with the **Capitao Rodrigo** (considered the city's best, *Moderate*) in the Plaza São Rafael Hotel, Rua Alberto Lins 514 (21–6100). Next try the always good **Mosqueteiro,** *Moderate,* near the Olimpico Stadium, Av. Dr. Carlos Barbosa (23–9210). Other top steak houses are the **Quero-Quero,** *Moderate,* Praça Otavio Rocha, 49 (21–8825), and the **Santa Teresa,** *Moderate,* Av. Assis Brasil, 2750 (41–2251).

In the unlikely event you tire of the succulent beef, try Italian food at **Bologna,** *Moderate,* Av. Coronel Marcos 2539 (48–4601). French and international at the panoramic **Everest Roof,** *Expensive,* Duque de Caxias 1357 (24–7355), or **Le Bon Gourmet,** *Expensive,* Av. Alberto Lins 514 (21–6100). German at the **Ratskeller,** *Moderate,* on Rua Cristovão Colombo 1564 (22–8409).

WHAT TO SEE. For a good introduction to the folklore and traditions of Gaucho Country, visit the **Estancia Santa Isabel,** a colonial-era ranch one hour from the city where regional dances are performed while you feast

THE SOUTH

on a hearty Gaucho barbecue. Make reservations 48 hours in advance by calling 36–0059.

MUSIC AND DANCE. Performances of the traditional dances and folk songs of Rio Grande do Sul may be seen at the **Teatro de Camara,** Praça de Republica 575, every Mon. evening at 9 or at the **Centro de Tradiçoes Gauchas,** Av. Ipiranga 5200, Fri. at 8:30 P.M.

CAXIAS DO SUL

HOW TO GET THERE. By plane, bus, or rental car from Porto Alegre, 80 miles to the south.

HOTELS. Good hotels are: **Alfred Palace,** *Moderate,* Rua Sinimbu 2302 (221–8655); the older **Alfred,** *Moderate,* next door at 2266 (221–2111); **Samuara,** *Moderate,* 12 miles from downtown on the Parque do Lago (221–7733); **Alfred Volpiano,** *Moderate,* Rua Ernesto Alves 1462 (221–4744); **Cosmos,** *Moderate,* Rua 20 de Setembro 1563 (221–4688); **Italia,** *Inexpensive,* Av. Julio Castilhos 3076 (221–1979).

RESTAURANTS. Don Jon, *Moderate,* in the Alfred Palace Hotel, Rua Sinimbu 2302 (221–8655), international cuisine; **Bellaria,** *Moderate,* Rua Pinheiro Machado 2007 (221–1316), Italian food; **Perini,** *Moderate,* Os 18 de Forte 965 (222–1388), steak house.

WHAT TO SEE. This is the capital of the wine country with a strong Italian influence. Every three years in February and March the city is host to the Grape Festival, the largest promotional event for Brazil's wine producers.

NOVA PETRÓPOLIS

HOW TO GET THERE. By bus or rental car, the city is located 60 miles from Porto Alegre and 25 miles from Caxias do Sul.

HOTELS. The city has three main hotels, all small and all with excellent views of the countryside: **Recanto Suiço,** *Moderate,* Av. 15 de Novembro 2195 (281–1229); **Veraneio dos Pinheiros,** *Moderate,* RS-235; **Veraneio Schoeller,** *Inexpensive,* RS-235 (281–1229).

GRAMADO AND CANELA

HOW TO GET THERE. By bus or rental car. The two cities are located 80 miles from Porto Alegre and 40 miles from Caxias do Sul.

BRAZIL

HOTELS. The growing fame of these cities as a tourist center plus the publicity given to the Brazilian Film Festival held each year in Gramado has led to a rapid growth of new hotels. Most are medium-sized to small and several offer chalets. All of the best hotels have excellent views from the rooms. The best hotels are: **Laje de Pedra in Canela,** *Expensive,* the largest and most luxurious of the hotels in the two cities, Av. Presidente Kennedy (282–1530); **Serrano Gramado,** *Expensive,* Av. Presidente Costa e Silva 1112 (286–1332); **Ritta Hoppner,** *Moderate,* Gramado, Rua Pedro Candiago 305 (286–1334); **Hotel das Hortensias,** *Moderate,* Gramado, Rua Bela Vista 83 (286–1057); **Gramado Palace Hotel,** *Moderate,* Rua D'Artagnon de Oliveira 237 (286–2021); **Grande Hotel,** *Moderate,* Canela, Rua Getulio Vargas 300 (282–1285); **Canto Verde,** *Inexpensive,* Gramado, Av. Coronel Diniz 5660 (286–1961); **Alpestre Hotel,** *Inexpensive,* Gramado, Rua Leopoldo Rosenfeld 47 (286–1311); **Alpes Verdes,** *Inexpensive,* Canela, Villa Alpes Verdes (282–1162).

RESTAURANTS. The mountain air will whet your appetite, which is just as well since the two cities have several excellent restaurants specializing in international, Swiss, and Italian cuisine as well as the ever present churrascarias. **Saint Hubertus,** *Expensive,* Swiss cuisine, Gramado, Rua de Carriere 974 (286–1273); **Panoramico** in the Hotel Laje de Pedra, *Expensive,* Parque Laje de Pedra, Canela (282–1530); **Le Petit Clos,** *Expensive,* Swiss, Rua Demetris Pereira dos Santos 599, Gramado (286–1936); **Bella Italia,** *Moderate,* Italian, Av. Borges de Medeiros 883, Gramado (286–1207); **Cantina d'Italia,** *Moderate,* Italian, Av. Borges de Medieros 543, Gramado (286–1600); **Steinhaus,** *Moderate,* steak house, Av. Coronel Diniz 707, Gramado (282–1252); **Bela Vista,** *Moderate,* steak house, Av. Coronel Diniz 3964, Gramado (286–1359).

WHAT TO SEE. The **natural attractions** of Gramado and Canela are the most compelling sights of the region, although if you happen to be in town in March don't miss the **Brazilian Film Festival.** English-language films are also shown during the festival, but even if the films don't impress you, you'll love the parties. Make hotel reservations well in advance as the cities fill up for the festival. Gramado also offers a **classical music festival** in July. **Hiking paths** are plentiful here and **horses** can also be rented. Ask at your hotel for directions on how to get to the many beautiful viewpoints in the area overlooking canyons and waterfalls.

SANTO ANGELO

HOW TO GET THERE. By car or bus from Porto Alegre, a 250-mile trip. By plane from Porto Alegre.

HOTELS. Unfortunately there is not much to choose from. All hotels are modest. Best bets are: **Avenida II,** *Inexpensive,* Av. Venacio Aires 1671 (312–3011); **Maerkli,** *Inexpensive,* Av. Brasil 1000 (312–2127); **Santo Angelo Turis,** *Inexpensive,* Rua Antonio Manoel 726 (312–4055).

WHAT TO SEE. Santo Angelo is the jumping off point for the **mission region.** The most interesting and best preserved of the mission ruins is São Miguel, 30 minutes from Santo Angelo. A light and sound show at the ruins gives the history of the mission and the region.

PARANÁ AND SANTA CATARINA

Iguaçu Falls

Paraná is home to one of Brazil's most unforgettable sights, the Iguaçu Falls. Eleanor Roosevelt remarked that: "Iguaçu Falls make Niagara look like a kitchen faucet." The water comes from some 30 rivers and streams from the interior of Paraná, and as it rushes toward the 200-foot precipice, it foams and carries huge trees it has uprooted. The volume of roaring, earth-shaking water has been estimated at 62,000 cubic feet per second. During the flood months of May to July the water plunges over at 450,000 cubic feet per second.

Brazilians and Argentines have each made national parks on their side of the falls and views from both countries are spectacular and different. Your hotel will take care of transportation to the Argentine side and all the necessary customs paperwork. You will be impressed by the Devil's Throat Falls, which must be seen by taking a highly adventurous outboard trip across the rapid currents to a trembling but secure little island. Don't wear your good clothes. The spray of this breathtaking portion of the fall is thrust 500 feet into the air.

Another view of the falls can be seen by taking a jeep to where a boat will carry you to the foot of the cascade for a really close-up view from below. During the jeep ride through dense forest, alive with colorful birds and butterflies, flowers, poisonous spiders, and wildlife, a guide will point out the highlights of the local flora and fauna, amidst lakes and lesser falls. Or skim down the river in a helicopter. As the water drops away beneath you, you will have the sensation that you too are going over the waterfall!

On the road to Iguaçu from Curitiba, capital of Paraná, is Vila Velha, a unique region of unusual rock formations carved by wind and water over millions of years.

Curitiba

Curitiba is a busy city of one million inhabitants standing some 3,000 feet above sea level on the plateau of Serra do Mar. For over a century, its bracing climate and picturesque location have attracted immigrants of Slav, German and Italian origin, who have imparted a few European characteristics to its buildings and surroundings. Formerly best known as the center of the *hervamate* industry, it has now acquired much greater importance as the capital of a flourishing and progressive state that derives its economic prosperity from extensive coffee plantations in the north and vast timber forests in the southwest, as well as fertile areas that produce abundant crops of cereals and other foodstuffs. In addition to being the capital of the State of Paraná, it is the headquarters of the Fifth Military Region and therefore the residence of many officers and their families, and there are barracks for infantry and artillery regiments. There is also a modern and well-equipped military air base. The University of Paraná attracts thousands of students from all over the states of Paraná and Santa Catarina as well as from more distant states of the union.

Along the coastline of Paraná are several historical cities from colonial times, the most interesting of which is Paranagua, founded in 1648 and today one of Brazil's most important ports. A three-hour train ride from Curitiba down the coastal mountains to Paranagua is one of the more spectacular journeys in Brazil, with breathtaking views of the coast and mountains at virtually every curve.

Cities of Santa Catarina

In Santa Catarina the accent is decidedly German, with graphic examples of German influence, especially in the architecture and food, found in the cities of Joinville and Blumenau. Blumenau is located in a valley reminiscent of the Rhine region of Germany and has recently carried this association one step further with an Oktoberfest. The state's coastline has the finest beaches in southern Brazil, a fact that is now attracting the residents of São Paulo to the beaches of Santa Catarina. Laguna, a colonial city founded in 1676, in addition to its picturesque narrow streets and colonial architecture, also has the south's best beach resort hotel, the Laguna Tourist Hotel.

Appropriately, for a state known for its beaches, the capital of Santa Catarina, Florianópolis, is an island city with fine beaches on the oceanside.

PRACTICAL INFORMATION FOR PARANÁ AND SANTA CATARINA

For definitions of price categories see *Planning Your Trip.*

CURITIBA

HOW TO GET THERE. By air. Daily flights from São Paulo and Rio via *Vasp, Varig-Cruzeiro,* and *Transbrasil.* **By bus.** Served by major bus lines from all of the country's large cities.

HOTELS. Numerous fine hotels here include the **Iguaçu Campestre,** *Expensive,* on the BR-116 Highway (262 –5313); **Iguaçu,** *Moderate,* Rua Candido Lopes 102 (224 –8322); **Del Rey,** *Moderate,* Rua Ermelino de Leão 18 (224–3033); **Mabu,** *Moderate,* Praça Santos Andrade 830 (222–7040); **Caravelle Palace,** *Moderate,* Rua Cruz Machado 282 (223–4323); **Deville Colonial,** *Moderate,* Rua Com. Araujo 99, downtown (222–4777); **Araucaria Palace,** *Moderate,* Rua Amintas de Barros, downtown (224–2822); **Guaira Palace,** *Moderate,* Praça Rui Barbosa 537 (232–9911); **Ouro Verde,** *Moderate,* Rua Dr. Murici 419 (224–1633); **Tibagi,** *Moderate,* Rua Candido Lopes 318 (223–3141); **Tourist Universo,** *Moderate,* Praça Osorio 63 (223–5816); the **San Martin,** *Moderate,* Rua Joao Negrão near Rua XV de Novembro (222–5211).

THE SOUTH

RESTAURANTS. You will find good food in the dining rooms of the better hotels and at the following restaurants (all are *moderate* in price, with the exception of the steak houses and Italian restaurants, which are *inexpensive*): For churrasco (steak)—**Pinheirao Campestre,** Rua Vitor do Amaral 1010 (262–3711). German foods—**Schwarte Katz,** Rua Franco Torres 18. French and international dishes—**Ile de France,** Praça 19 de Dezembro 538 (223–9962). Italian—**Bologna,** Rua C. Carvalho 150 (223–7102). Also numerous fine restaurants in the Santa Felicidade area, such as the Italian restaurants **Madalosso** (272–1014) and **Veneza** (272–1673) and the steak house **Churrascaria Colonia** (223–6522).

WHAT TO SEE. Places of interest include: the **Coronel David Carneiro Museum,** with a unique collection of objects of historical interest and the **Graciosa Country Club.** Also noteworthy are the modern buildings, especially the **Civic Center,** which houses in one homogenous group the **Governor's Palace, State Secretariats, House of Assembly, Treasury, Law Courts,** etc. There are two modern **theaters** (one for plays and revues, one for concerts and ballet) and a **library** in the center of the town.

IGUAÇU FALLS

HOW TO GET THERE. Most tourists arrive by **plane** from, Rio or São Paulo at the Iguaçu airport. There is, however, a land connection also on a paved highway from Curitiba with frequent **buses.**

HOTELS. Absolutely tops, even from the international tourist's point of view, is the Varig Airlines-owned **Hotel das Cataratas,** *Moderate.* The food is good and there are guides to take you to the falls. It's best to make a reservation with a Rio or São Paulo travel agent or call ahead for rooms (74–2666). Other good hotels are the **Salvati,** *Moderate,* Rua Rio Branco 951 (74–2727), in town, and, out of town headed toward the falls on the Cataratas Highway, the **Bourbon,** *Expensive,* (74–1313); the **Carima,** *Moderate* (74–3377); **San Martin,** *Moderate,* (74–2577); **International Foz,** *Expensive* (73–4240); and **Panorama,** *Moderate* (74–1200).

FLORIANÓPOLIS

HOW TO GET THERE. The state capital of Santa Catarina can be reached by air from all of Brazil's major cities as well as by bus.

HOTELS. The best hotels are: **Jurere Praia,** *Super Deluxe,* 30 beach houses for rent with minimum rental period of one week (66–0108); **Maria do Mar,** *Expensive,* Rodovia Virgilio Varzea (33–3009), on the beach; **Canajure Club,** *Expensive,* Estrada Geral de Canasvieiras, (66–0175), on the beach with tennis courts; **Florianópolis Palace,** *Expensive,* Rua Artista Bittencourt 2 (22–9633); **Querencia,** *Moderate,* Rua Jeronimo Coelho (22–2677); **Faial Palace,** *Moderate,* Rua Felipe Schmidt 89, downtown (23–2766).

Located on an island with many fine beaches, Florianópolis is a popular spot for camping. Permits are not needed.

BRAZIL

RESTAURANTS. Fragata, *Moderate,* seafood, Rua Henrique Veras, (32–0366); **Manolo's,** *Moderate,* international cuisine, Rua Felipe Schmidt 71 (22–4351); **Ataliba,** *Moderate,* steak house, Rua Jau Guedes da Fonseca (44–2364).

BLUMENAU

HOW TO GET THERE. A modern prosperous city of 150,000, Blumenau is served by *Varig* and *Cruzeiro* airlines. The best way to reach the city, however, is by bus from São Paulo. While the highway is not the best in Brazil, it passes through both Blumenau and Joinville, giving you a good look at the German origins of this region, visible in the homes as well as the features of the residents, many of whom are blue-eyed blondes.

HOTELS. Plaza Hering, *Moderate,* Rua 7 de Setembro 818, (22–1277); **Grande Hotel Blumenau,** *Moderate,* Alameda Rio Branco 21 (22–0366); **Garden Terrace,** *Moderate,* Rua Padre Jacobs 45 (22–3544).

RESTAURANTS. In German country there is nothing better than hearty German cuisine. Among the best are: **Frohsinn,** *Moderate,* Morro do Aipim, on top of a hill with a view of the city and surroundings (22–2137); **Moinho do Vale,** *Moderate,* Rua Paraguai 66, along the river that flows through the city (22–3337); **Cavalinho Branco,** *Moderate,* Alameda Rio Branco 165 (22–4300). The city also has a well respected French restaurant, **Le Foyer,** *Expensive,* Rua 7 de Setembro 1415 (22–5800).

JOINVILLE

HOTELS. Like Blumenau a city with a strong tie to Germany, Joinville's top hotels are: **Tannenhof,** *Moderate,* Rua Visconde de Taunay 340 (22–2311); **Anthurium Parque,** *Inexpensive,* Rua São Jose 226 (22–6299); **Joinville Tourist,** *Inexpensive,* Rua 7 de Setembro 40 (22–1288).

RESTAURANTS. For German food, try the **Tante Frida,** *Moderate,* Rua Visconde de Taunay 1174 (22–0558); **Bierkeller,** *Moderate,* Rua 15 de Novembro 497 (22–180); **Bavaria,** *Inexpensive,* BR-101 Norte, km. 28 (99–0353).

LAGUNA

HOW TO GET THERE. The state's top beach resort is reached by bus or car on a highway from Florianópolis 75 miles away.

HOTELS. The Laguna Tourist Hotel, *Deluxe,* is tops in the region and highly popular with international tourists, on the beach, Praia do Gi (44–0022). Make reservations well in advance. Other fine hotels are: **Itapiruba,** *Moderate,* on the beach, Praia de Itapiruba, BR-101 (44–0294); **Lagoa,** *Moderate,* Trevo BR-101 Sul (44–0135). The city also has several fine camping areas.

CENTRAL-SOUTH BRAZIL

To visit Brasilia, Brazil's capital, is more than a step into the future, it's a headlong leap into the 21st century. Rising amidst the scrawny jungle of the high red earth plateau, stands one of the most unusual, most strikingly different, most beautiful cities in the world.

There is nothing outdated about Brasilia. In fact, everything there, architecturally, is far in advance of its time. Like something out of Buck Rogers, the city's administrative buildings spread out along the ground, coil around, then leap up in a shaft of marble to capture the rays of the sun.

It was a city "they" said couldn't be done, but others, more dedicated and more determined, went ahead and did it. With a rare thrust of Brazilian energy, a city rose in just three years, in the very spot where once the jaguar roared.

No trip to this magnificent and confusing country is complete without a visit to this city. It's not quite the same as visiting Italy and not seeing Rome—but almost.

Yet all around this spanking new wonderland of modernity nestles the old Brazil—the land of coffee beans and beef cattle, of palm trees and sluggish rivers, of shoeless peasants and Indians.

While it would be unfair to say that the area neighboring the new capital hasn't progressed with the city, it is a gross exaggeration to say that it has greatly changed. Belo Horizonte, the most important interior city after São Paulo, has taken advantage of the geographical fact

134　　　　　　　　　　**BRAZIL**

that almost everyone and everything traveling by highway to the new capital passes through it. But it was a bustling and prosperous town before Brasilia, as its steel mills and hundreds of factories attest. Goiania, a vibrating little town that has sprung up in the past half century, was doing all right before Brasilia was even thought of. But it, too, has managed to cash in on the boom.

One city in the Belo Horizonte area but far enough away from any national progress not to be tarnished is Ouro Prêto. The sleepy, colonial prize still rings with the sound of hooves on its cobblestone streets, the sound of Latin chants coming from its thick walled churches, and the sad plaintive notes of a lover's guitar being strummed beneath a balcony. The city at one time (the 1700s) was a bustling capital state with gold, silver, diamonds, and slaves. But hemmed in by tall, almost impassable mountains, it slowly strangled in the commercial competition of the 20th century. In 1897, it lost its status as capital city of Minas Gerais, and Belo Horizonte came into prominence instead. Preserved by the National Patrimony, it stands as a proud reminder of the glory that was once Imperial Brazil. Here, too, are many works by Brazil's greatest colonial artist, the sculptor Aleijadinho.

BRASILIA

Brazil has had three capitals—Salvador, Rio de Janeiro, and, since 1960, the new city of Brasilia. The reason for the move from Salvador to Rio was that the Portuguese court wanted to be near the center of all the mining and exporting activity. The reason for the move from Rio to Brasilia was that the nation had stagnated for too long along the coast and officials wanted to waken the center of this sleeping giant.

It was not a new idea. As far back as 1808 newspapers were clamoring that Rio was not an adequate place for a capital and were proposing the construction of a city in the interior, where communications could be made with the rest of the country: "Our present capital is in a corner of Brazil and contacts between it and Pará or other far removed states is extremely difficult. Besides, Rio subjects the government to enemy invasion by any maritime power." In 1892, Congress authorized a special expedition to go into the backlands and study the terrain in the center of the nation where "a city could be constructed next to headwaters of big rivers and where roads could be opened to all seaports." After a three-month overland trip, the expedition leaders decided on the planalto area of Goias. They turned in their report and nothing was done with it.

It was not until 1956, when a sharp politician named Juscelino Kubitschek was elected president of Brazil, that the idea became a reality. He needed a campaign platform when he was running for President, and one night at a rally someone shouted to him about building a new capital. Immediately he took up the idea as his own and, as soon as he was installed as President, he set the wheels in motion.

It was a monumental undertaking, one without equal in the modern world. What had to be done was to build a totally new city that would

CENTRAL-SOUTH BRAZIL 135

become the center of government for the biggest nation in the Western Hemisphere—with all the conveniences of light, power, telephones, sewage, housing, streets, police protection, fire protection, schools, hospitals, banks, industry, commerce, ministries, churches, theaters, as well as all the necessary buildings needed by the Congress, Supreme Court, and the President to govern the country.

In the very beginning there was nothing there but scrub trees, red dust, and wild jaguars. President Kubitschek flew there, had Mass said, stayed the night, and set up a long list of work committees. Money came from all over the world in the form of loans and government grants. The Brazilians pushed the button on their printing presses and turned out billions of cruzeiros that inflated their economy as never before.

Very few of the raw materials needed for such a grandiose enterprise could be obtained in Brasilia and had to be contracted from outsiders. Airplanes flew in continually from Rio and São Paulo, loaded with steel bars and bags of cement. The roads to the new capital were still under construction, so all this heavy equipment had to be brought in by air.

Literally thousands of unskilled, uneducated workers, who needed money and were willing to face any hardship to get it, came from the northeast of the nation. They learned fast and worked hard. Living in wooden shacks and working as much as 15 hours a day, they built Kubitschek's dream city.

Back in Rio, opposition to the new capital was loud and heated. Debates in the senate turned into fistfights, and investigating committees were formed to see where all the money was going. Very few people wanted to move to Brasilia and they complained bitterly about the "lack of everything" there. They said their children would not have the proper schools, that they would be unable to pay the high prices that the artificial city was commanding, and that they would be separated from their families and friends. Actually, most of the big politicians were unhappy about being away from the beach and afraid that their investments in Rio apartment buildings and commercial shops would suffer once the city ceased to be the nation's capital. Kubitschek's government countered this with special inducements to civil servants of a 100 percent increase in salary for working in Brasilia, special tax considerations, and an earlier retirement age. He also promised free transportation of government workers and their household effects, commissioned furniture factories to manufacture modern styles to be sold to workers at wholesale costs, and put rentals on new houses and apartments at ridiculously low rates.

"Freetown," where most of the construction workers lived, had grown into a city of over 100,000. It was a rough, sprawling, dirty, vice-ridden place, where anything went as long as there was money to buy it. It was straight out of Hollywood. There were wooden store facades with false second stories. Instead of horses, men parked their jeeps in front of the 101 bars. Two movie houses did a roaring business.

Kubitschek had set the date for the inauguration of the city for April 21, 1960, and in spite of all odds it was ready. The inauguration itself was a memorable day that began with a Mass in the uncompleted

136 **BRAZIL**

cathedral and ended with a fireworks display, during which the name Juscelino Kubitschek burned in letters 15 feet tall.

For all of the troubles and haste that Brasilia generated, it is today a modern, comfortable, functioning capital city. It offers many things of interest to the visitor aside from its architecture and feeling of unreality. It has already started to do what those journalists of 1808 wanted. The area around the capital is being opened and a new era of pioneering and colonization has started. There are roads (the Brazilians call them highways) that stretch outward from the new capital to far off Acre, and upward to the coastal city of Belém, and others under construction will go to Fortaleza and Salvador, Bahia. All along these roads, families are coming in, clearing the land, and raising their children. Little communities are forming, and the poor of the big cities are finding out how much nicer life can be in the country than in a cramped favela slum. It will be a long time before the city really "works" or the interior of the country is really settled—maybe another hundred years —but there is no doubt that Brasilia has kicked off the much-needed social improvement.

In spite of its world fame and the fact that it is the capital of South America's largest nation, Brasilia is still a moderate-sized city, with a population of one million. Tourists can see it all in one day, if pressed for time, or two days if they are interested in the various architectural wonders or in studying more closely the mode of life of a group of people who have been recently uprooted from their original environment.

Exploring Brasilia

Most visitors to Brasilia take an early plane from Rio—there are flights from 6:30 A.M. onward—land in Brasilia before noon, take a sightseeing tour around the main buildings, and have lunch at one of the two good hotels; in the afternoon they continue their tour, this time visiting the old "free city," and are delivered to the airport in time to catch a flight back to Rio and dinner.

There is one treat that the linger-awhile type of tourist gets that the one-dayer doesn't. That is to see the city illuminated at night. There is probably no lovelier urban sight in all Brazil than the federal buildings, all white marble with reflecting glass windows, shimmering under dozens of huge, superbly placed spotlights, while the stars shine brightly out of a jungle sky of black velvet. As one old peasant woman told her daughter after she made the trip to the new capital in the back of an open truck: "It looked like I always expected Heaven to look at night. It was difficult to tell where the building lights ended and the stars began. They seemed to be put there to show off the other."

Another thing you'll notice about Brasilia is the sky. It is bluer than the sky in Rio and turns purple. There are always fleecy cloud formations decorating it. Another noticeable item is the red earth of the city. Not unlike the red soil of Georgia, it has stained the bases of the buildings, has tinted the carefully planted grass, and, in a sudden gust of wind, is just as liable to coat your face and clothes with a fine red

CENTRAL-SOUTH BRAZIL
137

powder. The earth is very poor in minerals; artistically, it looks as if it had been placed there on purpose for contrast.

Those with only one day to spend should be able to cover the most important points of the city by using this itinerary.

Leaving the airport, take a taxi (if you prefer to drive yourself, there are rental cars available at the airport, too) and watch for the white arrow-shaped signs saying "cidade" (city). If you turn right, take a dip curve, and come up again to where the sign says "Eixo Rodoviario," you will be on the main avenue of the south wing of the city. Along this avenue the luxury apartments are built, and since all rooms have huge plate glass windows onto the street, the Brazilians refer to them as "the Candango's television." The workers do spend a great deal of time looking up into the windows of the senators and ministers who live there. It's cheaper than the movies and much more eventful! The area through here has been planned into Super Blocks (Super Quadras) and each block was designed to be a complete unit in itself. There are high-class apartments in front, then middle-income apartment buildings in the rear. Each Super Block has its own shopping area, complete with supermarket and barber shops, etc., as well as a Catholic chapel. There is also a primary school for almost every Super Block, so that school-age children do not have to cross streets coming or going to class.

Brasilia, if you glance at a map, is built in the form of an airplane, a fitting symbol for a city in this space-minded age. The two "wings" are for commercial and residential areas. The fuselage, from propeller to tail blades, is for government, communications, and transportation centers. The city highways are so designed that there are almost no red lights or traffic signs. City planner Lucio Costa's wife was killed in an automobile accident and he vowed that he would make Brasilia as "accident free as possible," which it is.

As you go down this residential highway, turn off beneath another sign that directs you to a Super Quadra and explore the internal workings of community life there. Then, heading in the same direction, you'll come out onto Avenida W3, the commercial main street of the capital. Here you'll find the shops, both chic and mundane, the good restaurants, a movie house, the banks, the telephone company, and the post office.

After heading south on W3, turn around and go to the far north and, turning right onto the main highway by the Hotel Imperial, follow the directional arrows that will take you in front of Hotel Nacional, down a ramp under the monumental bus station (with music, shops, and perhaps some visiting Indians riding up and down the escalators), then make another right turn and you'll be on the Three Powers Square.

The first building of importance you'll pass is the national Cathedral, with clasped fingers of concrete reaching to the sky. Worshippers go in underground and come out to hear Mass in the center under the fingers, protected from the elements by huge panes of glass. Check with your hotel to see if there is a Mass on the Sunday or holiday you're visiting.

Besides the Cathedral, on both sides of the square, like huge glass-plated dominoes, are the 18 various government ministries. Functional,

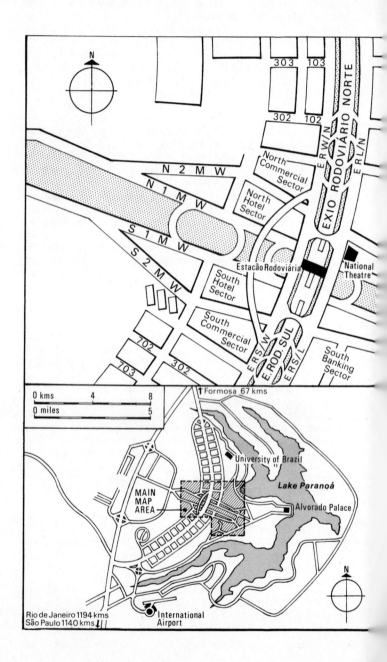

CENTRAL-SOUTH BRAZIL 139

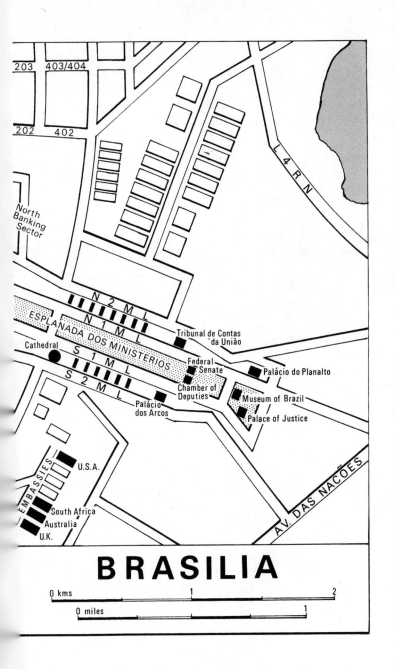

140 **BRAZIL**

but with a tendency to absorb the hot sun's rays, they take the place of literally hundreds of offices scattered around Rio when that city was the capital.

Beyond the last building on the right is what many people claim to be the most beautiful building in Brasilia, if not in all Brazil—the Ministry of Foreign Relations (Palácio dos Arcos on the map, "Itamaraty" to all residents), with its water garden and soaring concrete arches. Despite its extravagance—those arches support nothing but themselves—it's a must for the amateur photographer.

Across the way, almost floating on air and the shallow reflection pools, is the magnificent Congress building with its twin, 28-story towers where senators and deputies have their offices. The two orange halves, sitting on each side of the towers, are the Senate Chamber and the House of Deputies. The Senate is the smaller, inverted one. It is completely air conditioned and perfectly illuminated within. The building can be visited but permission must be obtained from the blue-uniformed guard at the desk just across the ramp on the upper level. If either of the houses are in session, the Brazilian flag is flying from either of their flagpoles.

Continuing down past the two houses of congress, you'll see the small but perfectly balanced Supreme Court on your right with a modern statue of Blind Justice in front. Further along, you'll come to a plump, oblong cement box, with a huge head of Juscelino Kubitschek in its courtyard; it is the Brasilia Museum.

Directly facing the Supreme Court is probably one of the most beautiful of all the buildings, the Planalto Palace, where the president has his offices. Guided tours can be arranged. Be sure to see the luxurious Hall of Mirrors, where state receptions are held, the severe but lovely room to the right where the President holds open conferences, and the sun-illuminated interior corridors on the second and third floors, where tropical plants grow in profusion.

Head east now, toward the lake, past what seems to be miles of modern lamp posts, until you come to the exclusive Alvorada Palace, official president's residence, at the "propeller" of the airplane. This was the first administrative building ready and the most expensive. Every inch of cement, all the steel girders, the pipes, the glass, tiles, everything had to be flown in, because there was no way to reach Brasilia by land. Beside this jewellike palace is a small circular chapel, where the presidential family attends Mass.

The long, low, burned-out building nearby is the Brasilia Palace Hotel, gutted in a fire in 1979.

After lunch, you will still have some three hours to see the other less important things or to go back for a closer look at what you saw that morning. You could visit the handsome national theater, a pyramid of weathered concrete near the bus station, head off in the same direction for the Yacht Club (where you get an interesting side view of the Three Powers Square), or continue way out on the as yet almost deserted North wing and arrive at the other side of the lake, where many expensive homes have been built or are going up.

For a sharp contrast of a "satellite city" to modern Brasilia—from the "architecture" of a dust town to the year 2,000—take a 20-minute

CENTRAL-SOUTH BRAZIL

drive beyond city limits to one of the communities settled by the Brazilian builders. You may want to hire one of a group of American guides, right opposite the Hotel Nacional.

If you will have an hour or so before your plane, take a quick look at the wild-west, clapboard satellite town called Free City. Though the bulk of Brasilia's working class now lives far out in the satellite towns of Gama or Taguatinga, the *Cidade Livre* (Free Town) still stands as a monument to those hardy northeasterners who built the 21st-century capital city.

PRACTICAL INFORMATION FOR BRASILIA

WHEN TO GO. The best time is probably the summer, from Nov. to around the middle of Apr. It gets chilly in Brasilia. Because the city is on a high plateau, some 3,500 feet above sea level, and in the direct path of winds from the moist warm jungles as well as those from the colder south, its climate is variable and invigorating. Sweaters at night during the winter months are almost a necessity, and no matter what the season, you'll probably want to sleep under a blanket.

HOW TO GET THERE. There are daily flights from Rio, São Paulo, and Belo Horizonte. Buses also travel the roads connecting these cities with the nation's capital on a daily basis.

HOW TO GET AROUND. Take a taxi. Many people prefer to have a guided tour by one of the registered agencies. If you only have time for a once-around-lightly view of the city, then *Ciclone-Hinterland Turismo* at the Seitor Commercial Sul, or *Trips, Toscano, Excelsior,* or *Presmic,* all located in the arcade of the Hotel Nacional, will give you the best service. They have their own cars, usually Brazilian-made Volkswagen "Kombi" station wagons, and their drivers speak English as well as half a dozen other languages. Prices are moderate but a little higher than in Rio for the same service, about $15.

You might, just for the fun of it, get on any of the buses that leave from the street level platform at the centrally located Highway Terminal ("Estação Rodoviaria") and stay on it till it takes you back to the terminal again. No matter which line you take, you'll get odd and interesting angles of the city that other tourists don't catch from the guided tour. But it's best to do this after you've seen Brasilia the regular way, so you can appreciate what you are seeing even more. Bus fares are about 10 cents.

HOTELS. Unfortunately, young Brasilia has never had a top-quality hotel. However, the Hilton chain is now building a hotel, and a Sheraton and an Inter-Continental are in the planning stages. In the meantime, the best is still the **Nacional,** Setor Hoteleiro Sul (226–8180), situated in the heart of the city with an incomparable view of the Congress, Ministries, and the banking section. Ten floors of comfortable apartments. Off the spacious lobby is an excellent restaurant where one of the daily specialties is a long smorgasbord table with 100 different dishes to choose from. The wine cellar is excellent and the European-trained chefs add a Continental touch. There is a small bar done in beautiful jacaranda wood paneling, and a pool. The basement is equipped with a modern Finnish-style sauna as well as steam baths and massage parlors.

For evening entertainment, one of the best nightclubs in town is on the ground floor, alongside a patio *churrascaria*. There is also a H. Stern store.

Other good hotels are the **Garvey Park,** Setor Hoteleiro Norte, Quadra 2, Bloco J (223–9800); **Carlton,** Setor Hoteleiro Sul, Quadra 5, Bloco G (226–7320); **Eron Brasilia,** Setor Hoteleiro Norte, Quadra 5, Lote A (226–2125); **Torre Palace,** Setor Hoteleiro Norte, Quadra 4, Bloco A (226–3360); **Phenicia,** Setor Hoteleiro Sul, Quadra 5, Bloco J (224–3125); **Aracoara,** Setor Hoteleiro Norte, Quadra 5, Bloco C (225–1650); **Saint Paul,** Setor Hoteleiro Sul, Quadra 2, Lote 5 (226–1515); **Bristol,** Setor Hoteleiro Sul, Quadra 4, Bloco F (225–6170). All these hotels are moderately priced ($15–$45).

RESTAURANTS. Brasilia does have some good restaurants. Price ranges used below: *Expensive,* $10–$15; *Moderate,* $5–$10. For good solid Brazilian beef, done "churrasco gaucho" style, pay a visit to the **Churrascaria do Lago** (223–9266) on the banks of the lake, within walking distance of the Hotel Brasilia. Their specialty is a "mixto," which is a little bit of everything, both beef and pork, served with rice, manioc flour, and a special barbecue sauce of raw onions, tomatoes, and vinegar. *Moderately* priced.

A good spot for international cuisine is the **Piantella,** *Moderate,* (224–9408) with live music. In the same commercial center (Comercio Local Sul) is the **Florentino,** *Expensive,* the favored eatery of the nation's congressmen and where political deals are always in the works (223–7577). The Centro Commercial Gilberto Salomao has a number of spots. This commercial center, where bureaucrats and diplomats of all levels gather nightly, is home to the **Gaf,** *Expensive,* for French food (248–1103), the **Bier Fass,** *Moderate,* German food and beer (248–1519), and the **Au Chalet,** *Expensive,* for Swiss (248–2897).

WHAT TO SEE. Everything. The two presidential palaces (the Alvorada where the man in power lives and the Planalto where he works), the twin-towered **Congress building** at the Praça dos Tres Poderes, the domino-placed **Ministry buildings** in the same area, the crown-shaped cathedral at the Eixo Monument, the national theater also at the Eixo Monument, the modern spacious apartments, and the bustling—almost small town—atmosphere of the business district. A visit should be paid to the yacht club and the area known as Embassy Row. A visit to the shrine of Dom Bosco is also in order, not just to pay him homage, but to get an over-all, complete view of the city. There are no museums as yet of any importance, nor any special collections. The exteriors of the buildings are more interesting than the interiors (with a few exceptions mentioned already), and don't forget to take note of the way the highways and by-passes have been laid out. Also study the faces of the "candangos," the dusty but courteous immigrant workers who built the city with almost nothing but bare hands and determination.

SPORTS. In Brasilia, there used to be such an exodus of governmental workers, especially such important types as congressmen and ministry directors, that weekend activities were limited. But the city is now developing a social life of its own, even on weekends. The one favorite focal point is the yacht club, on the artificially created Lake Pinheiro. Although open only to members, your travel agent or almost any Brazilian citizen can get you in. There is a nice big pool, a small but more than adequate restaurant, and if you look sad, and wistful, some friendly Brazilian is bound to ask you if you'd like

CENTRAL-SOUTH BRAZIL 143

to take a ride on the lake in his "yacht." There are about ten other good social clubs that have also sprouted up—all normally crowded and lively on sunny weekends.

People do go fishing some as far away as on Bananal Island in the surrounding state of Goias. Check with your tourist agent in Brasilia about this and see if they can arrange a two-day trip to the Carajá Indians, who will act as your guides. There is a hotel there; it was called the Juscelino Kubitschek until the latter's political disgrace, whereupon it became John Kennedy. Don't go there without a reservation. Andre Safari & Tours, in the Torre Palace Hotel, specializes in this trip.

MINAS GERAIS—BELO HORIZONTE
AND THE HISTORICAL CITIES

The third largest city of Brazil with a population of 1.7 million, Belo Horizonte is an airy modern metropolis nestled into the mountains of Minas Gerais, source of much of Brazil's vast mineral wealth. Although the city is relatively young, celebrating its 90th anniversary in 1987, it is the jumping off point for the fabled historical cities of Minas, colonial-era towns that dot the surrounding mountains and offer visitors a first-hand look at life in Brazil in the 18th century when the gold fields of this region attracted Portuguese adventurers and Catholic priests, a combination that gave birth to the area's famed baroque churches, rich in gold leaf.

But before taking off for a look at its historical surroundings, spend some time in Belo Horizonte itself. There are many things for the tourist to do. One of them is to stroll along the shady downtown streets and watch the new buildings going up all around. Another is to visit the municipal park located in the heart of the business area. Town fathers planned well, for should you become tired of cement and commerce, you can cross over into the well-kept park, with its tree-lined walks, its small lakes, its rustic bridges, and red flowered bushes. There is something going on there almost all the time, and it is a favorite spot for lovers, nursemaids, and photographers.

Another interesting place is the Minas Tennis Club, one of the biggest sports arenas in the state. Extremely modern in design, the gymnasium can hold 10,000 people. Its swimming pool is Olympic size and its separate courts for volleyball, basketball, and tennis have caused favorable comment from many international sports-minded figures.

Just as modern, but much more controversial, is the oddly shaped church at Pampulha, just outside the city. Designed by famed Brasilia builder Oscar Niemeyer, the church, once constructed, was refused consecration by Catholic authorities because both Niemeyer and Portinari (whose frescoes adorn it) were known Communist sympathizers. The battle raged for a number of years until the people of Minas put pressures to bear on the Bishop and the church was blessed.

The Tassini Museum has a collection of maps, crystal, lamps, work tools, photographs, and general miscellanea collected over a 30-year

144   **BRAZIL**

span by one Raul Tassini and donated to the city. It is devoted strictly to objects that figure in the history of Belo Horizonte and the early diamond mining days. Well worth a visit, it is open every day except Monday.

When you have finished with the sights of Belo Horizonte it will be time for you to travel back into the past of this fascinating region. Most trips to the historical cities can be handled on a one-day basis, using Belo as your starting and ending point. Your first trip should definitely be to Ouro Prêto (Black Gold, so-called because of the black coloring of gold in the area caused by iron oxide in the soil). Though still little known outside of the country, Ouro Prêto is one of the most unforgettable tourist attractions in all of South America. It is revered by Brazilians the way Italians revere Venice or the Americans, Williamsburg. Founded in 1711 with the name Vila Rica (Rich Village), it soon became the center of the gold, diamond, and semiprecious stone trading in the colonial era. So much gold came from the hills around Ouro Prêto that the area was named simply "minas gerais" or "general mines."

It became *the* place to live in those days, and the rich built fine houses and palaces, donated gold to construct churches, and hired the very best artists to decorate them. One of the most famous names to come out of this period was a crippled mulatto sculptor called Aleijadinho. The man could do no wrong when he was working with wood or stone, but arthritis turned him into a monster. His facial features became so deformed by disease that he put a sack over his head so that no one could be frightened by his ugliness. His legs refused to coordinate and his fingers and hands became so contorted that his assistants used to tie his hammer and chisel to his wrists with leather thongs so he could work. What he did with the beauty inside him is in evidence in Ouro Prêto and the surrounding area and is part of the rich Brazilian cultural heritage.

The Glorious Churches of Ouro Prêto

The best place to see Aleijadinho's artistry is the Church of São Francisco, located just down the hill to the left from the Praça Tiradentes. Note the twin towers in an almost salt-and-pepper-shaker form. Be sure and inspect the huge soapstone medallion high up over the front door, as well as the intricately carved doorway. Inside, the main altar with cherubic faces, garlands of tropical fruits, and allegorical characters is still fresh with the original paint. Also note the twin soapstone side altars. Just doing one of them is enough for a man to be hailed as a genius, and he did two for this church alone.

His work can also be seen in the impressive Monte do Carmo Church, in whose tall towers hang two bells that weigh 7,000 pounds. The altar dominating the church of São José was also done by Aleijadinho.

There are 11 churches in this one town in the Brazilian hills. If any were in Europe, they would be international "musts" on any tourist itinerary, but hidden away as they are here, they have preserved their

CENTRAL-SOUTH BRAZIL 145

charm and offer a new delight to the tourist with spirit enough to come this far to see them.

While in Ouro Prêto, don't fail to take a slow tour of the Museum of Inconfidência. Housed in an impressive baroque building that was started in 1748 and finished in 1846, it was at one time the home of the Municipal Congress. It was here that the first Brazilian rebellion against the Portuguese was started and here that the first rebel, a white-bearded martyr nicknamed "Tiradentes" (tooth puller), was captured, then taken to Rio and brutally executed. The museum is full of clothes, children's toys, slaves' manacles, firearms, books, and gravestones of the turbulent era. The director, who speaks English very well and is proud of his Brazilian past, will be delighted to show you around personally. Admission is free.

Many people stay two days in Ouro Prêto, savoring the winding old streets and the colonial buildings and dodging the donkeys and horses and carts that still move among the automobiles. Ever since 1933, when the entire city became National Patrimony, not a thing has been changed, and it is to the Brazilians' credit that many things have been restored and cleaned up. Tour buses are no longer allowed to transverse the city's narrow streets, in order to preserve the colonial-period buildings. The buses stop outside of the city from where taxis take you into Ouro Prêto. Whether you spend the night or not, try to stay at least until sundown, when you will witness the reflection of the sunset off the city's tiled roofs, the gradual darkening of the surrounding hills and mountains, and finally the cool mist that spreads across the city, evoking a sensation of distant times in Brazil's colonial past. If you decide to remain for a second day, you might hire a taxi and travel a few miles to the sleepy village of Congonhas. The main attraction there is the church of Bom Jesus de Matosinhos, where Aleijadinho sculpted 12 life-sized statues of the Prophets and placed them outside at the front entrance.

These works, breathtaking in their exact details and expressive faces, have been called "a genial mixture of Quasimodo, Beethoven and Michelangelo." Aside from a number of statues inside the church, he did the Stations of the Cross in life-size, using 66 different figures that are housed in six separate buildings. Rarely visited by the Brazilians themselves, these figures are "finds" for the really discriminating tourist.

Aleijadinho, deformed and crippled though he was, got around. His works can be seen in the churches of the nearby town of Mariana and São João Del-Rei. Baroque lovers should also visit the churches of Sabará.

Diamantina took its name from the diamonds that were extracted in great quantities from its soil in the 1700s, and even today the mines still supply gold, iron ore, and rock crystal. It was here also that the famous Chica da Silva, the mulatta slave who captured the heart of the wealthy Portuguese mine owner, lived. He showered her with gold and precious stones, built her a palace with hanging gardens and even transported a sailing yacht overland for her pleasure. Then he turned around and dug her a lake to sail it on.

The city looks very much like it did in the days of Chica. Be sure to note the covered overhanging roofs with their elaborate brackets.

PRACTICAL INFORMATION FOR BELO HORIZONTE AND THE HISTORICAL CITIES

For definitions of price categories see *Planning Your Trip.*

HOW TO GET THERE. Like the rest of the country, this area is no exception when it comes to distances. Belo Horizonte is 453 miles from Brasilia, 250 miles from Rio de Janeiro, and 360 miles from São Paulo. Ouro Prêto, the living museum city, is a full 75 miles away from Belo, but the people in the state capital consider it "a suburb." And Diamantina (another colonial jewel in the Minas hills), is 180 miles away, but citizens in Belo will calmly tell visitors who have nothing to do for the day, "Why don't you run over and see Diamantina?"

The city of Belo Horizonte is served by all of Brazil's major airlines, and there are daily flights between the city and Rio, São Paulo, and Brasilia. Bus service is also frequent and the roads are good. For trips from Belo to the historical cities, the best bet is by bus or car. The roads in the region are paved and in good condition. There is regular train service between Belo Horizonte and Diamatina. Day tours depart from Belo for all of the colonial cities in the region. Taxis will drive you to Ouro Prêto and back for $45 or so and a regular bus line charges about $4 for the same service.

BELO HORIZONTE

HOTELS. Othon Palace, *Expensive,* Av. Afonso Pena, corner Tupis e Bahia (226–7844). Newest, biggest, and most luxurious in the city, with 317 air-conditioned rooms, rooftop pool and bar, international restaurant, coffee shop, sauna, conference facilities for 800 persons. Overlooking trees and lakes of Municipal Park.

Brasilton Contagem, *Expensive,* Contagem industrial district on a hilltop near Belo Horizonte (351–0900). First Hilton Hotel in Brazil outside São Paulo, the Brasilton Contagem opened early in 1978. Rooms are built around central courtyard with pool and tropical gardens, and all have air conditioning, heat, color TV, well-stocked mini-bars.

Hotel Del Rey, *Moderate,* Pça Afonso Arinos 60 (222–2211). One of the best traditional hotels downtown; 270 non-air-conditioned rooms, private baths, 24-hour room service.

Normandy, *Moderate,* On Rua Tamoios 212 (201–6166). Service is very good; the rooms large and airy; modern restaurant and bar are fine. Located in the center of the city's business district, it is one of the most popular meeting places. Insist on an outside room.

The Amazonas, *Moderate,* On Av. Amazonas 120 (201–4644). New and small but service is very good. Excellent restaurant on the 11th floor.

Other hotels include the **Wembley Palace,** *Moderate,* Rua Espirito Santo 201, downtown (201–6966); the **Serrana Palace,** *Moderate,* Rua Goitacazes 450, downtown (201–9955); and the **Financial,** *Inexpensive,* Av. Alfonso Pena 571, downtown (201–7044).

CENTRAL-SOUTH BRAZIL 147

RESTAURANTS. As in most Brazilian cities, new restaurants are constantly opening with an increasingly international flavor. Tops among Belo's international eateries is the **Tacho de Ouro** in the Othon Hotel, *Expensive* with live piano music, Av. Alfonso Pena 1050 (226-7844). Also good is the **Nacional Club**, *Moderate,* Rua Bernardo Mascarenhas 77 (201-5007). But Minas is also rightfully famous for its own regional cooking, hearty meals perfect for the cool nighttime temperatures in this mountainous state. Specialties are suckling pig and sausages but any pork dish in one of Belo Horizonte's finer restaurants is recommended. A true Minas meal is always accompanied by tutu, a delicious black bean mash. One of the state's traditional dishes, a favorite throughout Brazil, is *tutu à mineira*—sausages, pork and tutu. In Belo, for regional cooking try **Pato Selvagem**, *Moderate,* on the highway to Nova Lima (541-1112); **Chico Mineiro**, *Moderate* Rua Alagoas 626 in the sophisticated Savassi neighborhood, home to the city's newest and liveliest night spots (224-5604); **Arroz com Feijão**, *Moderate,* Rua Antonio de Albuquerque 440, also in Savassi (221-1266); and **Jeca Tatu**, *Moderate,* Rua Pernambuco 1426, Savassi (225-9326). Best churrascarias are **Minuano**, *Moderate,* Rua Professor Morais 635 (225-3600) and **Rodeio**, *Moderate,* Av. do Contorno 8222 (335-7544)—not only is the food good here but the way it's served is spectacular, all the steaks and sausages you can eat. Called rodizio or rotation-style, this system has become popular in recent years—the waiters rotate from table to table carrying long skewers heavy with sizzling meat and sausages and stopping only when you say no more. Other conventional churrascarias are **O Laçador**, *Moderate,* Rua Gonçalves Dias 874 (224-3335); **Mangueira's**, *Moderate,* Praça São Francisco 30 in Pampulha (441-5766); and **Adega do Sul**, *Moderate,* Av. do Contorno 8835, (335-6550). The best Italian restaurant is **Tavernaro**, *Moderate,* Rua Antonio de Albuquerque 889 in Savassi (221-8283) and for German cooking try **Stadt Jever**, *Moderate,* Av. do Contorno 5771, Savassi (223-5056).

NIGHTLIFE. The nightlife in Belo has become concentrated in the Savassi neighborhood, with many outdoor bars, excellent restaurants, and a few night clubs with live Brazilian music. The "in" spots tend to change from season to season but try **Aloha**, Rua Pernambuco 1108 (226-6783); **O outro Lado do Moeda**, Rua Professor Morais 476 (223-1440); and **Era Uma Vez um Chalezinho** (with excellent fondue), Rua Paraiba 1453 (221-2170). All are located in Savassi, where you can't go wrong for nightlife.

Note: The **historical cities region** offers a range of hotels but most are quaint inns and pensions, some rather primitive in their basic comforts.

OURO PRÊTO

HOTELS. The best hotel is the **Estrada Real**, *Moderate,* located on the highway at the entrance to the city, Rodivia dos Inconfidentes km. 87 (551-2122). Like all the hotels in Ouro Prêto this one is small, with 30 rooms and 10 chalets. Other options are **Luxor Pousada**, *Moderate,* Rua Dr. Alfredo Baeta 16 (551-2244) **Grande Hotel Ouro Prêto**, *Moderate,* Rua Senador Rocha Lagoa 165 (551-1488); **Pouso Chico Rey**, *Moderate,* Rua Brigadeiro Mosqueira 90 (551-1274); **Pilão**, *Inexpensive,* Praça Tiradentes 57 (551-2057); **Colonial**,

148 BRAZIL

Inexpensive, Travessa Camilo Veloso 26 (551–1552); **Toffolo,** *Inexpensive,* Rua São José 76 (551–1385).

The best **restaurant** in town is the **Taberna Luxor** in the Luxor Pousada.

DIAMATINA

HOTELS. The **Tijuco Hotel,** *Inexpensive,* is really the only option in the city. Located on Rua Macau de Meio 221 (931–1022), it adheres faithfully to the historical atmosphere demanded by the visitor.

CENTRAL-WEST BRAZIL

While most visitors to Brazil have heard of the country's beautiful Atlantic beaches and the jungle attractions of the Amazon rain forest, few are aware that Brazil is also home to the last major ecological frontier on earth. Known as the Pantanal, this 140,000 square mile area covers a region the size of Holland, Switzerland, and Belgium combined. Once an inland ocean in prehistoric times, the Pantanal today is a giant plain with an average elevation of 400 feet that is cut by the basin of the Paraguay River. Just south of the Amazon watershed, the northern Pantanal is home to the headwaters of the rivers that form the Paraguay Basin. In the rainy season these rivers drain south, forming huge lakes throughout the region with only a few areas left above the level of the waters where the Pantanal's wildlife escapes from the floods. In the dry season, the water level subsides and the Pantanal's incredible variety of wildlife moves out to the now dry plain, accumulating along the banks of the many rivers that cut through the area. The dry season (usually May to September) is the best time to visit the Pantanal, a time of the year when visitors can see thousands of alligators, armadillos, monkeys, the capivara (the world's largest rodent), and if you're lucky the famed onça, the Brazilian jaguar. But the best sights are reserved for those who lift their gaze skywards. As birdwatchers throughout the world have long known, the Pantanal is world-class birding territory where in a single day you can see more species than you ever thought existed, such as the proud Tuiuiú, the

150   **BRAZIL**

elegant Heron, the Rhea (a Brazilian ostrich), the Siriema, Rose Spoon-
bills, the Baquari, Cabeças-secas, Anhumas, Cara-caras, parakeets, and
parrots.

For those who come to do more than watch the wildlife, the Pantanal
is also famed as one of the top fishing areas on the earth. It is practically
unbeatable for both variety and quantity of fish. Here you will find the
piraracu, at 600 pounds the largest fresh-water fish in the world. Other
top eating varieties are the pintado and the pacu and if you've ever
wondered what a piranha looks like close up, here is the place to find
out.

Unlike the Amazon, the Pantanal is not closed in by jungle; thus,
movement here, by river, road, or rail, is relatively unrestricted. In past
days the lack of facilities for tourists made a trip to the Pantanal a form
of Brazilian safari but today the region has received major investments
in tourism infrastructure. Comfortable fishing camps plus small hotels
for those who simply want to sit back and enjoy nature watching are
now scattered throughout the Pantanal. But while the comfort has
increased a sense of adventure still prevails, thanks to the as yet undisturbed natural setting where tranquil rivers with alligators sunning on
the banks cut through the vast sedimentary plain, leaving a sensation
that you have escaped the modern world and returned to prehistoric
times. A trip to the Pantanal is an unforgettable experience.

THE PANTANAL

The region has two main gateways, in the north via the city of
Cuiaba, capital of the state of Mato Grosso, and in the south by way
of the city of Curumba, in the state of Mato Grosso do Sul. These two
states contain all of the Pantanal as well as some of the largest cattle
ranches in South America. In this area a sense of frontier life still exists,
but the region's main cities are expanding quickly. Only ten years ago,
Cuiaba was a city where you could see roughened ranch hands walking
the streets wearing holsters and packing six-shooters. Today such
sights belong to folklore and Cuiaba is a bustling modern city with high
rises sprouting up at every downtown corner. The cattle ranches plus
an explosion of farming (especially soybeans, of which Brazil today is
the world's number two producer, behind the United States) have
brought new wealth to the city and region.

Once you've arrived in Cuiaba get in touch with a tour operator,
assuming you have not already taken this step in Rio or São Paulo. A
guide is highly recommended for the Pantanal. On your first day in
Cuiaba either join a tour or rent a van with an English-speaking driver
to take you on a drive on the nearby Transpantaneira Highway. The
Pantanal in this area is swampy, somewhat like the Everglades in
Florida, and the highway is built above the level of the swamps, giving
you an excellent view of the region and whatever wildlife is visible.
Some tours spend the night in small towns along the highway, returning to Cuiaba the next day. The city itself has few attractions. While
it was founded in the 18th century by Portuguese adventurers looking

CENTRAL-WEST BRAZIL 151

for gold, Cuiaba has preserved little of its heritage. The Indian Museum of the Federal University of Mato Grosso is of interest and Cuiaba is also home to a satellite tracking station maintained by NASA.

On day two, arrange to visit the Chapada dos Guimarães, a mystical rock formation located 40 miles from Cuiaba. This immense geological formation surges to a height of 2,400 feet with lush green forests and spectacular waterfalls as well as curious rock formations carved by the action of the wind over millions of years. The Chapada also possesses a strange magnetic force that reduces the speed of cars, even when they are going downhill.

Now you are ready for a full-scale trip into the Pantanal. From this point on you will have to deal with a travel agency or tour operator to arrange things for you. Most trips last three to four days and several begin with a drive or flight from Cuiaba to the city of Caceres, about 120 miles to the southwest. Here you will take a trip in an outboard motorboat down the Paraguay River for three hours until you reach the Jauru River. Going up the Jauru (always have your camera ready, especially for the birds and alligators), you will soon arrive at the Hotel Fazenda Barranquinho, one of the better hotels in the area, with room for 36 guests. Run by a tourism agency, the hotel provides horses and outboard boats for fishing and trips.

In this hotel, as in other fishing camps and hotels in the Pantanal, you will receive all the assistance you need from the staff to either fish or take trips to see and photograph the wildlife (there is no hunting allowed in the Pantanal). Accommodations tend to be comfortable but modest. Although the Pantanal today is no longer off the beaten track, it still has no luxury facilities for tourists. The food is included in the room rate and most of it comes from the region itself. Besides the fish from the rivers, you will have freshly-baked bread made by the hotel as well as such Pantanal delicacies as monkey meat and piranha soup. Be prepared to take things easy since there is virtually nothing to do at night except rest or talk to the other guests of the hotel. The hotels are isolated and it is not possible to travel from one to another at night since all travel in the Pantanal is by boat.

Similar excursions into the Pantanal are possible via the southern gateway city of Corumba, located on the Paraguay River. If you wish to get an idea of the immensity of this part of Brazil, there is a train ride from the city of São Paulo to Corumba. The one-and-a-half day trip is not known for its comfort but the final ten hours provide a spectacular view of the Pantanal. Once in Corumba, a sleepy river town with little to see, boat trips into the Pantanal can be arranged. For the truly adventuresome there is a two-day trip across the Pantanal on a supply boat that carries food and other necessities to small settlements located in the marshlands. The boat goes up the Paraguay and São Lourenço rivers, ending the trip at Porto Jofre, the last stop on the Transpantaneira Highway. The trip provides an excellent look at the Pantanal and the way its inhabitants live, but life on board is rustic to say the least. There are no cabins and passengers must bring their own hammocks to sleep in. To buy a passage go to the wharves in Corumba.

PRACTICAL INFORMATION FOR THE PANTANAL

For definitions of price categories see *Planning Your Trip.*

 WHEN TO GO. The dry season (May to Sept.) is the only time when it is practical to make a trip to the Pantanal. During the rainy season (Oct. to Mar. or Apr.), the Pantanal is mostly under water, which makes visits impossible although you may rent a plane to fly over the region. It is usually hot, except for June and July, and few of the hotels or fishing camps have air-conditioning so dress for warm weather. Also, mosquitoes are a constant nuisance—bring lots of bug spray.

 HOW TO GET THERE. Both Corumba and Cuiaba have airports that are served by Vasp, Varig-Cruzeiro, and Transbrasil airlines. There are also direct buses from São Paulo and Rio that make the trip to the two cities although the journey is long and tiring. The train ride from São Paulo to Corumba will provide you with a view of the booming interior region of the state of São Paulo, easily the most developed area of Brazil.

 HOTELS. In Cuiaba the best hotels are **Aurea Palace,** *Moderate,* Av. General Melo 63 (322–3377); **Excelsior,** *Moderate,* Av. Getulio Vargas 246 (322–6322); **Las Velas,** *Moderate,* Av. Filinto Muller 62 (322–4399); **Mato Grosso,** *Inexpensive,* Rua Comandante Costa 2522 (321–9121).

In Corumba there is little to choose from but try **Pousada do Cachimbo,** *Moderate,* Rua Guapore 4 (231–4833); **Santa Monica,** *Inexpensive,* Rua Antonio Maria Coelho 345 (231–2481); and **Beira Rio,** *Inexpensive,* Rua Manoel Cassava 109 (231–2554).

For accommodations in the Pantanal, the most recommended options are: **Hotel Fazenda Barranquinho,** *Moderate,* (279–0555 in São Paulo), for fishing and nature watching, near Cuiaba; **Hotel Cabanas do Pantanal,** *Moderate,* fishing and nature trips, northern Pantanal near Cuiaba (64–4245 in São Paulo); **Cabana do Lontra,** *Moderate,* fishing and nature trips, in the southern Pantanal near Corumba (283–5843 in São Paulo); **Fazenda Santa Clara,** *Moderate,* fishing and nature trips, southern Pantanal near Corumba (284–4877 in São Paulo); **Hotel dos Camalotes,** *Moderate,* fishing and nature trips, air-conditioning in the rooms, southern Pantanal near Corumba (231-1329 in São Paulo); **Pesqueiro do Severino,** *Moderate,* fishing and nature trips, air-conditioning in the rooms (258–4355 in São Paulo), southern Pantanal near Corumba; **Santa Rosa Pantanal,** *Moderate,* fishing and nature trips, northern Pantanal near Cuiaba (321–5514 in Cuiaba); **Boteis Corumbi e Amazonas,** *Moderate,* a boat converted into a hotel, air-conditioning, southern Pantanal near Corumba, (231–3016 in Corumba). All of these hotels have accommodations for 20 to 40 persons.

 RESTAURANTS. The best eating in this area is in restaurants specializing in river fish. At the hotels in the Pantanal, fish is the main course and in some cases the only course. In Cuiaba try **Flutuante,** *Moderate,* Rua Santa Baracat (321–9825)—the menu contains a wide choice of the best fish dishes of the region, which should give you a good idea of the flavor of the different species caught in the Pantanal; **Internacional,** *Moderate,* Praça Antonio Correia 74 (322–1849); **Aurea Palace,** *Moderate,* in the hotel of the same name, Rua General Melo 63 (322–3637); **Maria Taquara,** *Moderate,* in the Excelsior Hotel, Av. Getulio Vargas 246 (322–6322). In Corumba the best fish restaurant is the **Ceara,** *Moderate,* Av. Rio Branco 580 (231–1930).

TOURS. Getting to the gateway cities of Corumba and Cuiaba is not difficult, but from then on you will need the assistance of professionals to arrange visits to the Pantanal. Most large travel agencies and tour operators in Rio and São Paulo now offer Pantanal packages and you can get in touch with them through your travel agent at home. Plan a Pantanal trip well in advance since hotel space is limited and the best spots are always booked up ahead of time. Some persons, such as bird-watching enthusiasts, may want a special tour package to visit particular areas of the Pantanal. Your best bet in that case would be to get in touch with *Rio Custom Tours,* Travessa Madré Jacinta 25, Rio de Janeiro (274–3217), a Rio tour operator that specializes in Pantanal trips, especially for foreign bird-watchers.

GOIAS

The third state of Brazil's huge western hinterland is Goias, home to gold mines, cattle ranches, and one of the best rivers in Brazil for fishing and nature watching. Suspended like a giant teardrop in the very center of Brazil, Goias stretches from its southern border close to the Pantanal to its tip stuck sharply into the vast reaches of the Amazon jungle. In the immensely varied space in between are the federal district of Brasilia, hot springs resorts, and colonial towns. Like Brazil itself, Goias' south-north progression moves from urban sophistication to rural abandonment, ending finally in the dream world of Amazonia, where thousands of poor Brazilians have flocked in recent years in search of the region's latest El Dorado, the gold fields of the Serra Pelada mountain range.

It was gold, in fact, that first attracted settlers to what is now the state of Goias. The *bandeirantes,* or Portuguese adventurers who marched out from the state of São Paulo in the 18th century in search of gold and Indian slaves, quickly made Goias one of their favorite stopping points. Plunder, however, was of more interest to these raiders than colonizing and as a result, the state, like most of the vast area covered by Brazil's elevated central plateau, remained sparsely settled until the last 30 years. The turning point was really the building of Brasilia, which at last drew the attention of Brazilians away from the coastal beaches to the interior. With the construction of Brasilia, Goias' nearby capital of Goiania has enjoyed a boom cycle as the city's population has exploded to nearly one million. The remainder of the state, however, remains thinly populated, known mainly as the home of some of Brazil's largest cattle ranches plus rice plantations.

It is this more backwards area of the state, particularly its western border, that in recent years has become a mecca for tourists seeking

BRAZIL

something out of the ordinary. Their main discovery has been the Araguaia River, which forms the border separating Goias from Mato Grosso and the Amazon state of Rondonia. The Araguaia is famed for its white sand beaches and the excellent fishing available to anglers along a 270-mile stretch between the cities of Aruanã and Porto Luis Alves. Starting in May and continuing until September with the peak season running from May to July, the Araguaia is home to perhaps the best fishing in Brazil. Businessmen from São Paulo and Rio enjoy sneaking out of the office for an extended weekend on the Araguaia during this period when the river is low.

Goiania

The jumping-off point is Goiania, some 60 miles southwest of Brasilia. From here, a paved highway leads to the small town of Aruanã, five hours distant, and then to the capital of the Araguaia region. On the way you should stop for a short visit to Old Goias, the colonial capital of the state and its best example of colonial-period architecture. Aruanã itself is no more than a sleepy river town of 2,000—that is, except during fishing season. During these months, the town becomes a bustling center of activity for fishermen from throughout Brazil and abroad as well as the youth of Goias, who view the Araguaia's beaches as their answer to Rio's Copacabana and Ipanema.

For Araguaia veterans, the first step is to find out where the best beaches are located. Due to constantly shifting sandbars, this is not as simple as it sounds. The river's contour, and thus the sites of its beaches, undergo changes each year. Once the beaches have been uncovered, usually through a preliminary "exploration" of the river by boat, the next step is to set up camp. There are exactly three hotels in Aruanã, the main reason why a campsite on a beautiful beach is more contested than a cold beer on the Araguaia. By tradition, camps along the river are made up of hand-built tents of wood and palm fronds. Individuals invite their friends and in many cases, companies set up their own Araguaia headquarters for harried city-dwelling executives.

These encampments or tent cities are usually built around one large central tent which contains the essentials—kitchen and bar. The more sophisticated camps bring generators to provide electricity. All by necessity must bring basic provisions, since the nearest supermarket is five hours away. In July, the banks of the Araguaia are alive with up to 400 tent cities, many of them containing 100 to 200 persons. Once this river civilization has laid down its roots, the serious business of fishing, boating, and nature watching gets underway. Fishermen literally can not go wrong. River fish with romantic Indian names like the pacu, piau, and matrincha are found together with several varieties of catfish.

River Excursions

For those who are more interested in observing the region's flora and fauna, it is possible to rent a boat for $10 to $25 an hour to take a trip down the river. Along its banks you are likely to see wild pigs, tapirs,

CENTRAL-WEST BRAZIL

and deer. Swimming in the river is also a favorite pastime, but many Araguaia aficionados prefer simply to lie back in a hammock in this quiet, restful setting on the edge of the wilderness. (Fair-skinned tourists should be wary of the sun. The Araguaia region is close to the equator and even a short exposure to the sun's rays can be painful. Also, it is recommended that travelers to this part of Brazil take a yellow-fever vaccination before their journey.)

Most big-city Brazilians consider this part of their nation to be Indian country, but in fact the nearby tribes have been mostly assimilated. A small Indian village may be visited in Aruanã but is essentially there to be seen by tourists. The "real" Indians are too far off the beaten track to be visited by tourists.

Caldas Novas

Goias' other major tourist attraction is Caldas Novas, an entirely civilized warm springs resort in the southern part of the state, some 100 miles of Goiania. Here, in a spectacular setting surrounded by rugged mountains, tourists can enjoy naturally heated swimming pools in resorts that offer tennis, horseback riding, and hiking. In addition, the medicinal values of the hot springs in the area are highly touted, recommended for muscular pains.

PRACTICAL INFORMATION FOR GOIAS

For definitions of price categories see *Planning Your Trip*.

WHEN TO GO. For the Araguaia river region, the best time is between May and September, when the river is low. The most popular period among Brazilians is May to July, vacation time, when the few hotels in the area are filled. After September, the river level rises, overflowing its banks in many areas and making camping virtually impossible. The hot springs resort of Caldas Novas also fills up during vacation period, June to September. Not affected by seasonal changes, the resort can be visited at any time of the year.

HOW TO GET THERE. The capital of Goiania is a bustling modern city with an airport served by Brazil's major carriers, with connecting flights from and to Rio de Janeiro and São Paulo as well as nearby Brasilia. There are few highways in the state, but those that exist connect the main tourist attractions. You may travel by bus from Brasilia to Goiania, and bus lines connect the state capital to Aruanã in the Araguaia, passing through the colonial town of Old Goias. There is also a direct highway connection between Goiania and Caldas Novas. If you want to get a long, good look at the Brazilian hinterlands, you may want to take a bus from either Rio, São Paulo, or Belo Horizonte to Goiania. The roads are good by Brazilian standards (average by North American or European). The Belém-Brasilia highway also passes through much of the state, leaving Brasilia and heading through the more isolated northern part of Goias. The road, however, is poor and the trip only for the adventuresome.

GOIANIA

HOTELS. The state capital has little to offer tourists but is a good jumping-off point for visits to the Araguaia, Caldas Novas, or even Brasilia. The best hotels are: **Hotel Bandeirante**, *Moderate*, Av. Anhanguera 3278 (224–0066), 76 rooms in the downtown area with restaurant, bar, and nightclub. **Umuarama Hotel**, *Moderate*, Rua 4, No. 492 (224–1555), 136 rooms downtown with restaurant and bar. **Castro's Park**, *Expensive*, Av. Republica do Libano 1520 (223–7707), the closest the city comes to a luxury hotel with pool, restaurant, bar, and nightclub; 177 rooms. **San Conrado**, *Inexpensive*, Rua 3, No. 652 (224–2411), downtown, with 56 rooms, bar, and restaurant.

RESTAURANTS. Regional food other than fish tends to be heavy, with a strong accent on rice dishes. The best fish restaurant in Goiania is **Dourado**, *Moderate*, Rua 6–226 (223–1444). Also good is **Degrau 94**, *Moderate*, Rua 94–822 (225–4647). For international cuisine with live music, try **Cliff**, *Moderate*, Rua 23–72 (241–7888). The city's best steak houses are **Braseiro**, *Moderate*, BR–153 km. 1270 (261–0062), and **Serra Dourada**, *Moderate*, Rua 84–497 (241–5021).

NIGHTLIFE. The options are extremely limited, but the two best bars are located in the Cliff and Degrau 94 restaurants.

ARUANÃ

HOTELS. Since most of the fishermen who come to the Araguaia prefer to camp out along the river, there are only three hotels in Aruanã: **Hotel Recanto Sonhado**, *Moderate* (376–1290), best of the three, pool and air-conditioning. **Hotel Araguaia**, *Inexpensive*, (376–1251), 26 rooms with air-conditioning and pool and **Hotel do Sesi**, *Inexpensive*, (224–0324), 38 rooms, pool. All three offer meals with the room rate, a good thing since restaurants in the city are terrible and should be avoided.

TOURS. For non-Portuguese–speaking foreigners, getting to the Araguaia and arranging accommodations, fishing, and/or boat trips on the river can be an adventure in itself. If you are alone, without connections with Brazilians who know the area, it would be best to ask your travel agency to get in touch with professional tour operators who have experience with groups in this part of Brazil. The best operator for the Araguaia is **Transworld**, Rua 3,560, Gioania, Goias (224–4340), which offers a one-week group trip to the Araguaia River. In Rio, the agency **KR International Travel**, Rua Mexico, 11-Gr. 1701, Rio de Janeiro, RJ (210–1238), is run by a former Peace Corps volunteer and can provide reliable and up-to-date information on Goias or other adventure destinations.

CALDAS NOVAS

HOTELS. The best hotels are very good indeed, resort-style with a wide range of activities. Tops are: **Turismo,** *Expensive,* GO-507 (421–2244); 113 rooms, pool, tennis, restaurant, bar, and nightclub. **Parque das Primaveras,** Moderate, Rua do Balneario (453–1355); pool, restaurant, and bar; more secluded, with chalets and individual suites with thermal pools. **Pousada do Rio Quente,** *Moderate,* GO-507 (421–2244), 237 rooms with pool, restaurant, bar, horses for hire. Most of the hotels include meals in the room rate.

BAHIA

If you have only time to visit two cities in Brazil, make them Rio and Salvador, although, as residents of the latter will quickly add, once you've been to Salvador you won't need to visit Rio. With a rich colonial past evident in its historical churches, forts, and buildings Salvador is known to Brazilians as the most Brazilian of their cities. For this it draws not only upon its history (Salvador was Brazil's first capital) but also upon the colors, tastes, sounds, and aromas of this unique city that mixes old and new, black and white, religion and mysticism. A blend of African, Indian, and European cultures, Salvador moves to its own rhythm, slow and sensual, more at ease even than Rio and blessed with miles and miles of practically untouched beaches. The capital of the state of Bahia, with which it is so closely identified that Salvador is often called Bahia, Salvador is at once South American and African, a mix that makes it unlike any other city in the world.

There are red-tile roofs tacked atop white plaster walls. There are palm trees, baroque architecture, an abundance of churches, and happy carefree people. These are the expectable things. Then there are the thousands of black faces, with bodies swathed in cloth of neo-African styles. There are dishes of hot strange foods prepared nowhere else in the world. There is a strange drum beating voodoo ritual that mingles the best of the African and Christian ideals into a powerful, frighteningly personal religion. There is a fight dance called *capoeira* that originated in Bahia and is only practiced here. There are modern

159

BRAZIL

automobiles vying with plodding donkeys. There are sumptuous mansions vying for a place in the sun with mud-thatched shanties.

If you stay there for awhile, you'll find Salvador is not just a city but an entire way of life, where the arts and the human personality are more important than money or political ambitions. The city has been called the "Renaissance of Latin America," because of its attitudes toward beauty and self-expression and the number of artists from all over the nation (and the world) who have gone there for inspiration. But this does not mean that Bahia is all siestas in the sun. Far from it. One glance at the dozens of new office buildings and the hundreds of modern apartment houses will dispel that idea. It is simply that the Bahianos have found a way to live with the best of both worlds, and, like their hybrid religion, their city has become a surprising, fascinating experience.

SALVADOR

Salvador was the first city the Portuguese built up when they colonized Brazil. That was in 1549. Today this city spreads around the bay of Todos os Santos (All Saints), which is so wide (1,052 square kilometers) it could supposedly hold all the ships in the world. Salvador was built by the early settlers to keep the Spanish, French, and Dutch away from the new colony belonging to King Dom João III. The administration buildings and residences were built on the hills, the forts, docks, and warehouses on the beaches. To this day, it is still divided into upper and lower cities. From 1500 to 1815, Salvador was the nation's busiest port. The sugar from the northeast and the area surrounding All Saints Bay and the gold and diamonds from the mines in the south all passed through this town. It was a golden age for Salvador when magnificent homes and richly decorated churches were built. Its churches have few rivals anywhere in the world. Thanks to a federal commission called The National Historic and Artistic Patrimony Service, created in 1941, many of the city's old churches are the same today as they were the day they were built. Entire squares, such as Largo do Pelourinho, hundreds of private homes and even the hand-chipped street paving bricks have been preserved and restoration work is still continuing. Salvador counts 97,000 buildings and about 20,000 of them are over 250 years old. Yet there are brand new buildings going up everywhere to meet the living requirements of the progressive citizens of today.

Salvador may be seen, if necessary, in three days but only if you're pressed for time. The city really requires five days at the minimum. Save time for shopping and if possible one extra day to travel into the interior of the state of Bahia.

The first day: By now you've become intrigued by the history of Salvador, so plunge into the Upper City, home to Brazil's best preserved colonial architecture. If you wish to do this on your own it would be best to contact an English-speaking guide either through your hotel or the local tourism authority, Bahiatursa (see *Practical Information* below). Otherwise, there are several local tour operators that

BAHIA
161

can give you an excellent tour of the colonial Upper City and other sights in Salvador in air-conditioned mini-buses with English-speaking guides. For those of you on your own, start out at the downtown Praça da Sé. Remember, you should dress casually because of the heat but don't wear bermudas or swimming wear as some churches will not let you in. To the left of the Praça is the Archbishop's Palace, built in the 18th century and today used as the Catholic Law School. On the other side of the Tourist Office is the 18th-century Holy House of Mary church. Walking up Guedes de Brito Street, you'll see Saldanha Palace with its impressive gateway. The School of Arts and Crafts is there now. As you walk up Bispo Street you'll pass São Damasco Seminary, built in 1700, and will come to a little square and the Church of São Francisco Convent. It is one of Brazil's most famous and undoubtedly one of the most beautiful in the world. Hand carved in every nook and cranny and then covered with shining gold, it is so impressive that many tourists stay around all day just watching the play of light on the walls. It is especially beautiful during a High Mass. The image of St. Peter of Alcantara on the lateral altar on the right is so well done that church authorities had a battle with Emperor Dom Pedro II, because he wanted it for his private chapel. Only the men may visit the blue-tiled cloisters of the monastery; women must be content to peer through the grillwork. There are Franciscan fathers there who will show you around. When you leave drop some money into the poor box, for the church does an impressive job three times a day supplying warm meals for the poor. Right next door is the church of the Third Order of São Francisco. Inside there is a room that is worth seeing full of life-size statues. The intricate facade was carved in 1703 but hidden for many years by a thick coat of plaster. It was a major art find when it was uncovered recently. Now to the square of Terreiro de Jesus with the 16th century Basilica Cathedral, the church of the Third Order of São Domingos (1731), and the church of St. Peter of the Clerics. From here, up Alfredo de Brito Street you come to the architectural spectacle of the Largo do Pelourinho. It was here that thousands of slaves were chained together, then sold on that platform on the right side of the street. Note the typical old balconies, the tiles and the people who look as if they've stepped from a Debret engraving. The streets that lead into the Largo, all narrow and cobble-stoned, contain several fine shops for the purchase of the region's delicate lace work—blouses, dresses, table cloths, etc. Walk slowly down to Taboão Square where five streets cross and then up the Ladeira do Carmo. Now take a quaint flight of steps that leads to the Church of the Passo and continue to the top of the street. Here the Carmo Convent and the Church of the Third Order of Carmo stand side by side. The church is famed for its image of the crucified Christ. To enter the convent, you have to know the way. Beside the biggest door in the room hangs a cord. Pull it and from somewhere inside a smiling guard appears to escort you about. Be sure and tip him when you leave. Going up the Ladeira do Carmo, there is a corner of blue-tiled houses.

Tell the driver to take you to Baixa do Sapateiro, a street filled with shops and private homes that time has somehow forgotten. Afterward look at the Convent of the Desterro (1678), where the sisters have a

162 **BRAZIL**

well-deserved reputation as candy makers. It is Brazil's oldest and most beautiful convent. Go up Avenida Joana Angelica to the Tororó steps. Below them lies the Dique, an artificial lake made in the 17th century as part of the city's defense system. It is also considered by followers of candomblé, the African religion brought to Brazil by the slaves, to be the bay of Oxum, a river nymph who is the god of beauty and good fortune. At night presents are left on the banks of the Dique for Oxum. Also, no one swims in the Dique—these are sacred waters.

For the night of your first day in Salvador visit one of the many bars with live Brazilian popular music. Salvador is the birthplace of many of Brazil's top singing stars, such as Gilberto Gil, Gal Costa, Caetano Veloso, and Maria Bethania, and in the city's night spots you can listen to their songs and those of the other giants of samba and bossa nova. Nightlife is centered in the Barra neighborhood, along the beach of the same name. For your first night try Bistro 507 or Bistro do Luis in nearby Rio Vermelho.

The second day should be devoted to beaches and outdoor scenery. Rent a car and driver for the day and tell the driver to go *slowly* towards the Lagoa do Abaeté. The first impressive building you will pass is the white columned University Rectory. If you wish you may go in to see the blue tiles and the reconstructed auditorium. On the beachfront drive, called the Orla, you will see the results of the boom in tourism in Salvador in recent years. Anxious to compete with Rio, the city government has landscaped the beach area for a total of some 15 miles, turning this area of white sand beaches into one of the most beautiful beach drives in Brazil. Along the beach there are kiosks where you can savor a cold drink while you sample a seafood snack Bahia-style. (Although Bahian food has a reputation for being hot, in fact it is merely well-spiced. The hot sauces are served separately and if you wish to taste them, do so with caution. They are not really needed, though. Bahian food, especially seafood, is delicious and easily stands on its own, without the sauces.) Along the drive you will be impressed by the vast quantity of coconut palms as well as the little boys selling fresh coconuts. If you stop for one, watch how deftly a boy can nick off the top with his knife. The milk is warm and sweet. Ask him to split open the coconut and then go on and eat the soft white meat with your fingers. You will pass famed Itapuã Beach with its tall coconut trees and finally reach the lagoon. Brazilian composers have written dozens of songs about this strange inland lake with its contrast of white, white sand and black, black waters. Native women wash their clothes here, and there are some good restaurants in the area for lunch or a cooling drink. Take your bathing suit too, for you might like to sample one of the beaches on the way going or coming.

Once you've finished with the lagoon go back to the beaches and follow them out into the newest area where hotels and restaurants are now sprouting. The beaches here are even better than the stretch between Barra and Itapuã. Running on north of the Quatro Rodas Hotel are the beaches of Barra do Jacuípe, Itacimirim, Arembepe, Guarajuba, and Praia do Forte, where once a year great sea turtles return to lay their eggs. The drive is refreshing and the highway is flanked by coconut palms and white sand dunes. At Arembepe you'll find the remnants

BAHIA   163

of a 1960s colony of hippies once frequented by pop stars Janis Joplin
and Mick Jagger. Stop for lunch at Guarajuba and afterward continue
on to Praia do Forte, which is quickly becoming the most popular
beach in the Salvador area—it also boasts the ruins of Brazil's only
haunted castle.

For your second evening you should consider one of the three basic
nighttime activities that all first-time visitors to Salvador should take
in. First is a capoeira exhibition, where, at the best Salvador academy
in Brazil, you will witness the fascinating capoeira dance-fight. At first
glance it looks like an involved dance, with the two men rotating
around a small space flinging their legs into the air and seemingly just
missing each other's heads with their feet. In reality, though, capoeira
was invented as a karate-like fight—and was often a fatal one. The
slaves were not permitted by their masters to fight between themselves
but by disguising their struggle as a dance they were able to resolve
their disputes. Thus capoeira is accompanied by the strange-sounding
berimbau, a curving stick with a carved-out gourd at its base and a
single chord running from top to bottom which is stroked by the
musician. Together with drums, this musical background slowly builds
up with the tempo of the dancers until you become hypnotized by the
flying bodies in front of you and the eerie mystical sounds of the drums
and the berimbau. Although in today's capoeira no blows are struck
it is easy to imagine the force of the dancers' legs and feet should they
strike their mark.

If you decide to leave capoeira for another evening, you may opt for
a night of black magic, assisting a candomblé ceremony. Candomblé
is another example of how the African slaves fought to preserve their
own culture in the new world. Prohibited from practicing their native
religions, the slaves pretended to worship the saints of the Catholic
Church but in reality for each saint they substituted one of their native
gods. Over the centuries the Catholic priests grew to accept the fact
that for many of the worshipers who filled the churches, the symbols
of Catholicism were also symbols of candomblé. This duality of worship continues to exist today with the exception that while once it was
banned by the church, today it is accepted and even extolled as an
example of the blending of races and cultures in Salvador. Known as
the most deeply religious of Brazilian cities, Salvador has 166 churches
but it also has 4,000 candomblé temples. Bahians say: it's better with
both—if one doesn't work, the other will.

Several of the candomblé temples allow tourists to witness their
ceremonies and there is rarely a week that goes by without at least one
celebration for one of the many African gods. Each god has his or her
counterpart in the Catholic religion and each also wears a special color
and dresses and dances in a specific manner. Thus when a particular
god is being honored candomblé followers will wear his color that
day—even to work. You can arrange to visit a temple through your
hotel or a tour operator. Remember not to take photos unless the
permission of the Mãe do Santo (priestess) is given. Be prepared to be
separated from your friends once you arrive there. They will tell you
where to sit and it's always men on one side and women on the other.
There is nothing to be frightened of either, but don't be surprised to

164 BRAZIL

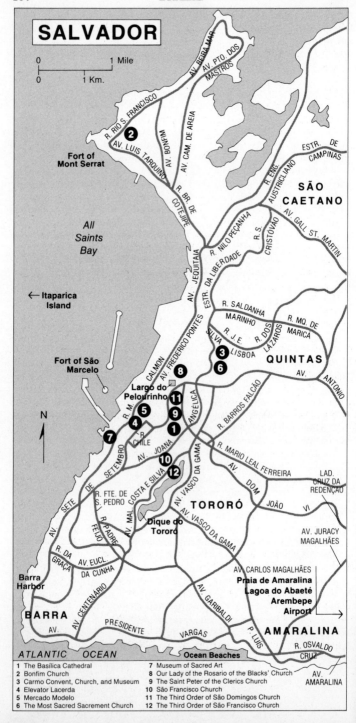

BAHIA
165

see the Brazilian beside you suddenly become "possessed" by spirits, fall onto the ground, roll his eyes, and then dance in a contorted, uncomfortable position. When you leave (sometime after midnight) show your appreciation by placing some money at the feet of the chief drummer.

One more thing you should be aware of. While most foreigners naturally associate candomblé with the voodoo ceremonies of the Caribbean, there is a major difference between the two. Unlike voodoo, candomblé is not aimed at producing bad luck for your enemies. Followers are forbidden to use the spirits convoked by the ceremonies to perform evil deeds. Candomblé is to be used only to produce positive results for the worshiper. There are no dolls with pins sticking out of them in candomblé.

Finally, if you don't feel you're ready for a night of either candomblé or capoeira, why not try a mixture of both as well as a sample of other Bahian dances and folklore? There are four restaurants and one theater in Salvador that offer Bahian folklore shows at night where examples of capoeira, candomblé, and the many other dances of the region are presented (see "Practical Information" below). All are good but the restaurants have the advantage of also offering you a sample of Bahian cuisine. The combination of food and folklore is the perfect match for a Bahian night.

The third day: Now you'll visit the other end of the city on the Itapagipe peninsula. If you leave about 9 A.M. from the Praça da Sé the car will go down commercially busy Rua Chile to Castro Alves Praça, then down the Ladeira da Montanha (where many accidents have happened when the brakes didn't hold) and reach the lower city. That big column of white cement rising to the upper city is the Lacerda elevator and is used to join the two levels of Salvador. Imagine if you had to walk up and down those steep hills every time! Taking Avenida Frederico Pontes, you'll pass the attractive Fort of Lagartixa and the Noble House of Jequitaia built in the 18th century and now used as an army officers' school.

Ask your driver to go to the Bonfim church, and on the way you'll pass the 18th-century Archbishop's summer palace, which is connected to the Penha church by a very interesting passageway. Now at Bonfim church, you are really in Bahia, for this church is the city's main sanctuary. It is not ornate or covered with gold, just a simple building with years of tradition among the faithful. It is said that the Lord of Bonfim never fails anyone and the room of miracles looks as if that might be so. Here you'll see wooden, silver, and plaster reproductions of parts of the human body hanging on the walls. These are there in gratitude for cures worked through prayers to the Lord of Bonfim. Almost always the cures are said to be miracles, as the many inscriptions indicate. It is here, on the Thursday before the third Sunday in January, that thousands of black women dressed in their colorful regional dress and carrying pottery jugs with flowers and water come to symbolically wash down the church steps. It is one of the most time-honored festas in Bahia. There is a spectacular view from atop this hill.

Back in the car, go to the Fort of Mont Serrat, named for the great shrine of the Black Virgin in Spain at Montserrat, near Barcelona. Its

BRAZIL

white walls rising from the seacoast, this 16th-century building looks like a giant bird ready for flight. There is the Mont Serrat Church nearby with its renowned carving of the Repentant St. Peter. If the church is closed, call the guard who lives at the back, and even though he grumbles, he'll show you the tiny jewellike interior. A tip calms him down amazingly. Now you can go to the Cacao Institute, where pictures and graphs tell the story of the chocolate industry from the planted seed to the finished foil-wrapped bar. More than $100,000,000 of cocoa is exported annually from Bahia's ports. Now you are ready for a visit to the Mercado Modelo. Recently reconstructed following a 1983 fire, the market is a Salvador tradition. Here in row after row of stalls you will find the best handicrafts of not only Bahia but all of northeastern Brazil. Although there are many fine shops specializing in specific products all over Salvador, the market has the advantage of bringing everything together in one place. Take your time and comparison shop. You will find the same quality handicrafts in several stalls but the prices are not always the same. Be prepared to bargain. The best price is seldom the first price. Many of the merchants now accept credit cards. Now take a boat at the Cairu docks for a quick look at the Fort of São Marcelo right in front of the market in the bay. It was built in 1650 and kept invaders away. Then it was used as a prison and now serves more for curiosity than anything else. Back in your car, go to the lovely Museum of Sacred Art on Ladeira de Sodré. You'll be impressed with the tiles and the silver altar. It is unquestionably the most beautiful museum in all Brazil. Then, if there is still time, visit the Museum of Bahian Art at Avenida 7 de Setembro 2340.

On this night, if you have not done so as yet, treat yourself to a Bahian meal. Most Bahian dishes are fish-based, with shrimp a favorite not only of the cooks but also of the customers of the city's better restaurants. The ingredients that add that special taste and rich coloring to Bahian food are coconut milk, peanuts, cashews, and dendé (palm) oil. The city's universally recognized best restaurant for traditional Bahian cooking is Casa da Gamboa, where you can't go wrong. The top seafood restaurant in the city is Bargaço. Either one will give you an excellent idea of what Brazilians mean when they say that only in Bahia can you find real Brazilian cooking.

EXCURSIONS FROM SALVADOR

If by now you have realized that three days is just not enough for Salvador, then you'll have time for one of the city's most pleasant day trips. The All Saints Bay is not meant simply to be seen but also to be experienced. In colonial times, Bahian-made boats called saveiros were used to transport goods back and forth between the city of Salvador and the outlying sugar plantations spread around the bay. Several of these boats have now been converted into modern schooners by wealthy Bahians and a few of them are rented out to tourist groups. Pioneer in this area and still the best is LR Turismo, one of Salvador's top tour operators. If you are traveling in a group it should be no problem

BAHIA 167

arranging a day's outing on the bay. If you are alone you will have to try to hitch a ride on somebody else's tour. If you want, you can rent the boat for yourself but be ready to pay a stiff price, at least $200.

The bay is filled with small islands but most boat trips stop at the largest of them, Itaparica. The island is a tropical paradise with beautiful white sand beaches on the ocean side. There are a few good hotels, and Club Mediterranée has established its only Brazilian club on the island. Looking back across the bay to Salvador gives you the best view available of the city. The day-long cruise on the bay is a delightful experience but if you want to spend less time on the water there is a launch that leaves from in front of the Mercado Modelo and in 45 minutes takes you to Itaparica where you can explore the island, then return by the same launch to Salvador. Either way, you shouldn't leave Salvador without having crossed the bay.

For a fifth day you should try to get outside of the city and into the country. Either by renting a car, taking a bus or joining a tour, you can make a lovely day out of an excursion to the nearby colonial city of Cachoeira. At one time the capital of the state, Cachoeira is considered by the citizens of Salvador to be the state's best example of colonial times. Founded in the 18th century, Cachoeira was the center of the booming sugar cane industry that made Bahia the wealthiest state of Brazil during the colonial period. Its richly decorated churches with beautiful ornaments and images show the affluence of the era. On the road to the city you will see sugar cane and cocoa plantations and some tours offer a visit to a distillery that produces cachaça, a potent Brazilian drink that is produced from sugar cane. The area also raises tobacco and the best cigars in Brazil are made here. You can visit an old cigar factory where the women who work there still hand-roll the cigars.

Carnival Bahia-Style

If by chance or good planning you happen to be in Salvador during carnival, you will witness one of the truly great spontaneous festivals on the face of the earth. Unlike Rio de Janeiro, where street carnival has been slowly fading away, replaced by the samba school parades and club balls, in Bahia 90 percent of the party is on the street, day and night. There is no starting gun for Carnival in Salvador but it seems that everyone realizes at the same moment that it is time to begin the celebration. The result is what will first appear to the uninitiated visitor to be pure pandemonium. The streets are packed with jumping bodies, chasing after giant sound trucks from which comes a nonstop ear-shattering flood of carnival music, some live from bands atop the trucks and some on tape. However it is presented you cannot help but hear it, even if you are 10 miles away.

The trucks, called trio electricos or electronic trios (although there can be anywhere up to a half dozen musicians and singers on board at any given moment), are Salvador's own contribution to Brazilian Carnival legend. No one can tell you exactly how this tradition started but clearly it is here to stay. After you have overcome your first shock, you should try gingerly to mix with the crowd. You will soon discover that the normally friendly and outgoing Bahians are ten times as much during Carnival. Before you know it you'll be swept along with the moving throng, jumping and laughing with all of them without the slightest idea of what is happening. This is the special joy of Carnival in Bahia—spontaneous, uninhibited, and pure fun. Leave your inhibitions back in the hotel room.

Center stage for Salvador's carnival is the Praça Castro Alves at the start of Avenida 7 de Setembro. If you saw it on a normal working day you would never believe the amount of people that can be squeezed into it for Carnival. Even more difficult to understand is how these people can go on dancing and jumping all day and most of the night.

But while Salvador's carnival is far more of a participatory event than that of Rio there are also parades to be seen. The most impressive is that of the Afroxés, particularly the Filhos de Gandhi. Afroxé is the sacred music of candomblé and around this theme several large associations have been formed to take part in Carnival. They parade through the city's streets dancing to the Afro-Brazilian beat of percussion instruments. The most striking are the Filhos de Gandhi (the sons of Gandhi), an all-male Afroxé with thousands of members, all of whom dress in white tunics and turbans. The turbans, worn in candomblé ceremonies and also by the elderly Bahian women you see in the city selling Bahian food on the sidewalks, are a result of the Moslem influence on the African slaves who were brought to Brazil. The passage of the long white file of the Filhos do Gandhi is always a moving experience and one further example of the mystical air that pervades the life of Salvador.

PRACTICAL INFORMATION FOR SALVADOR

WHEN TO GO. Because of its consistently warm climate, almost any time of the year is a good time to visit Salvador. But there are certain events that will make this attractive city even more interesting if you plan your trip to coincide with them.

January 1 has the celebration of Our Lord the Good Jesus of the Navigators. Hundreds of boats float offshore, decorated with flags and streamers. Later, there are exhibitions of drum beating and capoeira fighting. January 1, Festa de Nosso Senhor dos Navigantes takes place at Monte Serrat. On January 6, Festa dos Reis is celebrated in all parts of the city.

February 2 is devoted to Iemanjá, the goddess of the sea, who is also the Virgin Mary. In Rio Vermelho and Itapoan, celebrants make offerings all along the shores, and boats are gaily decorated. Festa de Rio Vermelho, in honor of Saint Anne, is held two Sundays before Carnival. Carnival itself is celebrated as in Rio and all business stops for four days. Must be experienced to be believed.

May 10 has the procession of St. Francis Xavier, a feast day in honor of the city's patron saint, held since 1686.

In *June,* twelve days after Holy Ghost, there is a Christian procession. At the same time candomblé worshippers hold services to Oxosse, the African God of the Hunt. Festa de Santo Antonio, a religious feast, takes place in June, while the 24th has the Festa de São João, a popular festival with local dances, entertainment and fireworks. On *June* 29 a twelve day and night candomblé celebration honors all the gods.

July 2 is devoted to the heroes of Brazil's fight for independence. Aside from parades, there are folklore dances and candomblé ceremonies.

BAHIA

On the second Sunday in *September* is held an impressive procession to the sea of Our Lady of Monte Serrat, while on the 27th the twin gods Cosme and Damião are honored with banquet tables loaded with rich regional cooking.

October, all month long, is devoted to the African gods Exú, Iabás, Ogum, Omulu, and Oxum.

December 4 is the Festa de Santa Barbara. Three days of festivities at Saint Barbara's Market, Daiza dos Sapateiros. *December* 8 has the celebration of Conceição de Praia, held in front of Our Lady of Conceição Church and includes candomblé, capoeira and folksingers. *December* 13: Festa de Santa Lucia, in front of the Pilar church.

HOW TO GET THERE. Salvador's 2 de Julho airport was classified as one of Brazil's international fields in 1975 and today there are regularly scheduled flights to and from Asuncion, Paraguay (*Aerolineas Paraguayas*); Frankfurt (*Lufthansa*); Lisbon (*Varig* and *Air Portugal*); Madrid (*Iberia*); and Paris (*Air France*). From Rio there are daily 90-minute flights (round trip costs about $250). There are also frequent flights from Brasilia and, of course, cities in the Northeast. Alternatives are driving or taking a 27-hour bus trip ($30 one way, or $45 on a "deluxe sleeper") up the good highway from Rio, or calling on one of the cruise or cargo ships that stops here.

HOW TO GET AROUND. Buses are overcrowded, dirty, and never on schedule. Taxis are plentiful and cheap, but bargain first if you're going to use one by the day. You should be able to make a deal for around $15 to $20. There are tourist agencies with cars for hire at $20 to $30 for the day, and your hotel can usually supply you with a limousine and an English-speaking driver. But the best way to see most of the city is just to get out and walk around the old streets. Nothing will happen to you. You're a lot safer in the back streets of Bahia than you are in New York or London. You can charter a native schooner for a day's cruise of the bay for $150 to $250, from either *L.R. Turismo* at Av. Sete de Setembro 540 or *Panorama Turismo*, Rua Marquês de Caravelas 110. Both have group rates for the bay trips and L.R. Turismo offers excellent tours of the old city during the day.

HOTELS. Outside Rio, Brazil's biggest spurt in construction of tourist-type hotels has taken place in Bahia. The Quatro Rodas Salvador is an excellent luxury hotel located near the beach on Rua Pasargada. Other top hotels are the Meridien and Othon Palace, which opened in 1976 and 1975. Alternate choices are the charming little (70 rooms) Pousada do Convento do Carmo downtown or the 164-room beachfront Salvador Praia, both also opened in 1975. Nearby Itaparica Island offers the Club Mediterranée in a secluded setting with nonstop activities and two other fine hotels. *Deluxe* hotels charge from $70 to $95; *Expensive* hotels range from $45 to $70, *Moderate* hotels range from $15 to $45, and *Inexpensive* hotels are $15 or less.

Deluxe

Bahia Othon Palace, Av. Presidente Vargas 2456 on Ondina Beach (247-1044). Built in a "Y" shape, with all 301 rooms facing the ocean. Swimming pool, nightclub, convention hall, sauna, and everything you'd expect in a modern new hotel. Pride of the Othon chain and one of Brazil's best.

170   BRAZIL

Club Mediterranée, (833–1141). The only Club Med in Brazil so far (another is now being built near Rio), it is located on the largest and most scenic of the many islands in Salvador's bay. The club follows the general style of Club Meds worldwide, with every type of activity imaginable. Reservations must be made in advance and can be made at offices in Rio (224–9337) or São Paulo (813–7311).

Meridien Bahia, Rua Fonte de Bahia 216 (248–8011). Overlooking the ocean, 30 minutes from the airport, 15 minutes from downtown Salvador, deluxe class, 502 rooms including 2 deluxe suites, 77 suites, and 27 cabanas. Conference and banquet facilities. Congress hall equipped with audio-visual aids and for simultaneous translation; 5 meeting rooms. Panoramic restaurants and bars at the top. Discothéque, beauty parlor, sauna, solarium, sea- and fresh-water swimming pools, tennis, marina, boutiques.

Quatro Rodas Salvador, Farol de Itapua on Itapua Beach (249–9611). Only five years old, this hotel is the latest addition to the Quatro Rodas chain, the best in the northeast. It has two excellent restaurants, an ocean-view rooftop nightclub, beach, pool, and a bar on the banks of a manmade lagoon. The hotel also possesses several tennis courts and an auditorium where many of Brazil's top singing stars perform. Like the other Quatro Rodas hotels in the northeast, the Salvador hotel also has a satellite dish for live reception of American television programs

Expensive

Enseada das Lages, Av. Presidente Vargas 511 (237–1027). Another new beachfront hotel with pool, bar, and restaurant.

Grande Hotel de Barra, Av. 7 de Setembro 3564 (247–6011). Beachfront at harbor entrance. Calm waters for swimming. Air-conditioned.

Luxor Convento do Carmo, (242–3111). Largo do Carmo, in the heart of the old section of Salvador. A restored former convent whose cells have been made into hotel rooms with wooden floors and ceilings lighted by rustic lanterns. Small swimming pool in inner courtyard. Chapel and art gallery in same building. Lots of atmosphere.

Marazul, Av. 7 de Setembro 3937 (235–2110). On the beach, this fine new hotel has a pool and one of Salvador's best restaurants.

Maritim Hotel Clube, at Praia do Forte (241–1184 in Salvador). On the beach, with many activities à la Club Med.

Salvador Praia, Av. Presidente Vargas 2238-Ondina Beach (245–5033). Pool, bar, restaurant, convention rooms. Mural by famous Brazilian painter Caribé and sculpture by Mario Cravo dominate the lobby.

Moderate

Bahia do Sol, Av. 7 de Setembro 2009 (247–7211). 84 rooms.

Bahia Praia, Av. Presidente Vargas 2483 (247–4122). 40 rooms, restaurant.

Belmar, Av. Otavio Mangabeira (231–2422). 48 rooms, pool, restaurant.

Galeao Sacramento, on Itaparica Island (833–1022). In the island's village known as Mar Grande, this small (12 rooms) hotel is new and spectacular. One of the best small hotels in Brazil. Pool, beach, bar, and restaurant.

Grande Hotel de Barra, Av. 7 de Setembro 3564 (247–6011). 120 rooms, pool, and restaurant. Near beach.

Hotel do Farol, Av. Presidente Vargas 68 (247–7611). Close to the beach, pool, restaurant.

Itapoa Praia, Rua Dias Gomes 17 (249–9988). 72 rooms with pool and restaurant.

Ondina Praia, Av. Presidente Vargas across from Ondina Beach (247–1033). Modern, with pool, bar, and restaurant.

BAHIA

Praia do Sol, Av. Otavio Mangabeira (231–0760). 84 rooms, pool, restaurant.
Praiamar, Av. 7 de Setembro 3577 (247–7011). 171 rooms, close to the beach, pool, and restaurant.
Vela Branca, Av. Antonio Carlos Magalhães on Pituba Beach (248–7022). Modern, motel-type accommodations with bar, restaurant, pool.
Vila Velha, Av. 7 de Setembro 1971 (247–8722). 98 rooms.

Inexpensive

Armaçao, Av. Otavio Mangabeira (231–2722). 58 rooms, restaurant.
Barra Turismo, Av. 7 de Setembro 3691 (245–7433), 60 rooms.
Paulus, Av. Otavio Mangabeira (248–5722). 77 rooms, pool, bar.
Pelorinho, Rua Alfedo de Brito 20 (242–4144). Restaurant. Located in historical old city.
Solar da Barra, Av. 7 de Setembro 2998 (247–4917). 18 rooms.
Villa Romana, Rua Professor Lemos de Brito 14 (247–6522). 52 rooms, pool, and restaurant.

RESTAURANTS. If you want to sample local dishes ask for: *Acaraje,* dumplings with bean mash; *vatapa,* a fish stew; *caruru,* a type of shrimp creole; *ximxim de galinha,* chicken cooked with peanuts and coconut; *muqueca de peixe,* fish creole; *Camaroes a baiano,* shrimp creole; *frigadeira de camarao,* spicy shrimp omelette; *efu,* stew with beef tongue and shrimp, traditionally served during candomblé (voodoo) services; *sarapatel,* a stew of pork intestines, tripe, brains, kidney cooked in a pig's blood—not for the weak of stomach; *cocada,* a dessert made of coconut; *quindins,* an egg and coconut dessert. Remember all Bahian dishes are spicy and the chile peppers and sauces are extremely hot. The leading alcoholic drink is called "a batida."

Besides the typical regional food, Salvador is also famed for seafood dishes in general. Northeast Brazil is one of the best parts of the world for fresh and tasty seafood.

Our restaurant grading system has four categories: *Deluxe,* $15 and up; *Expensive,* $10 to $15; *Moderate,* $5 to $10; *Inexpensive,* under $5. These prices are for one person and do not include wine, beer, or other drinks.

For regional food the best is **Casa da Gamboa,** *Moderate,* Rua Gamboa de Cima 51, (245–9777). Also good are: **Bargaço,** *Moderate,* Rua P Quadra 43, near the convention center (231–5141); **Agdá,** Rua Orlando Moscoso 1 (231–2851); **Praiano,** *Moderate,* Av. Otavio Mangabeira (231–5988); **Ondina,** *Moderate,* Alto de Ondina (245–8263); **Velhos Marinheiros,** *Moderate,* Av. da França, (241–7817); **Iemenja,** *Moderate,* Av. Otavio Mangabeira, (231–5069); **Xeiro Verde,** *Moderate,* Av. Otavio Mangabeira 929 (248–5158); **Senac,** *Inexpensive,* Largo do Pelourinho 13/19 (242–5503).

Don't fail to try a *muqueca mixta* (mixed seafood dish) at the **Limpião,** *Expensive,* at the Bahia Othon Palace, or almost any dish at the **Forno e Fogão,** *Moderate,* at the Pousada do Carmo. **Solar do Unhão,** on the shoreline of Av. do Contorno and expensive, was originally a slaves' quarters in the 18th century, and is worth a visit.

For international cuisine, try: **Le Saint Honore,** *Expensive,* French nouveau cuisine at the Meridien Hotel (248–8011); **Bernard,** *Expensive,* also French, Rua Gamboa da Cima 11 (245–9402); **Chez Bouillon,** *Expensive,* Av. 7 de Setembro, French (247–7947); **Cidade do Salvador,** *Moderate,* international, at the Quatro Rodas Hotel (249–9611); **Porto Seguro,** *Moderate,* international, the Salvador Praia Hotel, Av. Presidente Vargas 2338 (245–5033); **Chaillot,** *Expensive,* international, Av. Presidente Vargas 3305 (247–6309); **Di Liana,** *Moder-*

ate, Italian, Estrada para Arembepe, near the airport, (891–1007); **Don Guiseppe,** *Moderate,* Italian, Rua Marques de Leão 547 (245–4470); **Il Forno,** *Inexpensive,* a good pizzeria, Rua Marques de Leão 77 (247–7287). The Barra neighborhood, center of Salvador nightlife, has several pizzerias and snack restaurants.

For seafood: **Enseada das Lages,** *Moderate,* in the hotel of the same name (237–1027); **Byblos,** *Moderate,* Rua Barão de Sergy 156 (247–4025); **Frutos do Mar,** *Moderate,* Rua Marques de Leão 415 (245–6479).

While fish dishes are the top attraction in Salvador, if you want a break, the best churrascaria (steak house) is **Baby Beef,** *Moderate,* Av. Antonio Carlos Magalhães, near the Iguatemi Shopping Center (244–0811). Also **Roda Vida,** *Moderate,* Av. Otavio Mangabeira (248–3499).

USEFUL ADDRESSES. *U.S. Consulate,* Av. Presidente Vargas 1892, first floor (245–6691). In addition to the consulate there is a *U.S. Information Service Office* in the Edificio Casa Blanca, Av. 7 de Setembro 333. *The American Society of Bahia,* tel: 8–0073. *Police;* Radio Patrol: Dial 190. *Medical facilities:* Pronto Socorr, tel: 5–0000.

Bahiatursa (Bahia State Tourist Board) has several information booths at the airport, bus terminal, and Mercado Modelo, among others. Its main information center is at Belvedere da Se (241–4333).

WHAT TO SEE. Spread out over the length and breadth of this intriguing city are dozens of things that belong on your itinerary. The most important are: Agua de Meninos market, steep streets of Pelourinho, and Baixa dos Sapateiros, the Praça Terreiro de Jesus artisans market Sundays, the Lacerda elevator between the city's upper and lower levels, the harbor filled with multicolored sail fishing boats, the lighthouses and the old forts, the churches with special emphasis on São Francisco and Bonfim, the museums of Modern Art and Sacred Art, the beaches with the fishermen and their nets, the lagoon of Abaeté, the artists at work, a capoeira fight, and most definitely a candomblé ceremony

Candomblé is the term adopted in Bahia for the religious ceremony of African origin, which are called in Rio de Janeiro "Macumba," and "Xango" in Recife. In Salvador, these cults have been preserved in almost original form and are a vital part of the culture. Ceremonies honoring the various divinities, called "orixas," are held in temples called "terreiros." These consist of a large room for public ceremonies, with various smaller rooms or huts for other ceremonial purposes. Visitors may attend the public ceremonies, which are usually held on Sun. nights around 8:30 P.M. Some of the most important "candomblé" terreiros are: Federação de Culto Afro-Brasileiro, Rua Carlos Gomes 17, 2nd floor (241–0145); Bogum, Ladeira de Bogum 35; Menininha do Gantois, Alto de Gantois 23; Olga de Alaketo, Av. Alasketo 69. Call Bahiatursa for information on how to get to the temples and what god is being celebrated. It is always best to be accompanied by a guide and most tour operators offer a visit to a candomblé temple.

MUSEUMS. Museu de Arte da Bahia, located at Av. 7 de Setembro 2340 (235–9492), open Tues. to Sun., from 2 to 6 P.M. Ceramics, chinaware, ornamental tiles, antique furniture. **Museu de Arte Sacra,** Rua do Sodre (243–6310). Open Tues. to Sat., 10–11:30 A.M., 2–5:30 P.M. An outstanding

BAHIA

collection of figures of saints and other religious art. **Museu Carlos Costa Pinto,** Av. 7 de Setembro 2490 (247–6081). Open Wed. to Mon., 1–7 P.M. Antique furniture, Baccarat crystal, jewelry, china, silverware, and paintings. Also collection of "balangandães" (silver charms). **Museu de Arte Moderna,** at the Solar Unhao (243–6174). Open Tues. to Fri., 11 A.M.–6 P.M., Sat. to Sun. 1–6 A.M. Expositions of paintings only when announced—no permanent collection. **Museu do Carmo.** Located in the Convento do Carmo (242–0182). Open every day 8 A.M.–12 Noon, 2–6 P.M. Vestments and other religious art objects. **Museu Abelardo Rodrigues,** Solar do Ferrão, Rua Gregório de Mattos, 45 (242–6155 ext. 61). Open Mon. to Fri. 10–11:30 A.M.; 2–5 P.M.; Sat. and Sun., 2–5 P.M. Religious and folk art. **Museo da Cidade,** Pelourinho 3 (242–8773), open every day 8 A.M.–12 noon, 2–6 P.M., has an interesting collection of figures of Orixas or deities venerated in the *Camdomblé* rites with their costumes and weapons; also the world's largest collection of ceremonial women's headgear of African origin.

SPORTS. Salvador has miles of beautiful beaches. The cleanest and most attractive tend also to be the most distant, located beyond the district of Pituba. Because it is ideal for children, "Pla-K-For" is a favorite of Americans. This beach, like others, can be reached by bus. With luck you may see fishermen pulling in their big nets at beaches named "Praia Chega Nego," across the Aero Club, "Piata" and "Itapoa."

Capoeira, originally an African way of fighting with the feet, was developed in the days when slaves were forbidden to use their fists or carry weapons. Now it is preserved in a very acrobatic form of dance, accompanied by the typical instrument known as the "berimbau," tamborines, drums and other percussion instruments. Shows are given by the following "schools" under the direction of the Master, whose name the school bears: *Mestre Bimba* (located in the Nordeste de Amarlina) on Tues., Thurs., and Sat. at 8 P.M. *Academia de Capoeira Angola,* Rua Dr. J.J. Seabra 354, in the old colonial city. *Mestre Curio,* Tues.-Thur. and Sat. 7:30–9:30 P.M.

ART GALLERIES. Atelier Renot, Av. Sete de Setembro 437, Barra. Tapestries. **Galeria Canizares,** Av. Araujo Pinho 15, Canela. Works by students and other artists. **Kennedy Galeria de Arte,** Av. Sete de Setembro 283. Tapestries and paintings. **Sue Galeria de Arte,** Av. Sete de Setembro 30. Works of touristic subjects.

Many artists in Bahia maintain exhibits at their studios, although getting in touch with them can be difficult. Ask at the galleries about visiting a particular artist. A number of them speak English. **Carybe,** Rua Medeiros Neto 9, Brotas. Drawings and paintings. **Fernando Coelho,** Parque Florestal, Brotas, Rua Waldemar Falcao. Paintings. **Floriano Teixeira,** Rua Ilheus 33, Rio Vermelho. Paintings. **Hansen-Bahia,** Jardim Jaguaripe, Piata. Woodcut engravings. **Jenner Augusto,** Rua Bartolomeu de Gusmão 7, Rio Vermelho. Paintings. **Mario Cravo Jr.,** Rua Caetano Moura 39, Federacão. Sculptures in metal and plastic. **Mirabeau Sampaio,** Rua Ary Barroso 12. Sculptures and drawings. **Walter Sa Nenezes,** Av. Tiradentes, Roma. Paintings.

SHOPPING. The most typical souvenirs of Bahia are the "balangandães" (singular, "balangandã"), a macumba cluster of gourds, fruit, and a *figa* in silver or alloyed with tin. Also typical are the many items carved from "jacaranda," the Brazilian rosewood. For these try: **Gerson Artesanato de Prata Ltda.**, ground floor of the Convento do Carmo. **Penintenciaria do Estado,** Lemos Britto (State Prison), located in Mata Escura do Retiro, accessible by car or taxi only. All prices are clearly labeled at the **Instituto Maua,** Av. Sete de Setembro 261, while bargaining is widely practiced at other places. For antiques, wooden figures of saints, furniture, etc., walk along Rua Ruy Barbosa off Avenida Sete de Setembro, near the Cinema Guarani and the "A Tarde" building. Especially reliable are: **Casa Moreira,** Rua Visconde do Rio Branco 1, behind the City Hall, **José Pedreira,** Alameda Antunes 7, Barra Avenida, or any number of shops along Rua Ruy Barbosa, roughly between numbers 30 and 65. The modern **Shopping Center Iguatemi,** with all types of shops and restaurants, is well worth a visit. It is located at Largo da Mariquita 3 in the Rio Vermelho district.

NIGHTLIFE. The folklore of Bahia is rich and varied and Salvador has several fine folklore shows which will give you a good idea of what to expect should you later decide to visit a candomblé ceremony or a capoeira show. The best folklore show is at the **Solar do Unhao** restaurant, where you will also be treated to a delicious meal. Av. Contorno (245–5551), daily, with the show starting at 10 P.M. Other nightclubs and restaurants with folklore shows are: **Senac,** a vocational school for waiters and cooks that has a fine combination of good, inexpensive food, a folklore show, plus exhibits of Bahian artsts; Largo do Pelourinho 19 (242–5503); **Tenda dos Milagres,** restaurant with show, Av. Amaralina 553 (248–6058); **A Moenda,** restaurant with show, Rua P. Quadra 28 (231–7915); **Teatro de Ondina,** show, Alto de Ondina (247–4599).

Bahia is also home to some of the best Brazilian popular music and there are several small bars and nightclubs, especially in the Barra neighborhood, with live music—samba and bossa nova. The best for live music are: **Bistro 507,** Av. Sete de Setembro 507 (Barra); **Clube 45,** Rua Barão de Sergy 196 (Barra); **Bistro do Luis,** Rua Conselheiro Pedro Luis 369; **Kazebre 40,** Av. Otavio Mangabeira (Barra); **Queen's,** Rua Barão de Sergy 67 (Barra). Besides Barra, the nearby neighborhoods of Rio Vermelho and Pituba also have several fine bars with live Brazilian music, most of them located along the beach.

In Salvador as throughout Brazil, nightlife usually starts with a beer and conversation at an outdoor café. The top meeting places are **Berro d'Agua,** Rua Barão de Sergy 27-A (Barra); **Manga Rosa,** Rua Cezar Zama 60 (Barra); **Graffiti,** Rua Odorico Odilon 41 (Rio Vermelho); and **Bar 68,** Largo da Santana 3 (Rio Vermelho).

THE STATE OF BAHIA

For the moment tourism in the state is centered in Salvador, with day trips possible to the historical city of Cachoeira and the beaches north of the city. Beyond these two areas, any trips must be at least overnight. The best attractions are the Paulo Afonso Falls along the São Francisco River, the southern Bahia city of Ilheus, capital of the

BAHIA 175

cocoa market of which Bahia is the world's second largest producer, the hot springs resort of Caldas do Jorro, and the highlands area of Lençois.

Paulo Afonso

Paulo Afonso, besides the beautiful falls of the same name, also offers a look at an inland area of Brazil that is now being turned from desert into fertile farmland thanks to a massive irrigation project. The São Francisco River, Brazil's second largest after the Amazon, is to the country what the Mississippi is to the United States in terms of history and legend. Until the 1970s it was possible for tourists to book passage on the river boats that still ply the São Francisco, passing through most of the Northeast. Now, however, there is only one remaining boat trip for tourists, close to Paulo Afonso, which travels down the river on a day trip, passing through the locks in the area of the Paulo Afonso Falls and hydroelectric project. For information check with L.R. Turismo in Salvador. (See How To Get Around under *Practical Information for Salvador.*)

Ilhéus

In Ilhéus, besides the city's beaches, which are not quite as good as those of Salvador, the city is also a living monument to Brazil's greatest fiction writer, Jorge Amado, one of the giants of Latin American literature, whose best known novel *Gabriela* was set in this city.

Caldas do Jorro

Located three hours' driving time northwest of Salvador, the hot springs resort town of Caldas do Jorro is an oasis in the heart of the arid sertão region of Bahia. The springs and mineral water that have made Caldas famous in the northeast were discovered by accident when a Brazilian oil company was drilling for petroleum in the area in 1948 and instead of black gold hit a geyser of hot water. Word spread throughout the region that the water was miraculous, capable of curing all ills. The result was an invasion of tenant farmers and northeastern cowboys from the poor rural areas, all seeking miracle cures. Legends have since sprung up that paralysis victims have been cured by the magic waters of Caldas do Jorro. Today, Caldas retains its miracle image, but the hot springs have also attracted wealthy residents of Salvador and other cities in the northeast, giving it the air of a Bahian Lourdes. The poor mix with the rich at the city's Sunday outdoor market, where products of the rural area of the northeast and Bahia are sold.

Lençóis

Lençòis, on the high Chapada Diamantina plateau, was the diamond capital of Brazil in the 19th century. The city's name means "sheets" and comes from the observation that the first diamond prospectors' improvised tents seen from the surrounding hills looked like sheets stretched out to dry in the sun. Vestiges of the mining days are everywhere. The city's streets are paved with rock that was quarried in the search for diamonds and stone pathways lead up into the hills, where jumbled piles of broken rock and abandoned equipment are slowly being covered over by vegetation.

Fortunes were made and lost and when the diamonds were all mined out, those who had been lucky moved away, leaving behind the homes they had built—frequently out of material brought in by mule—in the Brazilian colonial style. Despite its distance from any larger city, in its heyday Lençóis had much contact with the outside world and its culture, fashion, and social life. But when the wealthy left, there was little contact with the "outside world" and for those who stayed, time stood still.

The city's decline preserved its old houses and stone streets until now and the government has made it a historical monument. Adding to the feeling that you have journeyed to a past era are the hospitable residents, who still lead a very simple traditional lifestyle and always seem to have time for a chat.

Besides the colonial charm of Lençóis itself, there is much natural beauty in the surrounding area. During the dryer winter months you can walk up the edge of the rock river bed, where women wash clothes and spread them out to dry on the rocks, to the ridge above, where the Chapada Diamantina National Park begins. Along the way are cascades and caves where artisans collect different colored sands, which they use to "paint" pictures in bottles. Day excursions can be made to several caves. Hiking in five miles from the nearest road, a local guide can take you to the spectacular Glass waterfall, which drops 1,330 feet amidst lush vegetation. Follow the stone trails that the miners and their mules once used, which will lead you to breathtaking lookouts, or drive to the Lagoa Encantada (Enchanted Lake).

PRACTICAL INFORMATION FOR STATE OF BAHIA

For definitions of price categories see *Planning Your Trip*.

PAULO AFONSO
(260 miles north of Salvador)

HOTEL. Grande Hotel de Paulo Afonso, *Moderate,* the best hotel in the city with restaurant, bar and pool (281–1914).

ILHEUS
(240 miles south of Salvador)

HOTELS. This city of 130,000 has three good hotels: **Ilheus Praia,** *Moderate,* bar, restaurant, and pool, Praça Dom Eduardo (231–2533); **Pontal Praia,** *Inexpensive,* bar, restaurant, and pool, Av. Lomanto Jr. 1358 (231–3033); **Britania,** *Inexpensive,* Rua 28 de Junho 16 (231–1722).

CALDAS DO JORRO
(153 miles northwest of Salvador)

HOTELS. Pousada do Jorro, *Moderate,* a resort-style hotel with pool, bar, and restaurant, Praça Antonio Carlos Magalhães (256–1146); **Caldas Palace Hotel,** *Inexpensive,* Av. José Carlos Arléo (256–1103); **Biliu,** *Inexpensive,* Praça Ana Oliveira, 27 (256–1148). All hotels include meals in their room rate.

LENÇÓIS
(240 miles west of Salvador)

HOTELS. Pousada de Lençóis, *Moderate,* Rua Altina Alves 747. Reservations in Salvador, (071) 233-9395. The hotel can provide transportation and guides for excursions.

THE NORTHEAST

The area known as the Northeast begins in Bahia and extends to the edge of the Amazon in the north, taking in that part of the nation that bulges out into the Atlantic Ocean up north. In addition to Bahia the region is composed of the states of Sergipe, Alagoas, Pernambuco, Paraiba, Rio Grande do Norte, Ceará, Piaui, and Maranhão. Although they are all part of the same region, the other states differ markedly from Bahia in that they have little of the African influence that makes Bahia so distinct. North of Bahia, the influence is predominantly European. With the passage of the centuries, however, even this influence has diminished and today the Northeast of Brazil has its own culture and characteristics, born of the geographical and climatic peculiarities of this region.

The main one of these is the tendency of the region to alternate between drought and flood. The arid interior area, known as the sertão, is prone to periodic droughts, which have driven many of its residents to the cities of the south in search of employment. The last, and worst, of these droughts ended after a five-year run in 1984. And when the rains come, they come in torrents—in 1985–86 the same area that had been stricken by drought was subject to massive flooding. Despite its problems, however, the interior of the Northeast may yet prove to be a vital food-producing area for Brazil. The success of irrigation projects in Bahia has encouraged the government to invest its money plus funds

BRAZIL

from the World Bank in a multi-billion dollar irrigation project for the rest of the Northeast in an effort to make the desert bloom.

But while the inland area of the Northeast is one of the poorest and most backward in Brazil, the coastal region is fertile and safe from drought. For the tourist this combination offers some of the most picturesque sights in Brazil. There are the jangada fishing boats, little more than balsa-wood rafts with a single sail, that brave the Atlantic with lone fishermen aboard, forts and churches, literally hundreds of miles of uninterrupted virgin beaches, women weaving fine lace, leather-clad northeastern cowboys who yearly face the searing heat of the interior, clay sculptors, and finally, for aficionados, the best shrimp, lobster, and seafood eating that you will find anywhere in the Americas.

Away from the state capitals, most located along the coast, you will find it rough going, but the recent discovery of the Northeast by European tourists—mainly the Germans, Swiss, French, and Austrians—has led to a building spree of hotels and restaurants of international quality on the coast. Here, mainly in the cities of Maceio, Recife, Fortaleza, and São Luis, you will discover an enchanting combination of warm weather, excellent beaches (the ocean water temperature in the Northeast is warm year-round), good hotels, and top quality restaurants, all at prices that today make the Northeast one of the great bargain destinations in the world.

Maceio

The present boom city in northeast tourism is Maceio, capital of the state of Alagoas. The state has long been famous for its 150-mile coastline, which the experts claim has the finest beaches in Brazil. Until recently, however, there was little in the way of basic comforts to greet the international tourist. Fortunately, things have changed, with new hotels already built and others on the way.

Like the other major coastal cities of the Northeast, Maceio combines its colonial past with the beauty of its natural setting. This is a place to relax and take it easy, enjoying the beaches and taking long walks through the city. On the mainland side of the city are several large, beautiful lakes which can be visited by taxi. This is a good outing for lunch as there are several fine restaurants along the Mundau Lake. The best beaches are just north of the city's limits and it is here also that the newest hotels have been built. Colonial buildings and churches can be seen in the center of the city around the Praça Dom Pedro II, a public square.

Recife

North of Maceio is the state of Pernambuco, whose capital Recife is also the true capital of the Brazilian Northeast. The sixth largest city in Brazil, with a population of 1.5 million, Recife is a vibrant metropolis whose spirit is halfway between the modern cities of the south and the more traditional centers of the Northeast, a combination of old and new that makes the city both an example of the past and a window on

THE NORTHEAST   181

the future. If you have time for only one stop in the Northeast, make it Recife.

Known as the Venice of Brazil because it is built on three rivers and connected by a host of bridges, Recife got its name from the reefs that line the coast and make the city's most popular beach, Boa Viagem, also one of the more unusual bathing spots in Brazil.

In the morning, when the tide is in, the waves come up almost to the road, then as the tide recedes, the rocks of the reefs slowly appear. Depending on the time of the day, individual swimming pools are formed, fish flap around the bathers, and the hidden rock formations dry into odd colors in the afternoon sun.

Another sight to see along this beach is the departure (about 6 A.M.) or the return (about 2 P.M.) of the *jangadas,* those crude, log rafts with the beautiful sails that local fishermen take out onto the high seas. Many stories and legends have been written about them, and they are as dangerous as they look. Only an expert navigator and swimmer should try one. It looks easy for the sunburnt men of Recife, but they have been working on them all their lives.

Boa Viagem for the residents of Recife is what Copacabana and Ipanema beaches are for Rio's citizens—the center of social life. On the weekends the beach is packed and at night the many restaurants, bars, and sidewalk cafes turn Boa Viagem into a glittering center of nightlife, the top spot in the Northeast for a night on the town.

Recife and Pernambuco were at one time part of the Dutch colonial empire until the Portuguese from the south of Brazil drove them out. The influence of the two European colonial powers is evident in the city's many fine churches. In the downtown area of Recife is the convent and church of Saint Anthony with the famed Gold Chapel, a baroque design covered in gold leaf and one of the most important and beautiful examples of religious art in Brazil. Other colonial-era churches in the center of Recife are the Church of the Blessed Sacrament, built in 1753, the Basilica of Our Lady of Carmo (1687), the Cathedral of the Clergymen of Saint Peter with the adjoining Saint Peter's Courtyard, where there are bars, restaurants, antique and handicraft shops (these three churches are all located on Av. Dantas Barreto), and the Basilica of Our Lady Penha (1656), on Rua da Penha. While you are downtown you should also visit the Cinco Pontas Fort, built by the Dutch in 1630 and today home to the city museum, and the Pernambuco Culture Center, built as a prison in the 19th century but now the best regional crafts center of the Northeast, offering a multitude of shops (located in the former prison cells) showing the wares of the region as well as performances of northeastern dances and music.

But the best of the old Northeast is preserved in the ex-colonial capital of Olinda, today a suburb of Recife, a half hour from downtown. In recent years Olinda has enjoyed a renaissance, taking on a life of its own after it was declared a world historical monument by UNESCO. Built on a series of hills overlooking the ocean, Olinda is remarkably well preserved, with its narrow, winding streets snaking up and down the hills and offering at every turn spectacular views of the ocean and Recife in the distance while up close you see the historical past of the Northeast in the colonial churches and homes of Olinda.

BRAZIL

The city was built by the Dutch during their brief turn at running Pernambuco in the 1600s. Many of the houses still have the original latticed balconies, heavy doors, and pink stucco walls, evoking the colonial period. Residents of the city are forbidden to change its architecture or to construct any new buildings that would not be compatible with the colonial motif. The result is a beautiful, compact city where the white, pink, and red of the homes and tile roofs stand against the rich green of the heavily landscaped hills and the blue of the ocean below. Give yourself plenty of time to explore Olinda by foot and if you can don't miss the sunset from here. You won't forget it.

The top attractions in Olinda are the Church of Our Lady Carmo, built in 1588; the Convent of Our Lady Neves (1585), the first Franciscan church in Brazil; the Seminary of Olinda, (1584), the Cathedral (1537), with an extraordinarily beautiful view; the Pernambucan Museum of Sacred Art; the Misericordia Church (1540), the best preserved and most impressive of Olinda's churches; the Ribeira Market, where handmade goods are sold; the Museum of Contemporary Art housed in an 18th century building; and the São Bento Monastery (1582), the first law school in Brazil. The highest point in Olinda, the Alto da Sé, is also the city's social center. Here, by day, several stands sell regional art and handicrafts, while at night on the weekends the square is packed with young people from Recife and Olinda and tourists attracted by the convivial nature of the milling crowds moving back and forth between several small bars that open at night on top of the hill.

At Alto da Sé and also at the downtown Culture Center, you will notice small clay statuettes for sale. Almost all of these are made in the interior town of Caruaru, considered the leading handicrafts center of South America. Reached by daily bus or special taxis on Wednesdays and Saturdays, the days of the fair, the trip is well worth it. Not only will you be able to see a very colorful interior market place, but you'll be able to rub elbows with the leather-clad cowboys of the harsh, dry region, see the way the people live on the parched soil, and be entertained by strolling musicians and dancers. Allow one full day for this.

Near the Recife-Olinda area is the historical city of Igarassu, which among its colonial buildings numbers the oldest church in Brazil, the Church of Saints Cosme and Damião. Also worth a visit is the island of Itamaracá, famed for its beaches and site of a fort built by the Dutch. Both Igarassu and Itamaracá can be visited in day trips from Recife or Olinda.

Farther away but just as interesting is the interior city of Nova Jerusalem, a replica of the city of Jerusalem of Biblical times that has been constructed to serve as an immense open air theater where, every Easter, the Northeast is home to one of the world's more remarkable passion plays. Nova Jerusalem is located 30 miles from Caruaru and is a must if you decide to visit the famous Caruaru fair; plan on spending the night in Caruaru. While in Nova Jerusalem you should also visit the Statue Park, where Northeastern artists have sculpted lifesize granite statues of typical and historical figures of the region.

Parties are also a part of the Northeastern lifestyle—the two biggest blowouts in the region are Carnival and the saints days during the month of June. For Carnival, Olinda has acquired a reputation as fun

THE NORTHEAST 183

capital of the Northeast. Each year through its narrow streets thousands of revelers dance all day and all night, performing the frevo, a regional dance that requires its performers to defy both gravity and human endurance. In the month of June on the days of the most popular saints, block parties are held throughout Recife, where a traditional dance called the *quadrilha,* similar to American square dancing, is performed.

João Pessoa and Natal

North of Recife is the city of João Pessoa, capital of the state of Paraiba and another site of fine beaches. The city has one of the best hotels in the region, the Tambaú, part of the excellent Tropical hotel chain owned by Varig Airlines. Beyond João Pessoa is the city of Natal, capital of Rio Grande do Norte. Besides warm water and good beaches, Natal is also known for its miles of sand dunes that run along the ocean.

Fortaleza

Capital of the state of Ceará, this city of 1.8 million, fifth largest in Brazil, has fallen on hard times lately, the result of the region's most recent drought which drove thousands of impoverished tenant farmers from the interior into the city. Because of this Fortaleza has not yet been able to live up to its tourism potential, but there is no question that in the near future the city will be making its name known outside of Brazil. The reason for this is that even in hard times, Fortaleza has excellent attractions—fine beaches and even better ones located nearby, the best lobster fishing and eating in Brazil, and the top lace industry in the country. The city is also on its way to becoming a world-class fashion center, thanks to the combination of abundant raw materials and cheap manpower. These two factors have already permitted Fortaleza fashion designers to challenge their big city rivals in Rio and São Paulo and today one of Brazil's most important fashion fairs takes place annually in Fortaleza in April.

Due south of Fortaleza on the coast is the city of Aracati, Ceará's most famed lace center where you will see little girls just three years old learning to thread a needle and unravel snarled thread, as well as aging grandmothers almost blind from the years of close, delicate labor. Close to Aracati are Ceará's best beaches, most notably Canoa Quebrada, with white sand dunes and crystal clear turquoise waters. This area is still little explored for tourism, a fact that complicates visits but also guarantees the survival for the moment of an area of rare primitive beauty.

São Luis

The last major city along the coast of the Northeast, São Luis, capital of the state of Maranhão, is also the poorest. While this does not detract from the beauty of its beaches, the biggest in the region, it has unfortunately complicated efforts by local officials to preserve the city's historical heritage. Many of the colonial buildings in the old part of the city, some of them still covered with 18th century French and Portuguese tiles, are today in desperate need of preservation, a fact recognized by local authorities who are, sad to say, handcuffed by a lack of funds. For that reason what is one of the largest areas of colonial buildings in Brazil is slowly wasting away. For the time being, however, it is still worth taking a walk through the old town, where you will see the colonial homes and buildings with their colorful tiles (all buildings in São Luis today have these tiles but most of them were added recently to maintain the colonial spirit of the city; only the historical buildings still have Portuguese and French tiles from the 18th century), as well as wrought iron balconies.

The city of São Luis is located on an island; on the mainland is another colonial relic, the city of Alcantara, today a national monument where the colonial ruins are maintained. Access to Alcantara, 15 miles away from São Luis, is by boat or private plane since the only road link is a precarious dirt strip that can take up to a day's journey. Boats leave daily from downtown São Luis but these are primitive fishing boats suitable only for the adventuresome. A catamaran also makes the trip and is far more comfortable and reliable, although the trip is made only with groups (contact Taguatur Turismo at 222–6658).

São Luis is known for its folklore presentations, which are considered the most authentic of the Northeast. The principal one is called *bumba-meu-boi,* an involved dance drama which reenacts a folk tale with colorfully costumed dancers. The same dance is performed throughout the Northeast but São Luis in particular is famed for the beauty of the costumes of the dancers. The city is also home to the *Tambor de Mina,* a voodoo ceremony that has generated a dance-ritual called *Tambor de Criolo.* These African religious rites were brought from the Caribbean by slaves and are the only ones in Brazil that are similar to the voodoo ceremonies of Haiti in their use of dolls and pins.

PRACTICAL INFORMATION FOR THE NORTHEAST

For definitions of price categories, see *Planning Your Trip.*

WHEN TO GO. The weather in the Northeast is good all year long, with the temperature and humidity increasing as you go north, nearing the equator and the Amazon. The rainy season usually begins in Apr. and continues through June, although in São Luis there is daily rainfall starting in Sept. Rains in the Northeast tend to be torrential and can lead to flooding in the downtown areas of the cities, so if possible avoid the rainy season. The best time to come is between Jan. and Apr.; for Carnival the top location is Recife-Olinda. Although the sea breeze keeps the temperatures of the coastal cities at pleasant levels, in the interior areas of the Northeast it can get extremely hot.

HOW TO GET THERE. The capital cities are all served by Brazil's major airlines, *Varig, Vasp, Cruzeiro,* and *Transbrasil.* The highways along the coast are also good up to Fortaleza. From Fortaleza to São Luis, however, you are better off flying, as the road connections are poor. Buses serve the entire region and bus transportation is the most popular way of travel from one capital to another. Recife has an international airport and receives charter flights from

THE NORTHEAST

Europe and Canada plus regularly scheduled flights from Miami *(Varig)* and Lisbon *(Air Portugal)*. For the adventuresome there is a highway that cuts through the jungle between Brasilia and Belem offering a fascinating look at the backlands of Brazil, including the state of Maranhão in the Northeast. There are daily buses in both directions and the trip takes three days. Comfort is minimal.

MACEIO

HOTELS. New and the best hotel in town is the **Jatiuca**, *Expensive*, Rua Lagoa da Anta 220 (231–2555). 96 rooms on the beach with pool, tennis court, restaurant and bar. Second best and also new is the **Luxor**, *Expensive*, Av. Duque de Caxias 2076 (223–7075), near the beach, pool, restaurant and bar. Other good hotels are the **Pajuçara Othon**, *Moderate*, Rua Jangadeiros Alagoanos 1292 (231–2200), with pool, restaurant, and bar; **Beira Mar**, *Moderate*, Av. Duque de Caxias 1994 (223–8022), pool, restaurant, and bar; **Enseada**, *Moderate*, Rua Antonio Gouveia 171 (231–4726), pool and bar; **Ponta Verde Praia**, *Moderate*, Av. Alvaro Octacilio 2933 (231–4040), pool, restaurant, and bar.

RESTAURANTS. Accompanying the arrival of tourism in Maceio has been the opening of several fine restaurants with excellent options for regional as well as international dishes. The best restaurants for northeastern seafood dishes are: **Restaurante das Alagoas**, *Moderate*, in the Hotel Jatiuca (231–2555); **Lagostão**, *Expensive*, Av. Duque de Caxias 1384 (221–6211) for lobster; **Restaurante do Alipio**, *Moderate*, Av. Dr. José Carneiro 321 (221–5186); **Bem**, *Moderate*, Rua João Canuto da Silva 21 (231–3316); **Peixada da Rita**, *Moderate*, Rus Antonio Baltazar, simple but excellent. For international cuisine try: **Forno e Fogão** in the Hotel Luxor, *Expensive*, (223–7075); **Aquarium**, *Moderate*, Av. Duque de Caxias 25 (223–2213); **Cactus**, *Moderate*, in the Beira Mar Hotel, Av. Duque de Caxias 1994 (223–8022); **Gstaad**, *Moderate*, Av. Robert Kennedy 2167 (231–1780), good for fondue.

RECIFE

HOTELS. Most of the top hotels in Recife are located along Boa Viagem beach, although the beach area of next-door Olinda has the new Quatro Rodas Hotel, best in the area. In Boa Viagem the newest and best is the just opened **Recife Palace**, *Deluxe*, Av. Boa Viagem 4070 (325–4044), owned and run by the same people who have Rio's excellent Rio Palace Hotel, with French restaurant and discotheque, on the beach; **Miramar**, *Deluxe*, Rua dos Navegantes 363 (326–7422), 120 air-conditioned rooms, swimming pool, bar, restaurant, and nightclub; **Internacional Othon Palace**, *Expensive*, Av. Boa Viagem 3722 (326–7225), pool, restaurant, and bar; **Mar**, *Expensive*, Rua Barão de Souza Leão 451 (341–5433), pool, bar, and restaurant, close to the beach; **Villa Rica**, *Moderate*, Av. Boa Viagem 4308, on the beach, pool, bar, and restaurant; **Boa Viagem**, *Moderate*, Av. Boa Viagem 5000 (341–4144), beach-front, pool, bar, and restaurant; **Jangadeiro**, *Moderate*, Av. Boa Viagem 3114 (326–6777), on the beach, pool, bar, and restaurant; **Savaroni**, *Moderate*, Av. Boa Viagem 3772 (325–5077), on the beach, pool, bar, and restaurant; **Park**, *Moderate*, Rua dos Navegantes 9 (325–4666), pool, bar, and restaurant; **do Sol**, *Moderate*, Av. Boa Viagem 978 (326–7644), bar, restaurant and pool, on the beach; **Casa**

BRAZIL

Grande e Senzala, *Moderate*, Av. Conselheiro Aguiar 5000 (326–0620), bar and restaurant; **Canto do Mar**, *Moderate*, Rua Barão de Souza Leão 400 (341–4400), bar and restaurant; **Coral**, *Inexpensive*, Av. Conselheiro Aguiar 4000 (325–3205), bar, restaurant, and pool; **Vela Branca**, *Inexpensive*, Av. Boa Viagem 2494 (325–4470), restaurant, on the beach; **Solimar**, *Inexpensive*, Av. Boa Viagem 1632 (326–5608), on the beach; **200 Milhas**, *Inexpensive*, Av. Boa Viagem 864 (326–5921), on the beach; **Saveiro**, *Inexpensive*, Av. Conselheiro Aguiar 4670 (325–3424); **Praiamar**, *Inexpensive*, Av. Boa Viagem 1660 (226–6488), on the beach.

In Olinda: **Quatro Rodas Olinda**, *Deluxe*, Av. José Augusto Moreira 2200 (431–2955), a top quality resort hotel on the beach with pool, tennis, two restaurants, bar, and nightclub. Best hotel in the area. Has a satellite dish for live reception of American television programs. Also **Marolinda**, *Moderate*, Av. Beira Mar 1615 (429–1699); **14-Bis**, *Inexpensive*, Av. Beira Mar 1414 (429–0409).

RESTAURANTS. Lobster and other seafoods are the highlight of Recife dining. Tops is a restaurant called, appropriately, **Lobster**, *Expensive*, Av. Boa Viagem 2612 (326–7593). Other fine seafood restaurants are: **Canto da Barra**, *Moderate*, Av. Bernardo Vieira de Melo 9150 (361–2168); **Costa do Sol**, *Moderate*, Av. Bernardo Vieira de Melo 8036 (361–1495); **Peixada do Lula**, *Moderate*, Av. Boa Viagem 244 (326–9420). For regional cooking, which in addition to lobster, shrimp, and fish includes manioc, tapioca, jerky, cornmeal dishes, chicken and sausages, try **Senzala**, *Moderate*, Av. Conselheiro Aguiar 5000 (341–0366); **Serido**, *Moderate*, Rua José Osorio 270 (227–1087); **Lapinha**, *Moderate*, Praça Boa Viagem 16, (326–1914); **O Buraco de Otilia**, *Moderate*, Rua da Aurora 1231 (231–1518); **Edmilson**, *Moderate*, Av. Maria Irene 307 (341–0644); **Chambaril do Fernando**, *Moderate*, Av. Antonio de Goes 14; **Ceia Regional**, *Moderate*, Rua Professor Andrade Bezerra 1462 (241–7664).

International cuisine is also well represented in Recife with the restaurant of the **Recife Palace Hotel**, *Expensive*, for fine French nouvelle cuisine; **da Nonna**, *Moderate*, for Italian food, Rua Cap. Fernando 198 (224–0093); **Genova**, *Moderate*, Italian, Rua Domingos Ferreira 1957 (325–4360); **Costa Brava**, *Moderate*, international, Rua Barão Souza Leão 698 (341–3535); **O Tocheiro**, *Moderate*, Praça da Bandeira 180 (227–3988), international; **La Fondue**, *Moderate*, Swiss, Rua Des. João Paes 186 (326–8659). For steak, the best are **Marruá**, *Moderate*, on the road to Olinda (241–2111); **O Laçador**, *Moderate*, Rua Visconde de Jequitinhonha 138 (326–3911); **Rodeio**, *Moderate*, Av. Boa Viagem 4780 (325–2276). The top spot for pizza is the **Pizza Pazza**, Av. Conselheiro Aguiar 2348 (326–5365).

In Olinda the best restaurants are: **Vila d'Olinda**, *Moderate*, regional and seafood in the Quatro Rodas Hotel; **L'Atelier**, *Moderate*, French, Rua Bernardo Vieira de Melo 91 (429–3099); **Mourisco**, *Moderate*, seafood, Praça João Alfredo 7 (429–1390); **Rei da Lagosta**, *Moderate*, seafood, specializing in lobster, Av. Beira Mar 1255 (429–1565).

NIGHTLIFE. Recife is easily the hot spot of the northeastern night, with the action centered on Boa Viagem beach and in Olinda. In Boa Viagem, the most popular nightspots are crowded side by side on Avenida Boa Viagem, the street that runs alongside the beach. Here you will find a wide variety of bars and sidewalk cafes that serve as the meeting places of Recife at night. In Olinda the same function is performed by the Alto da Sé, located at

THE NORTHEAST

the highest point of the hills of the colonial city, overlooking Olinda and Recife in the distance. The crowds begin gathering in the afternoon on Sat. and Sun. and the party doesn't stop until the wee hours. At Alto da Sé there are small bars, some with live music, plus tables scattered around the sidewalks where strolling vendors sell beer and snacks. The souvenir salesmen who work here during the day also stay around for the nightlife, creating a delightful bohemian mix, with artists pushing their paintings in the midst of the throngs moving constantly up and down the streets. The Northeast is also blessed with its own lively forms of popular music and folkdances but, unlike Salvador, Recife does not yet have a good restaurant-nightclub with folk shows. There is, however, an excellent dance troupe called the **Pernambucan Folk Dance Ensemble**, which has performed in Europe and the United States. Made up of young residents of Recife, the ensemble performs on the weekends at the theater of the Recife Convention Center. The lively one-hour show will give you a good idea of the variety of songs and dances that exist in the Northeast. With this in hand you should then head for what is called a forró, a nightclub that specializes in Northeastern song and dance. The best is the **Cavalo Dourado**, Rua Carlos Gomes 390. Loud and lively, forrós are Recife's answer to the fact that Carnival only comes once a year.

SHOPPING. Recife has several handicraft centers where you can find high quality leather goods, excellent ceramics, and fine lace, all at good prices. The largest handicraft center in the city is the **Casa da Cultura de Pernambuco** (Pernambuco Culture Center) at Cais da Detenção downtown. There are a multitude of shops selling products from throughout the state plus a theater, museum, and snack bars. Close by at Praça Dom Vital is the **São José Market**. Another downtown crafts center is the **Patio de São Pedro** with several shops, bars, and regional restaurants. On Sat. and Sun. starting at 1 P.M. a handicraft fair is held in the Boa Viagem Praça or square on the beach of Boa Viagem. In Olinda, the **Alto da Sé** and the **Ribeira Market** also offer a fine selection of handmade goods from the Northeast.

JOÃO PESSOA

HOTELS. Best here is the **Tambaú**, *Expensive*, 110-room circular hotel built into the sea at Av. Almirante Tamandaré 229 (226–3660). Two others with swimming pools are the **Tropicana Cabral**, *Moderate*, on Rua Alice de Azevedo (221–8445), and—on Cabo Branco (White Cape) 10 kilometers from town—the **Casa de Repouso O Nazareno**, *Inexpensive*, (226–1183). More modest is the **Aurora**, *Inexpensive*, Praça João Pessoa 51 (221–2238).

RESTAURANTS. For seafood try **Badionaldo**, *Moderate*, Rua Vitorino Cordoso (228–1441); **Peixada do João**, *Moderate*, Rua Coração de Jesus; **Elite**, *Moderate*, Av. João Mauricio 33 (226–3000); **Buzios**, *Moderate*, Av. Cabo Branco 2449.

NATAL

HOTELS. Here you'll want to stop at the **Reis Magos,** *Moderate,* half a mile from downtown on Av. Cafe Filho, on Praia (beach) do Meio (222–2055). Pool, nightclub, good restaurant. Acceptable downtown hotels are the **Ducal Palace,** *Moderate,* Av. Rio Branco 634 (222–4612); the **Sambura,** *Inexpensive,* Rua Professor Zuza 263 (222–0041); and the **Tirol,** *Inexpensive,* Av. Alexandrino de Alencar 1330 (231–4223). There are also the **Center Othon,** *Moderate,* Rua Santo Antonio 665, downtown (221–2355), bar and restaurant; the **Natal Mar,** *Moderate,* Via Costeira 8101, on the beach; pool, bar and restaurant.

RESTAURANTS. For seafood the best bets are: **Lira,** *Moderate,* Rua Pereira Simões 71 (222–6909); **Marinho,** *Moderate,* Rua do Areial 267 (222–1471); **Casa da Mae,** *Moderate,* Rua Pedro Afonso 153.

FORTALEZA

HOTELS. Most comfortable for the tourist are **Esplanada Praia,** *Expensive* (224–8555), the **Imperial Palace,** *Expensive,* (224–7777), and the **Beira Mar,** *Expensive* (224–4744), on Av. Pres. Kennedy in the Meireles district, or the **Colonial Praia,** *Moderate,* on Rua Barão de Aracati in the same area (226–7644). Closer to town is the **Iracema Plaza,** *Moderate,* Av. Pres. Kennedy 746 (231–0066). Downtown, the best is the 12-story **Savanah,** *Moderate,* Rua Major Facundo 411 at Praça do Ferreira (231–1077). Others nearby are the **San Pedro,** *Moderate,* Rua Castro e Silva 81 (231–0666); **Premier,** *Moderate,* Rua Barão do Rio Branco 829 (231–1166); **Excelsior,** *Inexpensive,* Rua Guilherme Rocha 172 (231–1533); and **Lord,** *Inexpensive,* Rua 24 de Maio 642 (231–6188).

RESTAURANTS. One of the best in town is at the **Ideal Club,** *Moderate,* on the beach. Old-world charm, with white columns and dark carved wooden balcony overlooking a grove of palm trees. The restaurant is part of the ultra chic Ideal Country club. Another private club with a good restaurant is the marble **Nautico Beach Club,** *Moderate,* Av. Abolição 2727.

Other good international restaurants: **Sandra's,** *Expensive,* Av. Perimetral; **Panela,** *Moderate,* at the Iracema Plaza hotel; the **Late** (Yacht) **Clube,** *Moderate,* Av. Matias Beck 4813 in Mucuripe. For seafood, try the following, all on Av. Pres. Kennedy along the beach: **Alfredo,** 4606, *Moderate;* **Tocantin's,** 4294, *Moderate;* **Peixada do Ceará,** 4632, *Moderate;* **Anisio,** 3990, *Moderate.*

In general the best hotels and restaurants in Fortaleza are located along the Meirelles beach on Av. President Kennedy. Bars and outdoor cafés are also here for nightlife. The nearby Praia do Futuro beach is being developed now for tourism and will offer some fine new hotels, restaurants, and bars in the near future. Unfortunately, the remainder of the city has suffered greatly from the recent economic problems of the state resulting from the last drought and today has little to offer except some rather depressing scenes of abject poverty.

THE NORTHEAST

SHOPPING. Fortaleza is famed for its lace work and here you will find intricate hammocks, lace blouses, tablecloths, and beautifully embroidered skirts, all at incredibly low prices. The best shopping areas are **Centro de Artesenato,** Av. Santos Dumont 1500 and the **Centro de Turismo,** downtown at Rua Senador Pompeu 350, open all day Sat. and until 1 P.M. on Sun.

SÃO LUIS

HOTELS. Easily the best hotel in the city is the **Quatro Rodás** *Deluxe,* Praia do Calhau (227–0244), located on the best beach in São Luis, with swimming pool, tennis courts, bar-nightclub, and one of the finest seafood restaurants in all of Brazil. Highly recommended as a getaway spot for complete relaxation. Other hotels are: **Vila Rica,** *Expensive,* Praça Dom Pedro II 299 (222–4455), downtown with pool, bar, and restaurant; **Grande Hotel São Francisco,** *Moderate,* Conjunto São Francisco (227–1155), pool, bar, and restaurant; **Panorama Palace,** *Moderate,* just opened, Rua dos Pinheiros (227–0067), pool, bar, and restaurant.

RESTAURANTS. Victor, *Moderate,* Quatro Rodás Hotel, excellent seafood, try their many varieties of white fish, all marvelous; **Ricardao,** *Moderate,* Praia do Aracaji, for lunch; **Solar do Ribeirao,** *Moderate,* Rua Issac Martins 141 (222–3068), famed for shrimp dishes.

THE AMAZON

The Amazon region has figured so prominently in novels and films that few people who come to see it don't have some preconceived notion of what they will find. Most often they expect an impenetrable jungle, herds of animals, flocks of swooping birds, and unfriendly Indians. In reality, there is little groundcover vegetation, the trees range from 50 to 150 feet in height, little animal life can be spotted, and the birds nest in the tops of the high trees.

Francisco de Orellana, a Spanish Conquistador, sighted the river in 1541 and was so taken by the size that he called it Rio Mar, the River Sea. Exploration was slow and arduous, and as explorers forged their way through unknown territory, they encountered and fought what they thought was a race of women warriors, whom they called Amazons. Whether they actually believed they were face to face with something out of pagan mythology is not known; but it is easy to imagine that they felt the name "Amazon" and its implications were pointedly appropriate to this hostile land, and this name came to refer to the entire region.

Most of the Amazon basin has been explored and charted. The river itself is 3,900 miles long, the second longest river in the world, and has 17 tributaries each over 1,000 miles long plus over 50,000 miles of navigable trunk rivers. Ocean-going vessels can travel 2,700 miles upriver to Iquitos, which is still about 600 miles from the origin of the river.

192 **BRAZIL**

About one-third the world's oxygen is produced by the vegetation, and one-fifth the fresh water in the world is provided by the Amazon. Although there are over 18,000 plant species in the basin, the extremely heavy rainfall leaches the soil of its nutrients and makes organized cultivation extremely impractical. Although poor in agricultural possibilities, the Amazon is rich in among other products, gold, diamonds, lumber, rubber, oil, and jute.

American travel firms began to make it more accessible in 1956. The region is now becoming increasingly open to tourism. Such cities as Belém, Manaus, Santarem, and Porto Velho in Brazil, Leticia in Colombia, and Iquitos in Peru, are easily reached by air and offer fine hotels, good food, excellent services, and fascinating sightseeing.

The main attraction in the Amazon is the jungle. It extends into nine countries of South America—French Guiana, Suriname, Guyana, Venezuela, Ecuador, Peru, Bolivia, Colombia, and Brazil. Most of these countries have developed tourism facilities—most of them new—enabling the visitor to explore the basin in reasonable safety and comfort. However, as it is a primitive area, many tourist facilities call for "roughing it."

The River and the Jungle

For both outsiders and inhabitants of the Amazon, there is a mystical attraction to this region summed up by the awesome size and impenetrable mystery of the area's two great constants, the river and the jungle. There is nothing that can prepare a first-time visitor to the Amazon for the sights that await. A flight over the jungle is an unforgettable experience—it goes on seemingly forever, with hours and hours of thick vegetation, a bright green, sometimes paling slightly only to deepen again, here and there an occasional clearing like an island in the middle of the ocean, no roads, no cities, just a seemingly endless green carpet sliced by the curving contours of the area's over 1,000 rivers. From the vantage point of the sky it is easy to see why the Amazon region accounts for 60 percent of Brazil's total territory, is larger than all of Western Europe, is the largest tropical jungle and rain forest in the world, and contains one-fifth of the world's fresh water reserves yet is inhabited by fewer people than live in New York City. This experience can be had on any of the flights linking Amazon cities or from the major cities in the south, Rio de Janeiro and São Paulo.

River travel is equally hypnotizing. Although the region contains hundreds of navigable rivers, commerce follows a few well-beaten paths, mainly the Amazon, the Negro, Solimoes, Madeira, Para, and Tapajos rivers. These are the options available to tourists, with the exception of those few intrepid souls who wish to organize their own expeditions. For most, their sensation of river life in the Amazon will be gained from a few hours on the Negro River in Manaus, on the Para in Belém, or the Tapajos and Amazon in Santarem. Longer trips are available on the Amazon and Madeira rivers and are highly recommended if you have the time.

As to be expected, the best experience is a trip on the mighty Amazon itself, between Belém and Manaus with a stop in Santarem. The

THE AMAZON

voyage lasts between four and seven days, depending on the ship you take, and will provide experiences and stories to recount for the rest of your life. By far the most enjoyable passage on the Amazon is offered by the Brazilian shipping company Enasa, which operates two catamaran-style vessels that ply the Belém-Santarem-Manaus route. They boast 53 double and 8 quadruple air-conditioned cabins with private baths plus a small pool, bar, dining room, and discotheque. The twice-monthly sailings are usually on Fridays from Belém, arriving in Manaus the following Thursday. Departures from Manaus are on Friday, arriving in Belém on Wednesday. Make your reservations well in advance.

For less comfort and more adventure, there are regular river boats that ply the Amazon carrying freight and passengers. These two deckers are romantic in appearance, but many are old and increasingly unreliable; as a result, there has been on recent average one major accident every two years, a factor that definitely should be taken into consideration before embarking on a river voyage in one of these vessels. On board, the boats have first-class cabins on the upper deck with meals prepared by the boat's staff. For third-class passengers on the lower deck, conditions are primitive, with no cabins (you must bring a hammock to sleep in) and little in the way of food (many experienced Brazilian travelers bring their own food together with gas-driven stoves, an indication of the quality of food in third class—not for the weak of stomach). The trip on the river boats between Manaus and Belém lasts four days. Check at your hotel for information on departures in either city.

By whatever class or boat you travel, the voyage is unmatched anywhere in the world. At some points the Amazon is so wide that you can see neither bank, giving the impression that you are traversing an inland sea. At night, the only light available in the vast darkness of the river and jungle is that of the moon and stars, reinforcing the sensation that you are indeed in the midst of the world's greatest wilderness.

By day, each sighting is an adventure in itself: Indians fishing in canoes, wooden huts on the banks of the river, small tributaries that flow into the Amazon, and throughout the voyage the extraordinary flora of the jungle. Although you may expect to see wild animals on the banks of the river, this is a rare occurrence. The denseness of the vegetation makes sightings of wildlife extremely difficult. Even inside the jungle, most tourists discover they can see very little except for the vegetation. To see wildlife, it is best to travel to the Pantanal.

At stops along the river, inhabitants of the villages and towns will come to the boat, their canoes filled with fresh fruits and other wares to sell. The river is their lifeline to civilization and their main source of customers. While passengers climb on and off, the incessant bartering goes on, particularly for fresh food.

You will quickly discover that on board any of the Amazon's boats, one of the most fascinating pastimes is meeting your fellow passengers. Adventurers, dreamers, romantics—all come to the Amazon, some to stay, others just to take a look and move on. Those who have been in the region before or who live there will be able to relate the legends of the Amazon. At times it seems as if there are nearly as many legends

BRAZIL

as there are trees. One of the most popular concerns the river's famed pink dolphin. According to legend, the dolphin is the Amazon's version of the mermaid: the female seduces men, while the male turns into an irresistably handsome youth on nights of the full moon. At outdoor markets in the Amazon, vendors sell amulets supposedly containing parts of a pink dolphin and guaranteed to attract the opposite sex.

The greatest legend of the Amazon is that which started it all, the myth of El Dorado, "the golden one." When 16th-century Spanish explorer Francisco de Orellano set out from Ecuador to explore the Amazon, he was after gold, enchanted by the stories of a kingdom ruled by an enormous king who each day covered his naked body in gold dust, the original El Dorado. Orellano found neither gold nor a lost kingdom but instead ran into hostile Indians, heat, disease, and the suffocating presence of the jungle from which he finally emerged one year later, telling tales of a race of women warriors, the Amazons.

Spanish historians did the rest, spreading the twin myths of the Amazon women and El Dorado while at the same time giving the river and the region its name. Two hundred years later, the Portuguese explorer Francisco Raposo claimed to have come across the ruins of a lost civilization in the Amazon jungle. Wrote the explorer: "We entered fearfully through the gateways to find within the ruins of a city . . . . We came upon a great plaza, a column of black stone and on top of it the figure of a youth was carved over what seemed to be a great doorway."

Whatever Raposo saw or imagined, it was never seen again—a fact, however, that has not prevented others from taking up the search. One of the most famous was British adventurer Colonel Percy Fawcett, who in 1925, after years of searching for The Lost City, started out on his final expedition. Fawcett disappeared in the jungle, adding one more chapter to the El Dorado legend. Even today, on board ships or in the bars and restaurants of the Amazon's cities, you will hear stories of lost civilizations hidden under the jungle's green canopy, or tales of extraordinary blond, blue-eyed Indian tribes who speak German or Swedish.

Far-fetched as many of the Amazon legends are, all of them gain some credence from the fact that 450 years after it was first seen by Europeans, the region has still not been thoroughly explored by land. In 1913, former U.S. President Theodore Roosevelt took part in an Amazon expedition which discovered a 1,000-mile-long Amazon tributary, immediately named the Roosevelt River. In the 1960s, two previously unknown Indian tribes were discovered, a major river was found, and what turned out to be Brazil's tallest mountain was uncovered hidden beneath the Amazon rain forest. Man may have gone to the moon, but he has still not found a way to penetrate the mystery of the Amazon.

Belém

The city of Belém is the gateway to the Amazon, 90 miles from the open sea. Ultra-modern high rises dot the horizon, mingling with older red-tile-roofed buildings.

THE AMAZON 195

Belém was the first center of European colonization in the Amazon. The Portuguese settled here in 1616, using the city as a jumping off point for the interior jungle region and also as an outpost to protect the mouth of the Amazon River. A river port with access to the sea, Belém developed over the years into the major trade center for the Amazon. Like the upriver city of Manaus, Belém rode the ups and downs of Amazon booms and busts, alternately bursting with energy and money and slumping into relative obscurity. All of this is evident in the architecture of the city where colonial structures survive along with rubber-era mansions and ostentatious monuments to the civic spirit of past magnates. This is most evident in the "old city" where you will find the Basílica de Nazaré church with its ornate interior replete with Carrara marble and gold, the former city palace, the Laura Sodre palace and the Bolonha Palace, the latter three examples of works by European architects brought to the city by the rubber barons.

While here, walk to the Praça da Republica, faced by the Municipal Theatre, to see the Victorian marble statues. The theatre is the third oldest in Brazil. Nearby are the handicrafts center run by the state tourism office, Paratur. In this daily fair you will find wood, leather, and straw objects plus handmade Indian goods and examples of the region's colorful and distinctive pottery, called marajoara.

Stop in the Goeldi Museum; in addition to an extensive collection of Indian artifacts and excellent photographs, there is a zoo with many local animals in their natural surroundings. In the Jungle Park, a large area of virgin forest has been preserved and traversed by trails, which lead to reflection pools with huge water lilies. Also worthwhile is the Agricultural Institute, where rubber and Brazil nut trees are cultivated. Or, delve into history with a visit to an old rubber plantation.

Although Belém today is a bustling, modern city, the influence of the Amazon river and jungle remains strong. Despite its international airport, the city still depends heavily on the river for contact with the outside world. The highway to Brasilia was built to end Belém's isolation from the rest of the country but it is still a seasonal highway, subject to periodic closures because of heavy rains and flooding along the route. Its main value to the city is in providing land access for farm products and manufactured goods from the south. Buses also ply the highway but the four-day trip is only for the adventuresome.

Because of its heavy dependence on the river, the port of Belém is today, as it was 300 years ago, an active trade and business center. Here you will find the Ver-o-Peso market (literally "see the weight," a colonial-era salespitch that has survived the passage of time). Dozens of boats of all types and sizes line up at the dock to unload their wares or haul on board Amazon goods destined for other ports. The market is a confusion of colors and voices with vendors offering medicinal herbs, regional fruits, miracle roots from the jungle, alligator teeth, river fish (both stuffed and for eating) and good luck charms for the body and soul. Here you will get a close-up look at many of the fish of the Amazon such as the pirarucu, the river's most colorful fish; the mero, which can come in at over 200 pounds; and the silver-scaled piratema. There are jars filled with animal eyes, tails, and even heads, plus snake skins and an endless variety of herbs, all with their own

196 **BRAZIL**

legendary powers. Lizard skins are sold to be ground into powder and then sprinkled over food, supposedly having the power to calm the high-spirited. Snake eyes are favorites for solving love or money problems. The tails, however, have a more prosaic purpose—they make excellent back scratchers. The market may be short on cleanliness, but it is long on local color.

A half block away from the market is the Castelo Fort, where in addition to a beautiful view of the Pará River (a tributary of the Amazon) from its parapets, you may also sample regional cooking at the fort's fine restaurant. The best-known dish is Amazon duck, or pato ao tucupi. In front of the fort is the Catedral da sé, Belém's cathedral, with images of Christ, Peter, and Paul carved in Carrara marble, an example of the extravagance that characterized rubber boom days along the Amazon.

Belém also has its own beaches, located on the Pará River's Mosqueiro Island, a short one-hour drive from the city. The string of 18 river beaches with hotels, bars, and restaurants are the meeting points for the city's residents during the summer months from May to October (the dry season). Several of them have spectacular views of the jungle, only a stone's throw away.

The port of Belém itself is best seen by boat. Paratur operates a sternwheeler that provides tours of the port and nearby islands. The oldtime river boat, with a bar on board, leaves from the Praça do Pescador at 9 in the morning on Saturdays and Sundays, returning at noon. Two private firms, Ciatur and Neytur, also conduct river tours, leaving from the pier at the Novotel Hotel daily. Both of these tours include a stop along the river with a short hike through the jungle. You can also arrange a boat trip to Jaguar Island, with its luxuriant vegetation and array of bird life. A small river cuts through the island; a short boat ride provides interesting insight into the lifestyle of the islanders.

Marajó

Just north of Belém and reachable by boat or plane is the island of Marajó, larger than Denmark and the world's largest river island. The island has two distinct zones of vegetation—forest and grassy plains—and is famed for its herds of water buffalo. The buffalo were imported from India at the turn of the century, although according to local legend their arrival was an accident, the result of a shipwreck of a boat going from India to the Guianas. Today the island is home to 70,000 head of water buffalo, which are raised for their milk, cheese, and meat.

Marajó is a vast, unspoiled tribute to the abundance of the Amazon region. Its only city, Soure, also has excellent river beaches. The trip to the island takes four to five hours by boat or 30 minutes by plane from Belém. The boats are double-deckers, with tourists usually preferring the cushioned seats of the upper deck while local inhabitants take over the lower deck, stretching out in their hammocks, a traditional feature of river-boat travel in the Amazon. The flight from Belém is not only faster and more comfortable but offers an incomparable view of the ocean's meeting with the waters of the Amazon and Tocantis rivers.

THE AMAZON   197

From the air you also get a good idea of the size of the island and see its pastures of cattle and buffalo herds.

Boat trips to Marajo leave from Belém's port area on Wednesdays and Fridays at 8 P.M. and on Saturdays at 2 P.M., with return trips leaving on Thursdays at 5 P.M. and Sundays at 5 P.M. and midnight. If you take the boat you will have to spend at least one night on the island, with the best option being the Pousada Marajoara, located on the riverfront and laid out in the form of an Amazon Indian village—just right for capturing the exotic spirit of the Amazon.

Unfortunately, getting around on the island is far more complicated than getting to it. There are only two taxis on the island, and bus service is spotty. Most tourists discover it is far easier and more enjoyable to arrange to accompany a group tour handled by experienced tour operators. A typical tour will include a visit to a buffalo ranch (sometimes staying overnight), canoe excursions, and demonstrations of the island's rhythmic local dance called the *carimbo,* a mixture of African and Indian rhythms.

The high point of a trip to Marajó is a visit to one of the island's buffalo ranches, where you get a close-up look at the unique lifestyle of the island's inhabitants. Everything, from transportation to food, is supplied by the buffalo. All tours give you a chance to experience this yourself, first by taking a ride in a buffalo-drawn cart, the primary means of transportation on the island, and then by tasting some of Marajó's distinctive delicacies such as buffalo steak, buffalo cheese, and desserts made with buffalo milk. You may also have the opportunity to witness a buffalo rodeo or to milk a buffalo.

In general, dining in the Amazon is as different as everything else in the region. Besides buffalo, you will have the opportunity to eat piranha fish, armadillo, wild Amazon duck and a wide variety of river fish with such exotic Indian names as *tucunaré, pirarucú, tambaquí, curimatá, jaraquí,* and *pacú* (beware of anyone offering you alligator or turtle—the killing of both is against the law). Also watch out for the region's famed hot pepper, the pimenta-de-cheiro. It is one of Brazil's most potent, the reason why even Amazon natives usually eat only sauces made with the pepper, avoiding putting it directly in their mouths. For dessert try some of the region's tropical fruits, found only in the Amazon, such as *cupuaçu, graviola, taperebá, pupunha, biribá, bacabá, burití, abio,* and *açaí.* To wash down Amazon food, there is nothing better than Belém's excellent Cerpa beer, mild and delicious.

Macapá

North from Marajó is Macapá, an Amazon river city of 95,000 and capital of the territory of Amapá. The city, one of only five in the world that lies directly on the equator, is 40 minutes flying time from Belém. Like Belém, Macapá was an Amazon outpost established by the Portuguese to develop the region and keep out invaders from Europe. To this end, the Portuguese built their largest fort in Brazil in the city. Its remains are today one of Macapá's main tourist attractions.

The top attraction, however, is provided by nature. Called the *pororoca,* this extraordinary natural wonder occurs when the incoming

198 **BRAZIL**

ocean tide crashes against the outflowing waters of the Amazon. The violent meeting produces churning waters and waves that reach 15 feet in height. The most remarkable aspect of the pororoca, however, is the sound that results. For nearly an hour before the final meeting of the waters, the air is filled with what sounds like a continuous crack of thunder, gradually building in intensity. At the end, the rushing ocean waves sweep into the forest along the river banks. The intensity of the pororoca is at its greatest during the months January to May when the Amazon is in flood stage. It is truly one of the most unforgettable sights in South America.

Santarem

Throughout modern times, the Amazon has been a magnet for adventurers and dreamers. First wood, then rubber and today gold have served as the lures for thousands of would-be millionaires seeking to carve their fortunes out of the jungle. Many have left behind rusted monuments to their dreams. The most noteworthy of these is Fordlandia, an Amazon boondoggle envisioned by Henry Ford, who poured $80 million over a period of 20 years, starting in 1927, into a vast rubber plantation destined to supply him with the raw material for the tires of his cars. The scheme failed primarily because of disease and Ford's eventual loss of enthusiasm for the enormous undertaking. Today the rusted remains of trucks and electric generators, together with abandoned American-style bungalow homes, can be seen in the jungle some 40 miles outside of Santarem, a city of 100,000 halfway between Belém and Manaus. Santarem is now enjoying unprecedented growth due to the latest Amazon boom cycle, this time built around gold strikes that have been made in the region starting in 1981. Originally settled by former soldiers of the Confederacy following the U.S. Civil War, Santarem boasts names like Higgins and MacDonald. The Tropical Hotel Santarem offers superior accommodations and arranges local boat trips on the Amazon and its tributaries.

The city is actually located on the Tapajos River at a point about two miles from where it flows into the Amazon. It is, however, the main port for Amazon ships traveling between Manaus and Belém. Besides the port activity, Santarem survives as a commercial center for individuals and companies engaged in lumbering and gold mining in the rain forest proper. There is also a nearby colony of Japanese farmers who raise peppers, one of the few agricultural projects that have succeeded in the Amazon.

During the 1970s the Brazilian government invested millions of dollars in the construction of two Amazon highways, one running north of the river and the other, south. The idea was to offer plots of land alongside the highways to poor tenant farmers in the northeast. Thousands accepted the government's offer of free land and moved to the region but quickly discovered the difficulty of raising crops in the mineral-poor soil of the Amazon. Today the highways, which never went beyond dirt tracks in the jungle, are abandoned, overgrown by the jungle in many places, and most of the settlers have left the region, giving up on an ill-conceived Amazon dream.

THE AMAZON 199

For the most part Santarem has escaped the dramatic ups and downs of Belém and Manaus, serving as a strategically located supply point independent of the booms and busts of the area's capital cities. Today tourists who visit the city will find it slow-moving and drowsy, as it has always been, even with the increase in population and activity that has been brought by the gold strikes of recent years. The best thing to do in Santarem is to take a one-day cruise on the river, a trip offered by the Tropical Hotel. The boat, like most of those used by tourists in the region, is specially outfitted to provide a maximum of viewing space with the decks open. The one-day cruise leaves Santarem, travels to the meeting point of the Tapajos and Amazon, then continues on the big river to a point called Pouso das Garcas, a beautiful region of small rivers, lakes, and forest and marked by the presence of hundreds of snow-white egrets who have made this spot their personal meeting point. You will also have a chance to try your hand at piranha fishing.

The Tropical also offers a second cruise, this time on the Tapajos, taking travelers to a spot called Alter do Chao, a small Amazon town on the banks of the Tapajos known for its sand beaches. If you are lucky, you may stumble on a group of Santarem natives organizing what is called a piracaia, a form of Amazon fish feed. Friends get together on a river beach, jump into their canoes, and spend the morning fishing, after which the results are brought back to the beach and char-broiled over hot coals.

Manaus

A sprawling city of nearly one million, built in the densest part of the jungle, Manaus has re-established its role as the key city of the Amazon basin after years of dormancy (the long-hoped-for expansion of the Amazon basin did not attain the desired results despite the inauguration of seasonal road connections with Belém and Brasilia).

Of all the Amazon cities and towns, Manaus is the most identified with what was the region's greatest boom. For a period of 25 years at the turn of the century, Manaus was the world's rubber capital. From here 90 percent of the world's rubber supply was shipped out on river boats that made the run to Belém, from where Amazon rubber traveled to the four corners of the earth. In return came millions and millions of dollars, an immense sum that was reaped by a handful of Amazon rubber barons, never numbering more than 100, who lived in Manaus and dominated the region like feudal lords.

The barons controlled huge plantations of which Indians and poor white laborers lived, virtually as slaves. Stories abound of the cruel whims of the rubber barons, one of whom is said to have killed 40,000 Indians during his 20-year "reign." Another boasted of having killed 300 Indians in one day.

Using their enormous wealth, the barons made Manaus one of the wealthiest and most ostentatious cities in the world. They had their laundry sent to Portugal and brought artisans and engineers from the Old World to construct their monuments. Manaus' famed opera house cost a reported $10 million and was completed in 1910, replete with French tiles and Italian frescoes, all ordered specifically for the Amazon's Opera House. French champagne ran from its fountains on opening nights and international stars such as Jenny Lind and the dancers of the Ballet Russe came to perform on its stage.

This fantasy world at last came to an end shortly before World War I, when a British businessman managed to smuggle several Amazon rubber trees out of the country. They were replanted in Malaysia, where they flourished. The arrival of competition brought the rubber boom crashing down on the heads of the barons. By 1925 the boom was bust, and Manaus slipped back into insignificance.

Vestiges of the opulent days of the rubber boom still remain in Manaus, particularly its main symbol, the Opera House, today restored to its former splendor.

The Custom House and Lighthouse were imported piece by piece from England and reassembled alongside the floating dock, built especially to accommodate the annual 40-foot rise and fall of the river.

Contemporary Manaus is a combination of modern high rise buildings scattered among lower, older stucco structures. It has staged a comeback over the past 20 years, partly due to the government's decision to make it a free port. Brazilians from the south now fly to Manaus to stock up on televisions, stereos, and video recorders without having to pay import taxes. The same factor has made the city the capital of Brazil's electronics industry. Television, stereo, and, most recently, microcomputer firms have their manufacturing bases in the city, taking advantage of fiscal incentives and the absence of import duties.

For tourists, the sights of the city are concentrated in the downtown area close to the port. Wander through the City Market Building, where caged animals and parrots are offered for sale alongside exotic fruits and vegetables.

For shopping, try the Credilar Teatro, an imposing edifice of native redstone and glass. Or, taxi to the suburb of Cachoeirinha to see the Little Church of the Poor Devil (Pobre Diabo) built by one poor laborer; it's only 12 feet wide and 15 feet long. While in the suburbs, stop at the Salesian Mission Museum to see a complete documentary of the now vanished "Floating City"; also, visit the Indian Museum operated by the same order.

River and jungle trips from Manaus vary from a few hours to several days and nights. The most popular is a six-to-eight-hour boat trip to the point where the Negro and Solimoes rivers join to form the Amazon. Here you can see the dark water of the Negro flowing into the muddy water of the Solimoes, with the two running side by side for 11 miles before becoming one. All "Meeting of the Waters" tours also include side trips, which vary from a visit to a rubber plantation to a motorboat ride through narrow Amazon tributaries that provides you with an excellent close-up view of the vegetation of the rain forest. Many of these tours stop at Lake January, an Amazon lake filled with giant Victoria regis water lilies and with a floating restaurant anchored in the middle.

Also popular are jungle walks and overnight boat trips that bring you into contact with the jungle. A typical overnight trip follows the Negro River, exploring flooded woodlands and narrow channels, stopping to permit you to walk along a trail in the rain forest during daylight hours.

THE AMAZON 201

At night, tour guides will take you by canoe on an alligator hunt. The guides shine flashlights into the eyes of the gators, hypnotizing them, after which they are grabbed and held for photographs and then released.

Variations on this theme exist for three days/two nights, four days/ three nights, five days/four nights, all the way up to a full-scale, custom-organized private expedition. There are several tour operators that offer jungle and river trips, and you should check what each one offers. Some include river fishing, while others schedule a stop at a native settlement to give you an idea of living conditions on the river. There are also options as to overnight accommodations. Some tours put you up in hammocks on board the boat beneath the Amazon sky and a short distance from the jungle, a singular Amazon experience. (Do not be worried about mosquitoes or other bugs. All boat trips out of Manaus are on the Negro River, whose dark color is due to the dissolving of humic acid, which has the unique and welcome quality of repelling insects. As a result, there are few pests on this river.)

On other tours you will sleep in a ship's cabin, either with air-conditioning or a fan. While this may seem more attractive, you should remember that one of the primary attractions of the jungle at night is its sounds. With air-conditioning you may sleep better, but you will miss a good part of the show.

Finally, there is also an Amazon lodge located on an island in the river where some tours stop. The lodge, Pousada dos Guanavenas, has 14 rooms with private baths. All meals are regional dishes, mainly river fish.

Porto Velho

Some 550 miles southwest of Manaus is the city of Porto Velho, a river port and capital of Brazil's newest and fastest-growing state, Rondonia. The city, like the state, is currently enjoying a major boom because of an influx of Brazilians from the states of the northeast, attracted by gold and the promise of good farmland made accessible at the start of this decade by the construction of a highway linking Porto Velho with Manaus and the paving of another road between Porto Velho and Cuiaba, capital of Mato Grosso, to the south.

These land links have ended the previous complete dependence of Rondonia on river or air transport to connect it with the rest of Brazil and also have made possible for the first time road travel between the cities of the south and Manaus by way of Cuiaba and Porto Velho. These highways are still subject to interruptions during the rainy season, mainly the first half of the year. It is possible, though, to travel by bus from Rio to Manaus, making connections along the route. The trip is long, tiring, and adventuresome, but if you are after unusual experiences, have a great deal of time to spare, and are not worried about lack of comfort or ease of travel, it may be of interest.

Porto Velho itself is another Amazon city that slipped into obscurity after the end of the rubber boom only to come back strong in recent years. The city, today with a population surpassing 150,000, became famous for one of the Amazon's most grandiose and tragic dreams. In

BRAZIL

the midst of the rubber boom, American entrepreneur and adventurer Percival Farquhar decided he could increase profits from the jungle rubber trade by building a railroad through the rain forest.

American and British engineers came to Porto Velho to plan the project, relying on local labor. What they did not count on, however, were the effects of disease, heat, and even hostile Indians, plus the sheer enormity of cutting a railroad through the thick vegetation of the Amazon, where it is sometimes necessary to carry a lantern to see during daylight hours.

A total of 225 miles of the Madeira-Mamore railroad, as it was called, was finally completed in 1913 but at a cost of $30 million, an enormous sum at the time, and the deaths of an estimated 1,500 workers. Shortly afterwards the rubber boom was over and the railroad, built at such great sacrifice, was gradually abandoned to the jungle. Some limited use of the railroad was made by the inhabitants of Porto Velho and nearby settlements, but there were no parts or replacements for engines, which eventually ground to a halt. In 1972 all operations stopped and today only nine miles of track survive, together with rusted locomotives and unused water towers. In 1981, the city renovated one of the locomotives and several cars, which now carry tourists on a five-mile journey three times a day on Sundays—a sad ending for this Amazon dream.

Other than the remains of the Madeira-Mamore railway, the main attraction in Port Velho is the Madeira River, one of the most important tributaries of the Amazon. River trips here, however, do not have the organization or sophistication of those in Belém, Santarem, or Manaus. The system is still one of walking down to the river bank and arranging your trip with a local boat owner, several of whom take tourists on short trips along the river.

The real adventure here, however, is a trip by boat from Porto Velho to Manaus on the Madeira River. The trip takes four days, the first half ending at Manicore, where you change boats for the remaining two-day journey to Manaus. There are only two aging river boats that still make the first part of the trip from Porto Velho to Manicore. Both are typical two-decker Amazon boats, transporting cargo and passengers. Unlike their sister ships on the Amazon, however, they have no cabins for first-class passengers. Here, hammocks and open-air accommodations are the rule for everyone, although first class offers a better view from the upper deck.

Since the Madeira is a narrower river than the Amazon, passengers on this trip get a sometimes better view of life on the river's edge. They also come into contact with the gritty existence of the gold prospectors who have flocked to the state of Rondonia in the past five years. Mechanized gold mining so far has been kept out of the Amazon, a decision taken by the government out of respect (some say fear) of the thousands of individual prospectors who have set up their own claims since the gold rush began.

On board ship you will hear endless stories about life in the gold camps and tales of overnight fortunes won and lost. In reality, most of the miners find only enough to live on for a short period, after which they grow weary of the work and risk and give up. At this point many

THE AMAZON

are contracted by gold field entrepreneurs, who have taken over and operate several claims, and become day laborers. Some of the gold fields seem like movie sets for biblical epics, with literally thousands of these laborers toiling up and down sometimes steep cavities dug into the earth, carrying sacks of dirt on their backs which will then be sifted in search of the evasive yellow metal.

Today, Brazil is the fifth largest producer of gold in the world, but most mining experts and government officials feel that if the true quantity of gold taken out of the Amazon fields—the main source—were really known, the country would probably be number two behind South Africa. Much of this gold is smuggled out through Brazil's northern border with Guyana, or to Bolivia on the west.

Although you probably won't see any gold aboard ship, the Madeira-Manicore voyage offers a rare chance to mingle with all of the varied types of adventurers, travelers, and simple river folk that inhabit or pass through the Amazon. Once you reach Manicore, this momentary classless society will break up: the boat that continues on to Manaus has a more respectable first class, with cabins. The city of Manicore is a river town built up around rubber and lumber, two activities that still support the majority of the city's 18,000 residents.

The Upper Regions

The upper reaches of the Amazon River are generally more interesting than the lower portions because the upper river is only one-half mile wide and the channel flows close to either shore most of the time. Indian life is far more evident.

There is weekly tour/cruise service on the upper Amazon between Iquitos, Peru and Leticia, Colombia. Reconstructed especially for cruising on the Amazon, the M/V *Rio Amazonas* sails from its home port of Iquitos each Wednesday and arrives in Leticia Saturday morning; return sailings depart Leticia Saturday afternoons and arrive in Iquitos Tuesday mornings. Sailing times in both ports are coordinated with air service to/from Bogotá, Manaus, Iquitos, and Lima.

The *Rio Amazonas* carries 55 passengers in 16 air-conditioned twin cabins with private bath and 10 non-air-conditioned twin/triple cabins with community bath facilities at half the cost. All meals, twice-daily shore excursions, lectures and films on the flora, fauna, and Indian life are all included in the cruise cost. Shore excursions are not duplicated on the in-depth roundtrip cruise, six nights from Iquitos back to Iquitos.

PRACTICAL INFORMATION FOR THE AMAZON

For definitions of price categories see *Planning Your Trip*.

WHEN TO GO. Since the Amazon Valley lies close to the Equator, winter and summer in the usual sense do not occur. High humidity is common only in the deep jungle, not in the cities or on the river. Average temperature is 80°F. Nights are always cool. Rainy Season—December to June (high water). Dry Season—July to November (low water). Travel in both seasons is good.

HOW TO GET THERE AND AROUND. From USA: Gateway is Miami, via *Lloyd Boliviano, Varig, Faucett,* and *Suriname Airways, Avianca* and *Aeroperu.*

From S.A. to Manaus: *Varig, Cruzeiro, Vasp, Lloyd, Boliviano.* To Belém: *Varig, Suriname Airways, Vasp, and Cruzeiro.* To Leticia: *Avianca* and *Cruzeiro.* To Iquitos: *Faucett, Aero Peru, Cruzeiro.* There are regular plane services that take you into Belém, the capital of the State of Pará on the mouth of the Amazon River. To get to Manaus, the capital of the state of Amazonas, you go by plane, boat, or bus from Porto Velho. *Cruzeiro* flies Manaus/Tabatinga/Iquitos and returns twice weekly; Tabatinga is one mile from Leticia by taxi. *Varig* and *Vasp* fly from Rio and Brasilia to Manaus, as well as to Belém and Paramaribo. Varig-Cruzeiro and Vasp also fly from Belém to Macapá and Santarem. The same airlines offer flights from Rio, São Paulo, Brasilia, Belo Horizonte and Porto Alegre to Macapá.

Enasa operates two catamaran-style vessels between Belém and Manaus with a stop at Santarem, usually twice a month. Sailings are usually on Fridays from Belém, arriving in Manaus the following Thursday. Departures from Manaus are on Fridays, arriving on Wednesday in Belém. Rates per person are $595 for an outside cabin and $495 for an inside double cabin. For reservations, contact Gran Pará Tourismo, Av. Presidente Vargas #679, Belém, Pará, Brazil. There is no land access to Belém, but you may now take a bus from Porto Velho to Manaus. The road, however, usually is open only in the dry season.

TOURS. There are three options for river and port tours in Belém: the **Paratur sternwheeler** leaves Praça do Pescador every Saturday and Sunday at 9 A.M. for a three-hour tour. Tickets can be bought at any travel agency or at the Paratur offices in Praça Kennedy (224-9633). Tickets also can be bought upon boarding. **Ciatur** provides daily tours leaving from the pier at the Novotel Hotel. Tickets may be bought at the pier or at the Ciatur offices, Av. Presidente Vargas 645, (222-1995). **Neytur** also offers daily tours leaving from Novotel's pier at Av. Bernardo Sayão 4804. Neytur's offices are located at Rua Carlos Gomes 300 (224-2469).

For river tours in Macapá, check at your hotel. The same is true in Porto Velho. In Santarem, the Hotel Tropical offers excellent river tours. In Manaus, several tour operators provide river excursions including walks in the jungle, some of them overnight on board the boat or in an Amazon lodge. Longer trips of up to a week are also available on request.

The best operators are the following: **Expeditours**—based in Rio de Janeiro, offering the widest variety of nature and river tours in Manaus, Rua Visconde de Piraja 414, Grs. 1005/6, 22410 Rio de Janeiro, RJ, tel: 287-9697, telex: 34727; **Amazon Explorers,** representatives in Manaus of Expeditours, 189 Quintino Bocaiuva, sala 22, 69000 Manuas, tel: 232-3052, telex: 2859; **Tropical Hotel,** the best hotel in Manuas, also offering river and jungle trips, in Manaus call 238-5757 or get in touch with the hotel's office in São Paulo, Rua da Consolacao, 368, 4th floor, tel: 231-5844, telex: 37790; Selvatur, located in Manaus' Hotel Amazonas, Praça Adalberto Valle, tel: 234-8984, telex: 277 HO AM BR; **Jungle Trips,** a Manaus operator at Rua Guilherme Moreira, 281, tel: 234-5864, telex: 2457; **Safari Ecologica,** based in Rio, Av. 13 de Maio 33, sala 2906, tel: 240-6785, telex: 31108; **Amazon Odyssey Tours,** Rua Guilherme Moreira 286-A, Manaus, tel: 234-2348, telex: 0922395; the **Pousada dos**

THE AMAZON

Guanavenas, an Amazon lodge, also offering tours, Rua Ferreira Pena 755, Manaus, tel: 233-5558, telex: 1101.

WHAT TO TAKE. Light summer clothing. Drip dry shirts and khaki slacks for the men. Cotton dresses for the ladies or skirts and blouses. Pants and pantsuits for women are also acceptable. All shirts and blouses should be long-sleeved. All colors may be worn with the exception of green. Very comfortable shoes are a must, and sneakers or tennis shoes will come in handy. In addition, for its jungle tours, *Amazon Explorers* has the following suggestions and comments: (1) Rubber boots (high) for walk through the jungles. A must. (2) Hat or head cover. (3) Flashlight—Since electricity is limited. (4) Insect repellent (for overnight trips a mosquito net will be supplied). (5) Knife, scissors, first aid kit, toilet paper, sewing kit, sunglasses. (6) Camera and *plenty* of film. Plastic bags to store exposed film. (7) All medications as needed. (8) Walking stick if needed will be supplied. (9) For fishermen: please bring variety of hooks and line. (10) Binoculars—good quality binoculars for bird and animal watching —500 varieties of tropical Amazon birds are constantly around you. (11) As the life on the Amazon is much more relaxed and primitive than anywhere else in the world, you must be prepared for constant changes, delays, or cancellations of flights or steamers according to the moods of the river. Should such changes occur while traveling, your guide will notify you immediately and make new arrangements accordingly.

SPORTS. Most popular sport in this area is *fishing*. *Selvatour* provides all services in Manaus. They are experts at arranging jungle expeditions.

BELÉM

HOTELS. Hilton, *Deluxe,* Praça da Republica (223-6500). Finest hotel in town, all rooms with private bath, air-conditioning; 2 bars and 2 restaurants.

Equatorial Palace, *Moderate,* Av. Bras Aguiar 612 (224-8855). One of the best in the city, with a bar, pool, and restaurant; the rooms have bath, air-conditioning, telephone, TV, and refrigerator.

Regente, *Moderate,* Av. Gov. José Malcher 485 (224-0755). Rooms with private bath, air-conditioning, and TV.

Selton Belém, *Moderate,* Av. Julio Cesar (airport) (233-4222). Rooms have private bath, air-conditioning, telephones, and TV; bar, restaurant, and pool.

Excelsior Grao Para, *Moderate,* Av. Presidente Vargas (222-3255). Rooms have bath, air-conditioning, and telephone; bar and restaurant.

Novetel, *Moderate,* Av. Bernardo Sayao 4804 (226-8011). 121 air-conditioned rooms near Rio Guama.

Central, *Inexpensive,* Av. Presidente Vargas 290 (222-3011).

Sagres, *Inexpensive,* Av. Gov. José Malcher (228-3999). 136 rooms, all air-conditioned, TV, bar, restaurant, and pool.

Vanja, *Inexpensive,* Rua Benjamin Constant 1164 (222-6457). Rooms with private bath, air-conditioning, and telephone.

RESTAURANTS. For international food try **Augustu's,** *Moderate,* Av. Almirante Barroso 439 (226-8317); **Well's,** *Moderate,* Av. Gov. José Malcher 2388; and **La em Casa,** *Moderate,* Av. Gov. José Malcher 982 (223-1212). Also the **O Teatro,** *Expensive,* at the Hilton (223-6500).

Avenida, *Moderate,* on Av. Gen. Deodoro 129 (223–4015), offers good regional food in comfortable surroundings.

For barbecue, **Gaucha,** *Moderate,* Av. Gov. José Malcher 2731 (226–8427).

Other specialties: Japanese food at **Miako,** *Moderate,* Rua Caetano Rufino 82 (223–4485) and Portuguese food at **Santa Rita Casa Portuguesa,** *Moderate,* Rua Manoel Barata 8907 (223–4871).

SHOPPING. The streets of Belém have a number of shops that sell jungle items; but remember that live animals or birds may not be imported into the U.S. Skins of protected animals such as alligators or crocodiles, or shoes/handbags or other articles made of these skins, are also not allowed into the U.S. and will be confiscated by the U.S. Customs. The Paratur handicrafts fair is located at Praça Kennedy near the Praça da Republica.

MANAUS

HOTELS. Tropical, *Deluxe,* (238–5757). Built and operated by Tropical Hotels, a subsidiary of Varig, on good beach overlooking the Rio Negro. 341 air-conditioned rooms, swimming pool, excellent restaurant, night club. About 10 minutes from the new airport and 45 minutes from town. Best buy.

Amazonas, *Expensive,* Praça Adalberto Valle (234–7679). Located in the center of the city, this 10-story building has 214 air-conditioned apartments and two elevators. All rooms have private bath, hot and cold water, and television. Permanent buffet service. Swimming pool.

Novotel, *Expensive,* Av. Mandii, 4. (237–1211). Newest in town. 111 air-conditioned rooms in commercial section.

Hotel Imperial, *Moderate,* Via Getulio Vargas 277 (234–4065). 100 air-conditioned rooms, TV and bar in every room.

Lord, *Moderate,* Rua Quintino, Bacaiuva 217 (234–9741). In the center of the city, this 6-story hotel has 53 apartments all with private bath, hot and cold water, and telephone. Restaurant.

Monaco, *Moderate,* Rua Silva Ramos, 20 (232–5211). 60 air-conditioned rooms with private bath, color TV, and pool. Downtown area.

Central, *Inexpensive,* Rua Dr. Moreira (232–7887). Centrally located, this 50-room, 3-story hotel has air-conditioning, private baths, and telephones.

Flamboyant, *Inexpensive,* Av. Eduardo Ribeiro, (234–0696). Mid-town, the 23 rooms all have private bath and telephone. Bar and swimming pool. Near the Opera House.

Rei Salomão, *Inexpensive,* Rua Dr. Moreira 119 (234–7374). In the center of the city, these 28 apartments have air-conditioning, private bath, and telephone.

National, *Inexpensive,* Rua Dr. Moreira 59 (233–0537). Also downtown, this small hotel has 16 rooms with private bath.

RESTAURANTS. River fish is the main meal at Manaus's restaurants, with the top specialties being the *pirarucú,* and *tucunaré.* While the fish are always fresh, the cooks of Manaus have not yet mastered the art of preparing them, with a few exceptions. The best one is the **Panorama,** *Moderate,* Rua Recife 900 (232–3177), followed by **Chapeu de Palha,** *Moderate,* Rua Fortaleza 619 (233–3607), and **Palhoca,** *Moderate,* Estrada da Ponta Negra

THE AMAZON

(238–3831). The Hotel Tropical has a fine international restaurant, the **Tarumá**, *Expensive*, (238–5757).

SHOPPING. Manaus, a free port, has hundreds of shops, stocked with goods from all over the world. *House of the Hummingbird*, which is owned and operated by Richard Melnyk, features rare and unusual artifacts handcrafted by Indians, caboclos (half-breeds) and regional artisans. Will ship anywhere without service charge.

NIGHTLIFE. The disco at the Tropical Hotel, *O Uirapuru*, is the hottest spot and the *Catedral* on Rua Saldanha Marinha 609, has a show and dancing. Manaus also has a casino. While supposedly illegal, this does not seem to bother the local authorities. Ask for directions at your hotel.

SANTAREM

HOTELS. Tropical, *Moderate*, Av. Mendonça Furtado 114 (522–1583). Offers 120 air-conditioned rooms with refrigerators. One of finest hotels in the region.

Nova Olinda, *Inexpensive*, Av. Adriano Pimental 140 (522–1531). A small hotel with local flavor but no air-conditioning.

MACAPÁ

HOTELS. Novotel, *Moderate*, on the river, downtown (222–1144). Restaurant, bar, and tennis court. New and very good. By far the best in town.

Amapaense Palace Hotel, *Inexpensive*, downtown. Rua Tiradentes, (222–3366). Old and no frills.

RESTAURANTS. The best restaurants in the city are the **Novotel,** *Moderate*, in the hotel of the same name, international cuisine, the **Piraque,** *Moderate*, Rua Iracema Carváo Nunes 102 (621–4828), regional cuisine, and the **Boscão,** *Moderate*, Rua Hamilton Silva 997 (231–4097), regional.

MARAJÓ

HOTELS. Pousada Marajoara, *Moderate*, located on the river in the island's capital city of Souré (741–1472). The only hotel that can be recommended on the island. Fortunately it's very good, built in the form of an Amazon Indian village. Best meals on the island are in the hotel's restaurant.

Porto Velho

HOTELS. Vila Rica, *Moderate*, Av. Carlos Gomes 1616 (221–2286). Restaurant, bar, and pool, 53 rooms with air-conditioning, best bet in town.

Rondon Palace, *Inexpensive*, Av. Gov. Jorge Teixeira (221–3166). Restaurant, bar, and pool.

TOURIST VOCABULARY

TEN-MINUTE PORTUGUESE

Glossary of often-used terms and phrases

ENGLISH	PORTUGUESE	PHONETIC PRONUNCIATION
Good morning (afternoon). (evening) (or good night).	Bom dia (boa tarde), (boa noite).	Vone dee'-uh (bo'-uh tar'-dee) (boh'-a noy'-te)
I don't speak Portuguese.	Nao falo portugues.	Now faw'-loo Por'-too-gays
I don't understand.	Nao compreendo.	Now comb-pree-en'-doo
How are you?	Como está?	Comb-oo ess-taw'
Very well, thank you.	**Man's answer:** Muito bem, obrigado.	Mwee'-too bain, oh-bree-gaw'-doo
	Lady's answer: Muito bem, obrigada.	Moo'-ee-too baying, oh-bree-gah' da
Where are you going?	Onde vai?	On'-djee vie'?
When are you returning?	Quando volta?	Kwahn'-doo vohl'-ta?
Many thanks.	Muito obrigado. (Lady: Muito obrigada).	Moo'-ee-too oh-bree-gah'-doo (Lady: Moo'-ee-too oh-bree-gah'-da)
More slowly.	Mais devagar.	My'-ees de-va-gahr'
Pardon me.	Desculpe-me.	Dis-kool'pe me
I don't know.	Nao sei.	Nah'-oong say
Do you know?	O senhor (a senhora), (a senhorita), (voce) sabe?	Oo se-nyohr (a se-nyor'-a), (a se-Nyoh-ree'-ta) (Voh-say') sah'-be?
Today	Hoje	Oh'-jee
Tomorrow	Amanha	Ah-mahn-yah'
Yesterday	Ontem	On'-tain
This week	Esta semana	Es'-ta se-mah'-na
Don't forget.	Nao se esqueca.	Nah'-oong se is-kay'-sa
All right.	Muito bem.	Moo'-ee-too bayng
See you later.	Até logo.	A-tay' loh'-goo
Goodbye.	Adeus.	A-day'-oos
Come here, please.	Vehna ca, por favor.	Vayng'-ya kah, poor fah-vohr'
It doesn't matter.	Nao tem importancia.	Nah'-oong tayng eem-poortahn see-a
Let's go.	Vamos.	Vah'-moos.
Very good (bad).	Muito bem (mal).	Moo'-ee-too bayng (mah'-l)
Where can I change my money?	Onde posso trocar meu dinheiro?	Ohn-de po'-ssoo troo-kahr' may'-oo-dee-nyay'-roo?
Monday	Segunda-feira	Se-goon'-da fay'-ra
Tuesday	Terca-feira	Tayr'-sa fay'ra
Wednesday	Quarta-feira	Kwahr'-ta fay'-ra
Thursday	Quinta-feira	Keen'-ta fay'-ra
Friday	Sexta-feira	Ses'-ta fay'-ra
Saturday	Sábado	Sah'ba-doo
Sunday	Domingo	Doh-meeng'-goo
Black	Preto, negro	Pre'-too, nay'-groo
White	Branco	Brahng'-koo
Red	Vermelho	V-mel'-yoo
Green	Verde	Vayr'-de
Blue	Azul	A-zool'

TOURIST VOCABULARY

ENGLISH	PORTUGUESE	PHONETIC PRONUNCIATION
Yellow	Amarelo	A-ma-re'-loo
One	Um (uma)	Oong (oom-a)
Two	Dois (Duas)	Doys (Doo'-as)
Three	Tres	Trays
Four	Quatro	Kway'-troo
Five	Cinco	Seeng'-koo
Six	Seis	Say'-ees
Seven	Sete	Se'-te
Eight	Oito	Oy'-too
Nine	Nove	Noh'-ve
Ten	Dez	Dayz
Eleven	Onze	Ohn'-zay
Twelve	Doze	Doh'-zay

Index

Map pages are in **boldface**.

Accommodations, 34
 in Amazon, 205–207
 in Angra dos Reis and Paratí, 98
 in Bahia, 169–171, 176–177
 in Belo Horizonte, 146
 in Brasilia, 141–142
 in Cabo Frio and Búzios, 94
 in Central-West Brazil, 152
 in Goias (state), 156–157
 in Northeast, 185–189
 in Ouro Prêto, 147–148
 in Paraná and Santa Catarina, 130–132
 in Rio de Janeiro, 72–75
 in Rio Grande do Sul, 126–128
 in São Paulo, 109–110
 in São Paulo (state), 119–122
 in Serra do Orgãos, 92
Agriculture, 13–15
Aguas da Prata, 118, 121
Aguas de Lindoia, 121
Air travel, 29–31, 43
 to São Paulo, 108
Alagoas, 180
Alcantara, 184
Amazon, 191–207
 accommodations in, 205–207
 restaurants in, 205–207
 tours and sightseeing in, 204–205
Amazon River, 13, 191–194
Angra Dos Reis, 95–96, 98
Anhembi Park (São Paulo), 105
Aquariums, in São Paulo, 104
Aracati, 183
Araxá, 121
Architecture, 18. *See also* Historic sites and
 houses
 in Belem, 195
 in Brasilia, 133, 135–137, 140
 in Salvador, 160–162, 165
 in São Paulo, 100, 102, 105
Art galleries
 in Bahia, 173
 in Rio de Janeiro, 83–84
 in São Paulo, 105–106, 114
Aruanã, 154, 156
Atibaia, 122
Automobiles, 32
 rentals, 44, 108

Bahia, 159–177
 accommodations in, 169–171, 176–177
 entertainment in, 174
 excursions from Salvador, 166–167
 museums in, 172–173
 restaurants in, 171–172
 Salvador, 159–166, **164**
 shopping in, 174
 transportation to and in, 169
Balls (during Carnival), 64–65, 69–70
Bar do Arnaudo (Rio de Janeiro), 56
Beaches
 in Angra Dos Reis, 95
 in Cabo Frio and Búzios, 92–93
 on Guarujá, 117
 in Laguna, 132
 in Recife, 181
 in Rio de Janeiro, 50, **62**, 81–82
 in Salvador, 162
 in Santos, 117
Belem, 194–196, 205–206
Belo Horizonte, 133–134, 143–144, 146–147
Blumenau, 130, 132
Botafogo (Rio de Janeiro), 50
Botanical Gardens (Jardim Botânico)
 in Rio de Janeiro, 54–55
 in São Paulo, 105
Brasilia, 18, 134–143
 map of, **138–139**
Brazil
 agriculture of, 13–15
 Brasilia, **138–139**
 economy of, 11–12
 ethnic diversity in, 6–7
 geography of, 12–13
 health and safety in, 39–40
 history of, 2–6, 8
 immigration to, 10–11
 Indians (natives) of, 8–10
 language of, 36
 map of, **vii**
 music of, 17–18
 religion in, 15–17
 Rio de Janeiro, **59, 62**
 Salvador, **164**
 São Paulo, **107**
 tours and sightseeing in, 26–29
 transportation to and in, 29–33, 43–44

211

212 INDEX

British travelers, 29
Buses, 33, 43–44
  in Rio de Janeiro, 71–72
Búzios, 93–95

Cabo Frio, 92–94
Cachoeira, 167
Caldas do Jorro, 175, 177
Caldas Novas, 155, 157
Campos do Jordão, 118, 121–122
Candomblé, 163, 172
Canela, 125, 127–128
Capoeira, 42, 163, 173
Caraguatatuba, 120
Carnival, 25, 61–70
  in Olinda, 182–183
  in Salvador, 167–168
Cas Rui Barbosa (Rio de Janeiro), 51
Catholicism, 15–16
Caxambu, 118, 122
Caxias do Sul, 124–125, 127
Ceará, 183
Central-South Brazil, 133–148
  Belo Horizonte, 133–134, 143–144,
    146–147
  Brasilia, 18, 134–143, **138–139**
Central-West Brazil, 149–157
Children's activities, during Carnival, 68
Churches. *See also* Historic sites and houses
  in Olinda, 182
  in Ouro Prêto, 144–145
  in Salvador, 160–161, 165–166
Climate, 25
  in Northeast, 184
Clothes and packing, 25–26
Copacabana (Rio de Janeiro), 73–74, 86
Corcovado (Rio de Janeiro), 57
Corumba, 151, 152–153
Costs, 23
Credit cards, 33
Crime, 41
Cruises, 31–32
  on Amazon, 192–194, 200–201
Cuiaba, 150–151, 152–153
Curitiba, 129–131
Currency, 33
Customs, 24, 44–45

Dance, 83, 127
Diamatina, 145, 148
Discotheques, 89, 115
Drinking water, 40

Economy, 6, 11–12
Electricity, 39
Entertainment
  in Amazon, 207
  in Bahia, 174
  in Belo Horizonte, 147
  Carnival, 61–70
  music, 17–18
  in Recife, 186–187
  in Rio de Janeiro, 83, 87–89
  in Rio Grande do Sul, 127
  in Salvador, 162, 174
  in São Paulo, 115–116
Ethnic diversity in Brazil, 6–7
  immigrants in, 10–11
  Indians in, 8–10
  in Rio de Janeiro's slums, 60
  in São Paulo, 101
Exotiquarium (São Paulo), 104

Favela (slums), of Rio de Janeiro, 58–61
Fishing, 42
Florianopolis, 131–132
Food and drink, 34–35
Fordlandia, 198
Fortaleza, 183, 188–189
Free City (Brasilia), 141
Freetown (Brasilia), 135, 141

Gafieiras, 89
Gaucho country, 123
Gems and jewelry, 84–85
Gloria Church (Rio de Janeiro), 52
Goiania, 154, 156
Goias, 153–157
Golf, 82
Gramado, 125, 127–128
Guarujá, 117, 119–120

Handicapped travelers, 28–29
Health and safety, 40–41
Historic sites and houses. *See also*
    Architecture
  in Belo Horizonte, 143–144
  in Brasilia, 142
  in Manaus, 199–200
  in Olinda, 181–182
  in Ouro Prêto, 144–145
  in Paratí, 96
  in Rio de Janeiro, 51–54, 57, 80–81
  in Salvador, 160–161
  in São Luis, 183–184
  in São Paulo, 102–106
Holidays, 36–37
Horse racing, 42
Hotels. *See* Accommodations
Hours of business, 36

Ibirapuera Park (São Paulo), 104
Igarassu, 182
Iguaçu Falls, 129, 131
Ilha Bela, 120–121
Ilha Grande (Angra dos Reis), 95–96
Ilheus, 175, 176
Indians (natives), 3, 8–10
  Museum of (Museu do Indio), 50–51
Information sources, 23, 39–40
  for Rio de Janeiro, 79
  for Salvador, 172
  for São Paulo, 113
Instituto Butantãn (São Paulo), 102–103
Ipanema (Rio de Janeiro), 74, 86
Itacurucá, 98

Japanese immigrants, 10
João Pessoa, 183, 187
Joinville, 130, 132

Karaoke, 89

Laguna, 132
Languages, 36
Leblon (Rio de Janeiro), 74
Lençois, 175–176, 177

Macapá, 197, 207
Maceio, 180, 185
Mail, 37
Manicore, 203
Manaus, 199–200, 206–207
Marajó, 196–197, 207
Maranhão, 183

INDEX

Medical treatment, 40–41
Metric conversion charts, 38
Minas Gerais, 143–148
Mineral water resorts, 118
Museums. *See also* Art galleries
  in Bahia, 172–173
  in Belo Horizonte, 143–144
  in Ouro Prêto, 145
  in Rio de Janeiro, 50–51, 53–56, 80–81
  in São Paulo, 102–106
Music, 17–18
  in Bahia, 174
  of Carnival, 61–67
  in Rio de Janeiro, 83, 87–89
  in Rio Grande do Sul, 127
  in Salvador, 162, 174

Natal, 183, 188
Newspapers and magazines, 37, 39
Nightclubs and bars
  in Amazon, 207
  in Rio de Janeiro, 56, 88–89
  in Salvador, 174
  in São Paulo, 114–115
Nightlife. *See* Entertainment
Northeast, 179–189
  accommodations and restaurants in,
    185–189
North Shore (near Rio de Janeiro), 92–95
Nova Friburgo, 91–92
Nova Jerusalem, 182
Nova Petropolis, 125, 127

Olinda, 181–183
Ouro Prêto, 134, 144–145, 147–148

Pantanal (Central-West Brazil), 149–153
Paraná, 129–132
Paratí, 96–98, 117–118
Parks, in São Paulo, 102–106
Passports and visas, 23–24
Paulo Afonso, 175, 176
Pernambuco, 180
Petropolis, 90–92
Photography, 39
Poços de Caldas, 118, 122
Porto Alegre, 124, 125–127
Porto Velho, 201–202, 207
Portugal, 2–4
Portuguese language, 35–36, 208–209

Rail travel, 43
Recife, 180–183, 185–187
Religion, 15–17
  candomblé, 163, 172
Rental cars, 44, 108
Resende, 98
Restaurants, 34–35
Rio de Janeiro, 49–50
  accommodations in, 72–75
  architecture in, 18
  art galleries in, 83–84
  beaches of, **62**, 81–82
  Botafogo and Sugar Loaf in, 50–52
  Carnival in, 61–70
  entertainment in, 83, 87–89
  excursions from, 90–98
  favelas (slums) of, 58–61
  Gloria Church in, 52–53
  information sources for, 79
  Jardim Botânico and Santa Teresa in,
    54–58

map of, **59**
museums and historic sites in, 53–54,
  80–81
music in, 17
restaurants in, 75–79
shopping in, 84–87
sports in, 82–83
tours and sightseeing in, 79
transportation in, 71–72
Rio Grande do Sul, 124–129

Salvador, 159–166, **164**
  accommodations in, 169–171
  Carnival in, 167–168
  entertainment in, 174
  excursions from, 166–167
  museums and art galleries in, 172–173
  restaurants in, 171–172
  shopping in, 174
  transportation to and in, 169
Samba
  parade and schools (Carnival), 61–67
  shows, 88
Santa Catarina, 129–132
Santarem, 198–199, 207
Santa Teresa (Rio de Janeiro), 55–56
Santo Angelo, 128–129
Santos, 117, 119
São Francisco, Church of (Ouro Prêto), 144
São Francisco River, 13
São Lourenço, 122
São Luis, 183–184, 189
São Paulo, 99–102
  accommodations in, 109–110
  art galleries in, 114
  entertainment in, 115–116
  information sources for, 113
  map of, **107**
  parks, museums and sights of, 102–106
  population and economy of, 11
  restaurants in, 110–113
  shopping in, 114–115
  sports, 113–114
  transportation to and in, 108–109
São Paulo (state), 117–122
Seasonal events, 26, 36–37
  Carnival, 61–70
Sepetiba Bay, 95
Serra do Orgãos (near Rio de Janeiro),
  90–92
Ship travel, 31–32
Shopping
  in Amazon, 206, 207
  in Bahia, 174
  in Fortaleza, 189
  in Recife, 187
  in Rio de Janeiro, 84–87
  in Salvador, 174
  in São Paulo, 114–115
Sightseeing. *See* Tours and sightseeing
Snake museum and institute, 102–103
Soccer, 41–42
South, 123–132
  Paraná and Santa Catarina, 129–132
  Rio Grande do Sul, 124–129
Southeastern Brazil, 117–122
  hotels and restaurants in, 119–122
  transportation to, 118–119
South Shore (near Rio de Janeiro), 95–98
Souvenirs, 85
Special-interest tours, 28

INDEX

Sports, 41–43
  in Bahia, 173
  in Brasilia, 142–143
  in Rio de Janeiro, 82–83
  in São Paulo, 113–114
Sugar Loaf (Rio de Janeiro), 51

Taxis, in Rio de Janeiro, 71
Telephones, 37
Tennis, 82
Teresópolis, 91, 92
Tijuca Forest (Rio de Janeiro), 58
Tipping, 19–20, 35
Tours and sightseeing, 26–29
  of Amazon, 192–194, 204–205
  in Central-West Brazil, 153
  in Rio de Janeiro, 79
  in São Paulo, 113
  of Sepetiba Bay, 95
Transportation
  to and in Amazon, 204
  to Belo Horizonte, 146
  to Brasilia, 141
  to and in Brazil, 29–33, 43–44
  to Cabo Frio and Búzios, 94

to Central-West Brazil, 152
Goias (state), 155
to Northeast, 184–185
to Porto Alegre, 126
in Rio de Janeiro, 71–72
to and in Salvador, 169
to and in São Paulo, 108–109
to São Paulo (state), 118–119
to Serra do Orgãos, 92
Travel documents and customs, 23–24
Traveler's checks, 33

Ubatuba, 120

Vidigal-São Conrado (Gávea; Rio de Janeiro), 72

Water-skiing, 42
Women, 7

Yachting, 42, 83

Zoos
  in Rio de Janeiro, 57
  in São Paulo, 103–105

FODOR'S TRAVEL GUIDES

Here is a complete list of Fodor's Travel Guides, available in current editions; most are also available in a British edition published by Hodder & Stoughton.

U.S. GUIDES

Alaska
American Cities (Great Travel Values)
Arizona including the Grand Canyon
Atlantic City & the New Jersey Shore
Boston
California
Cape Cod & the Islands of Martha's Vineyard & Nantucket
Carolinas & the Georgia Coast
Chesapeake
Chicago
Colorado
Dallas/Fort Worth
Disney World & the Orlando Area (Fun in)
Far West
Florida
Fort Worth (see Dallas)
Galveston (see Houston)
Georgia (see Carolinas)
Grand Canyon (see Arizona)
Greater Miami & the Gold Coast
Hawaii
Hawaii (Great Travel Values)
Houston & Galveston
I-10: California to Florida
I-55: Chicago to New Orleans
I-75: Michigan to Florida
I-80: San Francisco to New York
I-95: Maine to Miami
Jamestown (see Williamsburg)
Las Vegas including Reno & Lake Tahoe (Fun in)
Los Angeles & Nearby Attractions
Martha's Vineyard (see Cape Cod)
Maui (Fun in)
Nantucket (see Cape Cod)
New England
New Jersey (see Atlantic City)
New Mexico
New Orleans
New Orleans (Fun in)
New York City
New York City (Fun in)
New York State
Orlando (see Disney World)
Pacific North Coast
Philadelphia
Reno (see Las Vegas)
Rockies
San Diego & Nearby Attractions
San Francisco (Fun in)
San Francisco plus Marin County & the Wine Country
The South
Texas
U.S.A.
Virgin Islands (U.S. & British)

Virginia
Waikiki (Fun in)
Washington, D.C.
Williamsburg, Jamestown & Yorktown

FOREIGN GUIDES

Acapulco (see Mexico City)
Acapulco (Fun in)
Amsterdam
Australia, New Zealand & the South Pacific
Austria
The Bahamas
The Bahamas (Fun in)
Barbados (Fun in)
Beijing, Guangzhou & Shanghai
Belgium & Luxembourg
Bermuda
Brazil
Britain (Great Travel Values)
Canada
Canada (Great Travel Values)
Canada's Maritime Provinces plus Newfoundland & Labrador
Cancún, Cozumel, Mérida & the Yucatán
Caribbean
Caribbean (Great Travel Values)
Central America
Copenhagen (see Stockholm)
Cozumel (see Cancún)
Eastern Europe
Egypt
Europe
Europe (Budget)
France
France (Great Travel Values)
Germany: East & West
Germany (Great Travel Values)
Great Britain
Greece
Guangzhou (see Beijing)
Helsinki (see Stockholm)
Holland
Hong Kong & Macau
Hungary
India, Nepal & Sri Lanka
Ireland
Israel
Italy
Italy (Great Travel Values)
Jamaica (Fun in)
Japan
Japan (Great Travel Values)
Jordan & the Holy Land
Kenya
Korea
Labrador (see Canada's Maritime Provinces)
Lisbon
Loire Valley
London

London (Fun in)
London (Great Travel Values)
Luxembourg (see Belgium)
Macau (see Hong Kong)
Madrid
Mazatlan (see Mexico's Baja)
Mexico
Mexico (Great Travel Values)
Mexico City & Acapulco
Mexico's Baja & Puerto Vallarta, Mazatlan, Manzanillo, Copper Canyon
Montreal (Fun in)
Munich
Nepal (see India)
New Zealand
Newfoundland (see Canada's Maritime Provinces)
1936 . . . on the Continent
North Africa
Oslo (see Stockholm)
Paris
Paris (Fun in)
People's Republic of China
Portugal
Province of Quebec
Puerto Vallarta (see Mexico's Baja)
Reykjavik (see Stockholm)
Rio (Fun in)
The Riviera (Fun on)
Rome
St. Martin/St. Maarten (Fun in)
Scandinavia
Scotland
Shanghai (see Beijing)
Singapore
South America
South Pacific
Southeast Asia
Soviet Union
Spain
Spain (Great Travel Values)
Sri Lanka (see India)
Stockholm, Copenhagen, Oslo, Helsinki & Reykjavik
Sweden
Switzerland
Sydney
Tokyo
Toronto
Turkey
Vienna
Yucatán (see Cancún)
Yugoslavia

SPECIAL-INTEREST GUIDES

Bed & Breakfast Guide: North America
Royalty Watching
Selected Hotels of Europe
Selected Resorts and Hotels of the U.S.
Ski Resorts of North America
Views to Dine by around the World

AVAILABLE AT YOUR LOCAL BOOKSTORE OR WRITE TO FODOR'S TRAVEL PUBLICATIONS, INC., 201 EAST 50th STREET, NEW YORK, NY 10022.